Praise for *From the Heart*

From the Heart, by Canadian trailblazer Dr. Mary Anne Chambers, takes you through the fascinating journey of her lifetime of faith, humility, and service to others. Mary Anne's uniquely Canadian journey demonstrates the power of belief in oneself, excellence, and determination. Whether as a senior executive at Scotiabank, a member of provincial parliament and cabinet minister, a dedicated volunteer, or chairperson of numerous public, private, and not-for-profit organizations, her wisdom, grace, and humanity shine through as a source of hope and encouragement to others. Yet, what's clear from these pages is that her greatest source of pride comes not from her many accolades, as impressive as they are, but from being a wife, mother, and grandmother to her loving and supportive family and a mentor, friend, and sponsor to so many others. *From the Heart* is a timely, refreshing, and authentic memoir of Mary Anne's pathway to success from Jamaica, the land of her birth, to her chosen home of Canada, and inspires readers to be the best that they can be.

— DR. PAMELA APPELT, O.D., retired judge,
Court of Canadian Citizenship

From the Heart confirmed my earlier impressions of Mary Anne based on encounters from numerous community events. She is an accomplished person of integrity. I found myself totally engaged as she revealed how her experiences emanating from positions of privilege served to tackle both personal and societal issues in a practical and caring way.

— BERNICE CARNEGIE, author, speaker, storyteller,
co-founder of the Carnegie Institute and the
Herbert H. Carnegie Future Aces Foundation

From the Heart speaks to the heart, opens the mind, and challenges one to be and do better. Dr. Chambers reflects on her full and impactful life, gently sharing wisdom and insights from her personal and professional achievements and learnings. Her journey of caring, commitment, and courage — indeed all that she has done and will continue to do — is characterized by genuine humility, profound gratitude, and unshakeable integrity. Reading her book is not only solace for troubling times, it also gives one hope for creating a happier future.

— LOUIS CHARPENTIER, former secretary of the
Governing Council, University of Toronto

In the well written biography *From the Heart*, we meet Mary Anne Chambers, daughter, wife, mother, banker, politician, community supporter, grandmother. Mary Anne excels in each of those roles. As a banker, despite the odds, she rose to become a senior vice president at Scotiabank. The trajectory was fast because she was efficient, generous, went beyond expectations, and kept her Jamaican grounding principles always close at hand. She respected and was respected by colleagues and met negativity with positivity and innate resilience. As a politician her legislations and the causes she committed to were influenced by her natural empathy. She listened. She heard and then went into action to influence and create legislation helpful to all people of Ontario. She was responsible for two portfolios in the four years she was in government: training, colleges and universities, and children and youth services. During her tenure both those services saw advancements that were directly aimed at enhancing the lives of Ontario's population.

— PAULA DE RONDE, author, founder of Arts and Culture Jamaica, and past president of the Toronto Library Association

Remarkably inspirational, especially for women and girls of colour. Dr. Chambers breaks a triple glass ceiling in not one, but two, of the most restricted areas women of colour face: politics and finance. She outlines her path in these extraordinary challenges while maintaining the highest degree of humanity, compassion, and enthusiasm in the midst of building her community.

— DR. B. DENHAM JOLLY, C.M., businessman, publisher, author, broadcaster, human rights activist, philanthropist, and community leader

In her autobiography, Mary Anne Chambers writes "from the heart," revealing to us her true soul — a leader with the power of conviction, fearless in her pursuit of justice and equality for all. Her journey of self-discovery emboldens each of us to become the best we can be, persons audacious enough to dedicate our lives to love and service. Thank you, Mary Anne.

— DR. FRED W. KENNEDY, educator and author

In *From the Heart*, Mary Anne Chambers does us all the favour of detailing her life's journey — from high school in Jamaica, to senior leadership roles at Scotiabank, to cabinet minister in Ontario and significant roles in community service. Our community and Canada need stories of Black accomplishment told by Black leaders, and the author delivers with a heartfelt, easy-to-read story of grit, determination, and inspired leadership. This book is a must read for anyone seeking inspiration and encouragement in making a difference.

— TREVOR L. MASSEY, chair, Lifelong Leadership Institute

The opening chapter is titled "Walking Humbly." Given Mary Anne's Christian background, I thought that it might be taken from the scripture in Micah. "What does the Lord require of thee? To act justly, to love mercy, and to walk humbly with thy God." As a long-time friend and fellow political traveller, I can say with confidence that Mary Anne absorbed the Christian lessons of her childhood and walked the difficult road of humility, justice, and mercy in business, politics, and life. A delightful and thoughtful read.

— THE HONOURABLE JOHN MCKAY, member of
Parliament for Scarborough Guildwood

This is no ordinary autobiography. Mary Anne sets out a clear choice for each of us to make — to be either an advocate or an observer. Central to her life journey and now shared with us in engaging detail is what caused her to be an advocate for good from childhood through to the present. Integrity, passion, and loving your neighbour shine through every page. Mary Anne, thank you for showing the power of not sitting passively on the fence but instead demonstrating the rewards of taking action at every opportunity.

— THE HONOURABLE DOUGLAS ORANE, C.D., LL.D, author,
philanthropist, retired chairman and CEO of
GraceKennedy Ltd, and former senator in the
Government of Jamaica

A wonderful book full of wisdom and hope. A fresh and unpredictable memoir by a remarkable woman who recognized from an early age her obligation to share the privileges and benefits she enjoyed growing up in Jamaica, as a senior banker in Canada, as a cabinet minister in the Ontario government, and as a volunteer and philanthropist. Mary

Anne's life story makes a potent case for what can be accomplished when we work together in shared dignity and mutual respect. A tonic for our times.

— JUDITH WRIGHT, retired deputy minister,
Government of Ontario

I am drawn to calm and strong, and Minister Chambers (I still call Mary Anne "Minister") personifies that. I did not know the foundation of love, empathy, and compassion that is within her until I got to know her better. I hope this book encourages all of us to use whatever influence and power we all possess for good as she has done, for it is not our obligation to change the world, yet we are not exempt from trying.

— IRWIN ELMAN, former provincial advocate for children
and youth in Ontario

From the Heart

From the Heart

Family. Community. Service.

MARY ANNE CHAMBERS

DUNDURN
PRESS

Publisher and acquiring editor: Scott Fraser | Editor: Julie Mannell
Cover designer: Karen Alexiou
Cover image: photo taken at The Photo Company
All images courtesy of the author except folio page 4 (bottom) Stefan Chambers; folio page 5 (top left) Marilyn Chambers; and folio pages 13–15 Ron Fanfair.

Library and Archives Canada Cataloguing in Publication

Title: From the heart : family, community, service / Mary Anne Chambers.
Names: Chambers, Mary Anne, author.
Identifiers: Canadiana (print) 20220206554 | Canadiana (ebook) 20220206880 | ISBN 9781459749832 (softcover) | ISBN 9781459749849 (PDF) | ISBN 9781459749856 (EPUB)
Subjects: LCSH: Chambers, Mary Anne. | CSH: Jamaican Canadians—Ontario—Biography. | CSH: Black Canadian women—Ontario—Biography. | CSH: Black Canadian businesspeople—Ontario—Biography. | CSH: Black Canadian legislators—Ontario—Biography. | LCSH: Women bankers—Ontario—Biography. | LCSH: Bankers—Ontario—Biography. | LCSH: Women legislators—Ontario—Biography. | LCSH: Legislators—Ontario—Biography. | LCSH: Catholic women—Ontario—Biography. | LCSH: Catholics—Ontario—Biography. | LCGFT: Autobiographies.
Classification: LCC FC3100.J27 C43 2022 | DDC 971.3/00496972920092—dc23

We acknowledge the support of the Canada Council for the Arts and the Ontario Arts Council for our publishing program. We also acknowledge the financial support of the Government of Ontario, through the Ontario Book Publishing Tax Credit and Ontario Creates, and the Government of Canada.

Care has been taken to trace the ownership of copyright material used in this book. The author and the publisher welcome any information enabling them to rectify any references or credits in subsequent editions.

The publisher is not responsible for websites or their content unless they are owned by the publisher.

Printed and bound in Canada.

Dundurn Press
1382 Queen Street East
Toronto, Ontario, Canada M4L 1C9
dundurn.com, @dundurnpress 🐦 f ⓞ

For my mother,
whose dignity, wisdom, and strength
continue to guide me

How we define "meaning well" is influenced by what we understand to be true — and this is shaped by our experience, our social circles, our work and, crucially, whom we listen to.
— MARY ANNE CHAMBERS
Excerpt from "Speaking the Truth. It Matters Now, More Than Ever," *University of Toronto Magazine*, Spring 2020 Issue

Contents

Preface

THIS BOOK IS NONFICTION AND conveys my life as best I can re-
collect from my imperfect memory. Certain events, dialogue, and
names are too blurry to be exact, but I have tried, as far as humanly
possible, to remain truthful to my lived reality and to author this
memoir with integrity and sincerity.

A former Scotiabank colleague told me that I shouldn't be surprised if I didn't get very far. She had reasoned that I was a woman,
a Black woman, not Canadian-born, Jamaican, married, a mother,
and Roman Catholic. My colleague shared just two of those identities, woman and mother, but she believed she could anticipate the
challenges I would face. The year was 1976 and I had only recently
made Canada my home. My colleague was ahead of her time. In more
recent years the term *intersectionality* has surfaced in reference to how
overlapping social identities can impact an individual's life experiences. The identities that my colleague had observed were all accurate,
but the conclusion that she had formed did not become my reality.

It has taken me more than a decade to succumb to the wishes of
all who believed I should tell my story. Yet most know so little of my
story. They want to know more, I guess, and they want others to know.

After I left government in 2007, friends offered their help to record my memories. I said I would think about it. I didn't.

No one except Chris, my husband for the past fifty years, knows my story well enough. And even he sometimes wonders about me.

Chris said I was being given a message when someone at the University of Toronto gave me a beautiful leather-bound notebook engraved with my name and lots of blank pages for notes. I didn't get the message ... until one morning while I was doing my daily yoga stretches, after which I would no longer be in pain.

There is so much more to my life than what everyone thinks they know. Some, who know things about my life that they want me to share, know it has not always been easy. They are the ones who have seen me cry. They are the ones who have also heard me laugh as I would rise to live another day and to fight some more, fight harder, for what I believed mattered.

Some, who have seen me smile while under the bright lights receiving another award for doing what I have considered to be something quite ordinary, have asked me to share my story so that others might see a path for themselves. They don't know that even as I am being recognized, I am always thinking of the many people whose selfless and tireless contributions toward improving the quality of life for others often go unrecognized. I find that humbling.

I am well aware that my life experiences have influenced how I remember and present the stories that I tell. Stereotypes and pre-conceived notions of who or what is of value can confuse us and conflict with reality; not only our reality, but also the reality that others experience. Policy-makers make decisions based on what they believe to be true. There is also a healthy skepticism of how history is recorded, and how that record depends on who is doing the recording. My experiences are my "truth" and I know that my life has been one of great privilege in its broadest sense.

The *Oxford Dictionary* defines privilege as "a special right or advantage that a particular person or group of people has." I believe each of us is privileged in some way. How we choose to use that privilege is what defines us.

As you read *From the Heart*, it is my hope that while you are taking a look at life through the lens of my experiences and my perspectives, you will also appreciate and celebrate others whose actions have truly inspired me. It is with great admiration and appreciation that I dedicate this book to all whom I have had the privilege to encounter, whether specifically referenced in my writing or not, especially those who might have no idea how their lives have impacted and enriched mine.

Chapter 1

Walking Humbly

CONTRARY TO THE ADVICE OF more experienced members of my campaign team that I should never go out campaigning by myself, I decided that I needed to do exactly that. I was nervous about what the experience would be like. This was a self-imposed test and I hoped to be able to control how things went, to any extent I could. Most of all, I wanted to avoid embarrassing myself in the company of members of my team.

I had never, ever been in this kind of situation before. I felt vulnerable. I felt anxious, uncomfortable, even a bit afraid. I thought of how I felt when strangers came to my door, uninvited and without warning. They always wanted something. My reception could never be described as warm, under those circumstances. Yet here I was, exposing myself to the possibility of precisely that kind of response, and to think, I was going to be doing this, a lot, for the next few months. I had obviously not given enough thought to what I was agreeing to when I agreed to run for political office.

I couldn't have had a more perfect day for a walk in the riding of Scarborough East. The sky was almost perfectly clear, the day sunny but not too warm. The few clouds appeared distant and destined to stay intact. There was no sign of rain and there was little movement in the air. I had chosen a Saturday morning hoping that would improve my chances of finding people at home.

I parked my car some distance away from the first house that I would visit. I had selected an unfamiliar street where I didn't expect to encounter anyone I knew. Although the particular street was unfamiliar, it was close to the University of Toronto Scarborough (UTSC), a place I knew well from my many years as a student there.

With some candidate cards and the voters' list for that area in hand, I approached a man who was standing outside the house. He wasn't working in his garden, and he didn't seem to be working on the car that was parked in the driveway. He was by himself, but he looked preoccupied. Maybe around five and a half feet tall, he looked to be in his sixties, maybe early sixties. I thought, or perhaps I hoped, that he wouldn't see my presence as an intrusion.

"Good morning, sir," I said, choosing that greeting as a good balance between being pleasant and seeming too familiar. I didn't think that "Hi, how are you?" would have been appropriate given the reason I was there, although under normal circumstances, I would have felt comfortable greeting him that way.

"Are you Mr. ... ?" I asked, referring to the name shown on the voters' list for that address.

"I am," he said blandly, not hinting as to whether or not I was imposing myself on his morning.

"I am Mary Anne Chambers, the Liberal candidate for this riding," I said, following the sequence that the team had determined for our door-knocking outings, and I handed him my candidate card.

Then I mentioned that I'd noticed from the voters' list that someone by the name of ... also lived at this location. It was a woman's name, with the same last name as his. My heart sank to somewhere close to the ground when the man told me that person was his wife but she had passed away three weeks before. My first house! I told him I was very sorry to hear about his loss, asked him if he was doing okay, and wished him well. I then turned to leave, at which point he asked me what I had wanted to speak to him about.

"It's not important," I told him. "It can wait for another time." I asked him to take care of himself and I moved on.

I crossed the road in a semi-conscious attempt to move as far away from the first house as possible, quickly walking past eight or nine houses while I tried to compose myself. I then took a deep breath, turned onto a driveway, walked up a few steps to a front door and rang the doorbell. A man opened the solid door but left the storm door closed while saying, "I am tired of people trying to sell me stuff."

I cringed and heard my voice say, "I am not trying to sell you anything, sir. Wait, I am. I am actually selling myself!"

The kind man obviously saw how embarrassed I was, opened the storm door, and said, "Speak to me." I went through the motions and left as quickly as I could. My second house!

I did a few more houses without incident before deciding that I had had enough for my first outing, turned around and headed back in the direction of my car, still on the other side of the road from the first house. As I got closer, I noticed the man at that house was still in his driveway and he was looking in my direction. I then heard him calling out, "Hello, hello." Wishing I could disappear, I tried to pretend he was calling out to someone else. He crossed the road to meet me, his arm outstretched, holding my candidate card.

"This is you, right?"

"Yes, it's me," as if acknowledging guilt.

He then said that after I left his place, he had taken the card to some of his neighbours and told them about me. He said he told them I was the kind of person they needed in government. He believed I would look after their interests.

He told me he was sure that he had secured seven votes for me. I thanked him most sincerely.

When I got to my car, I sat still for several minutes, trying to breathe normally, processing all that I had just experienced.

Chapter 2

A Grateful Daughter

MY PARENTS HAD FOUR CHILDREN. My brother Keith, who was the eldest, was followed by my sister Kathleen (Katie). I am the third child, and my sister Patricia (Pat) is the youngest.

I was born on September 8, 1950, at St. Joseph's Hospital on Deanery Road in Kingston, Jamaica. I gather my parents named me Mary Anne Veronica with the hope that I would live up to the symbolism of the names they chose for me. That date in September is when the Catholic Church celebrates the birth of the Blessed Virgin Mary, the mother of Jesus. According to the holy teachings, Anne was the mother of Mary, and Veronica was the name of the compassionate woman who wiped the face of Jesus as he carried the cross on which he would soon be crucified.

According to my official certificate of birth, my father, Sibert Constantine Brown, was thirty-six years of age, as was my mother, Dolce Brown. I would later learn that both ages were wrong. Other documents show that my father was forty-one and my mother was thirty-nine when I was born. My father's profession was shown as accountant. There was no place on the certificate for the mother's profession.

On September 28, 1950, I was baptized at the Church of St. Theresa, Little Flower. At the bottom of my baptismal record there was a note that said, "N.B. This child must be brought up Catholic." St. Theresa's Preparatory School, the elementary school that I attended, was attached to the church.

I believed and memorized the catechism lessons from Sunday school, a regular feature of my childhood. *God loves me and made me in his likeness. God made us to love each other, not to live in isolation of each other, but as social beings.* I readily bought into the idea that God had made me.

As a child, going to confession every Saturday was a ritual that I embraced. It hardly seemed to matter whether or not I believed I had sinned during the preceding week. I had to go to confession. Going to confession was not only an expectation, it would also mean I could receive communion on Sunday. That also meant I could not sin between confession on Saturday and mass the following day. I had a notebook and in that notebook I wrote, just to ensure that I would always have something to confess....

"Bless me, Father, for I have sinned. It has been a week since my last confession. I disobeyed my mother three times, and I told an untruth once."

In response to my confession, the priest would tell me to say one "Our Father" and three "Hail Marys." I would do as I was told, knowing that all would be well after that. Before leaving the church, I would sometimes piously light a couple of votive candles — to seal the deal, I guess. On occasion, I might have had a special item to add to my standard list of sins, but not often. That didn't concern me because I figured that when the priest forgave my sins and I did the penance he assigned me, that would take care of everything, including anything I had not remembered to record in my notebook.

I still find it easy to believe in the concept of a supernatural be-ing, perhaps because I need to believe that there is someone much wiser and a lot more powerful than me. I am critical of those who use religion to exploit others, or to position themselves as better than others, or in other ways that I consider hypocritical. I don't try to impose my spiritual beliefs on others, but I have often relied on what I believe to draw strength for myself, to provide me with reason to be hopeful, to help me to see the good in others, to main-tain my sanity when sadness or feelings of helplessness could have overcome me, or simply as a source of inspiration. I also fell for the idea that God expected something from me. I was fine with that. I actually liked that idea. I have always liked that idea.

Our parents' home, where I spent my first fourteen years, was immediately across the road from our church and elementary school. The hospital where I was born was on the same road, al-though farther away. The Dominican Order of Nuns who ran my school also ran the hospital. There seemed to be a lot of them in those days, mostly from Ireland and the U.S.A. The pastor of our church, Father Thomas Glavin, was a Jesuit and an American. There was always scotch whisky in our home that only he drank, as I recall.

Our home had a large yard in the front and an even larger back-yard. Not long ago, when I drove by, I saw that another house had been built in front of the house where I grew up, the front of the property being large enough to accommodate that. We had lots of fruit trees, including a few varieties of mangoes, great for shade, and one special one that my brother, my two sisters, and I enjoyed climbing and in which we would hide when we had made Mommy angry. There was a drawer in which she kept one of our father's old leather belts. I don't recall anything else being kept in that drawer. We could always hear when the drawer was opened. That would be our signal to head for the mango tree. We also had avocados, bananas, plantains, breadfruit, ackees, sour sop, sweet sop, limes, pineapples, and other fruits, and there was a rose garden on the front lawn. There were benches and chaise longues in the backyard, great for taking naps in the gentle breeze on warmer days.

I had a happy and carefree childhood. On weekends I would go with my brother and sisters on the drive to National Bakery. We knew when we were close from the delightful smell of freshly baked bread that filled the air. There were no seat belts in our car in those times. The four of us would squeeze into the back seat of the car, leaving my father alone in the front to drive us home. Along the way home, slices of soft, warm bread would be formed and flattened into communion-like hosts, which we would ceremoniously place on each other's tongues, just as the priest did during mass at our church on Sundays. In no time at all, the bread would be finished, and my father would have to turn the car around and return to the bakery. I don't recall my father being upset with us, at least not for long. I sometimes wondered why he didn't simply buy more loaves in the first place, some for us to eat in the car and the rest for us to eat at home.

My mother did not work outside the home. I always knew her to be busy, but it seems she would always be there when I got home from elementary school. The blender would spring into action as she made punch — a raw egg, condensed milk, and a bottle of Guinness Stout with a dash of nutmeg poured over cracked ice. Mommy's punch always went down smoothly, replenished my energy and put me in a "good place" for getting my homework done.

Mommy had the help of a maid and a gardener. We called them by their first names. They called me Miss Mary Anne. Keith was Mas (for Master) Keith, and my sisters were Miss Kathleen and Miss Pat.

At an event in Toronto, when I was much older, Mrs. Leah Tutu, wife of Nobel Peace Prize laureate Archbishop Desmond

Tutu, told us a story about growing up in South Africa. The event was hosted by an organization, founded by Carole Adriaans, called South African Women for Women. Mrs. Tutu's mother would get young Leah and her siblings ready for school each morning, ensuring they had breakfast, before going off to her job. The children had no idea what kind of work their mother did, but they knew it had to be important because their mother always left home very well dressed. One Saturday, when they accompanied her to the market, some children ran up to their mother, hugged her lovingly, and called her by her first name. Seeing that as disrespectful, Leah and her siblings were mortified by the realization that their mother obviously worked in the home of the children's family. They begged their mother to give up that job. In response, their wise mother told them that it is how we treat others, not how they treat us, that defines us. A truth as important today as it was in the dark era of apartheid in South Africa.

I have no recollection of when Vera, one of my mother's helpers, started working in my parents' home. It seemed she had always been there, a fixture in our family.

Vera kept our house clean and did the laundry. Sometimes she helped my mother with the cooking. My mother always did most of the cooking. It was she who taught me to cook, something I still enjoy doing. Vera was not our nanny, but I felt close to her. She was quite the character, always cheerful, never sick, a hustler, always on the go. "Foot, whey yu deh?" is what I remember she would say when her work at our home was done, and she would be getting ready to leave for the day. She might have had another job. I didn't know. She obviously had other responsibilities. In the mornings, after our family moved to a new house on a hill with an even larger property, Vera would walk at a moderate pace, making her way up the driveway. At the end of the day, she would run down the hill, and that seemed more in line with her personality.

Vera seemed to me to be in her forties, but when I was a child, every adult seemed older than they probably were. She was short and chubby. I was tall and wouldn't have been described as chubby, but somehow, my clothes fit Vera and she would determine when I had worn some items enough. At that point they would become hers. I smile even now as I think of her.

I do remember that Vera left us when, at the age of nineteen, I married Chris and moved out of my parents' home. I remember her saying that she was no longer needed. She didn't leave only my parents' home, she left Jamaica. Vera moved to Canada.

Growing up in Jamaica, I had no sense that as a girl, there were any different expectations of me. I was known to be a leader at my co-ed Catholic prep school. That meant, for example, that the nuns relied on me to ensure that the orders for lunch for all students were collected each morning and conveyed to the caterer and that any problems with the fulfillment of the orders were my responsibility to resolve. It also meant that when the contest for which class could sell the most raffle tickets was winding down, I would be the one who would make the extra effort to ensure that my class won. I was also the student who, in the summer break, accompanied the nuns to parts of Kingston that Bob Marley wrote songs about, to teach the children who could not afford to attend school to read and write and do arithmetic. I recently found myself having to explain to some children that arithmetic was what they now know as mathematics. When I was a child, mathematics was known to encompass arithmetic, algebra, and geometry.

It helped that I was a cute little girl. I could sell raffle tickets faster than I could write the names and addresses of the purchasers on the stubs. At St. Theresa's Preparatory School, the class that sold the most raffle tickets got a picnic at the beach on a school day.

Every Roman Catholic student learned fundraising, I think. Garden parties. Bingo. Raffle tickets. Grab bags. I had worked at my mother's cake stall for the garden party at St. Theresa's Church in Vineyard Town each year. My mother asked other ladies at our church to bake cakes and we sold them whole, in quarters, or by the slice. And there were always a few of the most nicely decorated ones along with one or two Christmas puddings that we would raffle. Mommy's cake stall raised a lot of money for our church. We sold dozens of cakes and I sold hundreds of raffle tickets.

One Saturday just before the deadline for my school's raffle ticket sales, I decided to make sure that my class would win the day at the beach. I had taken a few dozen books of tickets home with me on the Friday, and on the Saturday, without my parents' knowledge, I took the bus downtown and positioned myself on the sidewalk outside the entrance to the Myrtle Bank Hotel, a popular upscale choice for businessmen. It is only in later years that I have realized the risk that I had taken. A little girl, alone on a downtown Kingston Street, asking strangers to purchase my raffle tickets and collecting lots of cash. I didn't know fear then. I had absolutely no sense of my vulnerability.

It wasn't unusual for me, even as a young girl in my pre–high-school years, to go out by myself on a Saturday. I often went to my father's office downtown on Harbour Street, where I would "help out" for a few hours. On those days, I would also visit a few of the larger stores on nearby King Street. Sometimes I would go into a sound booth in the music section of one of those stores, put the large headphones on, and listen to records.

On the Saturdays when I didn't go to my father's office, I would take the bus to the public library on Tom Redcam Drive. I loved to read, and I loved going to the library. I sometimes sat at a table with a short stack of books, but often I just sat on the floor in a corner with my head buried, in heaven, reading for hours at a time. At home, my favourite chair for reading was one of my family's rocking chairs. I sometimes ate a jam sandwich while I read and rocked. What more could a young girl need in life? For me that was bliss.

But that fateful Saturday, ensuring that my class would win the day at the beach was the only thing on my mind. And I sold every raffle ticket that I had. The day had gone exactly as planned, just perfect, until I got home.

My mother had always told us that she would know when we had done something that we shouldn't have done. I have never figured that out. In later years, I would tell my sons the same thing. It had worked for my mother. Maybe it would work for me with my sons. I don't think it did. I am still hearing stories about incidents twenty or thirty years after the fact that I had no knowledge of before.

I knew I was in trouble when my mother asked me where I had been. She didn't usually ask me that. I lied. She knew I was lying. So, she asked me a few more questions, maybe to help with her investigation, maybe to torture me, or maybe to give me a chance to come clean. That was the day that I learned it's not easy for me to lie. That was the day my mother told me that unless I was good at keeping track of the lies I would need to tell to make the earlier lies sound true, it would be best to simply avoid lying in the first place. I had never felt so ashamed. I was mortified. That lesson continues to serve me well.

I guess I should also tell you that I didn't give any thought whatsoever to the fact that I am Black. My father was Black. I have no recollection of how old I was when I learned that an executive from the head office of Pan American Airways, my father's employer, who was visiting Jamaica and had apparently had too much to drink at a company reception, was heard proclaiming that no other Black man would ever be allowed to reach the senior level in management that my father had achieved. That man was swiftly sent back to the U.S. and separated from the company. Those were not the days of political correctness, so he had obviously been seen as a liability because my father was very popular with the company's Jamaican customer base.

Mommy told us that her mother was Portuguese and her father was from Scotland. I am not sure about either of those claims. My maternal grandmother, Catherine Gomez, died of pneumonia at the age of twenty-nine, shortly after arriving by ship in New York, where her older sister lived. The year was 1920. Mommy was nine years old when she lost her mother. I don't recall meeting my maternal grandfather although I do believe he was a part of my mother's life even after she got married. His name was Archibald Parkin. Mommy had two younger siblings, a sister, Evelyne, and a brother, Morris. I remember a little about my father's parents, including visiting his mother at her stall at the large Victoria Craft Market by the pier in downtown Kingston. His father's name was Samuel Brown. Daddy didn't have any siblings.

My mother was the epitome of the perfect housewife who also did volunteer activities for our church, which I enjoyed doing with her. She dreamed of me becoming a physician. Mommy introduced me to community service and wanted me to be influential. I have always attributed to her far greater wisdom, strength, and success than her limited formal education might have prepared her to achieve. Her expectations of me were very high.

My father, who introduced me to the world of business, just wanted me to be happy. He also introduced me to the banking world and, in my mid-teens, took me along to a meeting with his branch manager, where I learned that it was possible to negotiate better interest rates than those generally available. Daddy introduced our family to the world of travel. Benefits associated with his position at Pan Am allowed me to fly for free until I was thirty-five years old. Travel became and still remains one of my favourite hobbies, not just for the different places and cultures that I could experience, but for what I could learn about other people's lives.

Being accepted by a high school meant having to pass the Common Entrance examination in the final year of elementary school. The headmistress at my school called my parents to say that they needed to hear about the results of my Common Entrance exam. Sister Marcella told my parents that the school had not seen results like mine before. I had earned a scholarship that, in addition to covering tuition, included an allowance for books, uniforms, lunch, and transportation from home to school, or boarding if I preferred to live at school. My parents were very pleased but because they had already been prepared to pay all of those expenses for me to attend the high school of my choice, they decided to open a bank account for me and deposit the scholarship funds from the government for me there. I saw that account as untouchable, a longer-term investment in my future.

At Immaculate Conception High School, an all-girls Catholic school, I was chosen to be a house captain and would also be chosen as head girl. I never actively competed or asked for those responsibilities. It just seemed to be the way it would be. I think the respect I had received from others might have had something to do with my self-confidence. Perhaps it also had something to do with the fact that I was tall for my age. Psychologists have theories about that kind of thing. Tall people cast long shadows, seem more mature and more authoritative, I gather.

My personal definition of leadership meant having the ability and the responsibility to help others to succeed. It never seemed to have anything to do with my personal interests or ambitions.

I didn't know there was anything particularly special about being a girl, although in high school, the nuns insisted that we could do anything we set our minds to do. They tried very hard to isolate us from boys, almost going as far as to suggest boys were unnecessary evils.

We wore white blouses with blue ties and white box-pleated skirts that had to hang below the knees unless we wanted to receive detentions or demerits. For sports, we wore unattractive, white, loose-fitting bloomers, which some of the girls would try to shorten by rolling the fabric under the elastic on the legs, especially for sports competition days when the nuns would reluctantly allow boys to be on the school grounds. Finishing off our uniforms were brown socks, brown loafers, and starched straw hats with brown bands that carried the initials "ICHS," for our school, in white.

ICHS was viewed as an elite school. The students were expected to carry themselves with pride and behave in a ladylike manner. The school grounds also depicted that kind of character with sprawling acres of lawns, landscaped gardens, and huge trees that offered generous shade. Tennis and netball courts, a softball field, a swimming pool, a circular pavilion that we referred to as the summer house, and a music hall that housed several pianos were all included in the experience that students enjoyed. The buildings were painted pink and well maintained. The student population was between eight and nine hundred in size when I was there in the 1960s. It has doubled since then, requiring additions to the buildings that have been done in a way that has maintained the original look of the school. It remains the most beautiful high-school campus that I have ever seen.

I wasn't good at sports. I enjoyed singing in the glee club and did well in my piano lessons. Those were my extracurricular activities throughout my high school years. Miss Lisa Narcisse was director of the glee club and my piano teacher. The glee club would always perform at school concerts and special events like graduation, and I would often be one of the students on the program to play piano selections. I preferred playing solo because when I played duets, I would usually be paired with a student at a level junior to mine. I once complained to Miss Narcisse about that. That complaint developed into a learning opportunity. Miss Narcisse asked me if I could play at the more junior level. Then she asked me if the other girl could play at my advanced level. The conclusion was simple. I would have to be the one to make the adjustment. I had no trouble grasping the fairness of that and the importance of making space for others to shine.

The nuns who ran our high school were from the Franciscan Order. Father Mathias, a Franciscan monk, was the only male teacher. Sister Maureen Clare, a Jamaican, was twenty-nine years of age when she was appointed headmistress. Her beauty and her youthfulness were striking, but more significant was the formidable reputation that defined her relationships with students, staff, and parents.

As an Immaculate girl, I was taught that there was absolutely nothing that I could not achieve. The expectation was that we should be successful at whatever careers we chose to pursue. Our school motto, "Ad astra per aspera," was intended to be taken seriously. We were proud of ourselves and our school, and we knew that we were being groomed to achieve big things.

We knew that being girls did not mean that we were less than or even equal to the boys. We were expected to excel, and we were expected to be leaders.

I was fourteen when our family moved to our new home, a manageable walking distance from my high school, but either my father or my mother would usually drive me to school. My mother had supervised the construction of our six-bedroom, four-bathroom, three-storey home on a two-acre hillside property in a residential area aptly called Stony Hill. The other properties on our road were of similar size. A limestone curb, about two feet in height, lined the long driveway from the road up to a large parking area by the house. High retaining walls of limestone stood behind the parking area, and in front of and at the back of the house. Mommy, also an avid gardener, kept the three or four clumps of bamboo plants that grew below the wall in front of the house and planted citrus trees, bananas, and plantains elsewhere on the property. There were service quarters at the back of the house, two bedrooms separated by a bathroom attached to the back of the house behind the laundry, but our household helpers never stayed there overnight.

It was not uncommon for homes and properties in Jamaica to be given a name, which would appear at the entrances to the property, close to the street number. Our family's home was named Dolcebert, a combination of Dolce, my mother's first name, and Sibert, my father's first name.

My recollection of what my parents most had in common was that they both agreed that I was wonderful. I grew up believing that I was their favourite. I knew that my parents had high expectations of me not only in terms of what I could achieve, but also in terms of the kind of person I should become. Their love reinforced my self-confidence and instilled in me a certain amount of invincibility. I will also be forever grateful for the wisdom of their support for my curiosity about, and respect and compassion for, people who were not as fortunate as we were.

Rather than aspiring to a career that involved leadership, I was determined to be independent. I am still fiercely independent.

Throughout high school I received a generous amount of pocket money from my father. I was a conscientious saver. I was also paid well for bookkeeping jobs that I did for my father and sought his help in securing jobs in department stores owned by people he knew, during summer and Christmas school breaks. My need for independence was very likely influenced by my observation that when my parents were having their disagreements, my mother would refuse to open the envelope that contained house money that my father would provide each pay day. Instead, she would sell mangoes and other fruits from our property to market women who would come with large, empty baskets and leave with them filled. And whenever my mother was leaving the house-money envelopes unopened, I would give her the money I had earned so that she could continue her protest.

I wasn't familiar with the word *feminist* at that time, but I was convinced that financial security would be essential to my own independence and peace of mind. And when my mother would observe how well I could do on our shopping trips to Miami, she would reinforce my desire for independence by telling me that I would need to have a career that paid well. She never, ever suggested that I should marry someone who could support me financially.

As a teenager in the mid to late sixties, being comfortable on shopping trips to Miami on long weekends was a sign that important progress was being made. My mother had experienced no barriers when she would go shopping or eat in restaurants during her trips to Florida. But on one occasion in the early 1950s, she had taken my older sister along and they were refused service in a restaurant that my mother had often patronized when she was by herself. The manager of the restaurant told my mother he could serve her but could not serve her little girl. Jim Crow laws on racial segregation were enforced in southern American states until 1965. Discrimination like my mother and older sister experienced, as well as other such atrocities, existed with the permission of the laws of the land of the free.

Chapter 3

I do

MY APPLICATION TO THE UNIVERSITY of the West Indies for undergraduate studies, intended to lead to medical school, was accepted. My mother had always dreamed of me being a physician. I didn't share that dream.

Feeling uncomfortable with the prospect of having to depend on my parents for financial support for the several years that a medical degree would have required, I sat aptitude tests for computer programming at two well-known computer companies, NCR and IBM. I earned full marks on both. I was fortunate that aptitude had the kind of respect that it did in those days. Specialized training and experience seem to be valued more by employers than aptitude, now.

Summer jobs were hard to come by in Jamaica, so I applied for jobs without revealing that I had been accepted to pursue studies at the university. That turned out to be a good strategy. I was successful. My new employer immediately enrolled me in a computer programming course at IBM. I had no idea that would change my life completely and forever.

Chris and I met in August 1969 while I was on the computer programming course. He was then a computer programmer/analyst at IBM. The first day I showed up for the course, he was working in the same room where I would be studying. It was a large room, laid out seminar style with tables and chairs forming an empty square in the centre. Chris was already seated in the room, alone, when I arrived. I chose a chair at the opposite end of the room, directly across from where he was seated. We faced each other. He was wearing dark pants, a white short-sleeved dress shirt, and a slim black tie. He sat leaning to the side of his chair, with his legs crossed just above his ankles. He looked youthfully charming. We said "hello" somewhat shyly as though we had not expected to see each other. I thought he might also be there for the same course but soon discovered that he had left his normal workstation to work quietly in the conference room that day.

I recognized him as the one, immediately. For me, it was love at first sight.

I had none of the experience that would have come from having already had boyfriends, or even really knowing boys other than my brother, Keith. I didn't know what to expect from serious romantic relationships. My attraction to Chris came naturally, as if it was simply supposed to be.

He was handsome, tall, and slender. I loved his smile and the way he walked with long, unhurried strides. The solid, dark rims of the glasses that he wore, all the time, made him look smart. I knew he was respected by his colleagues. They often sought his advice and, as a result, so did I. He seemed patient and eager to share his knowledge of computer systems.

I was young, a teenager. I suspected he was probably a few years older than me, not old enough to be so much more experienced that I would have felt intimidated, smothered, or controlled. I certainly wasn't interested in being controlled. Chris was soft spoken and polite, my idea of a gentleman. He held the door for me and treated me respectfully. I felt comfortable and safe around him, so when he invited me to go out with him, I didn't hesitate to accept. It hardly seemed to matter where he was taking me. I knew I would enjoy being with him and he seemed eager to impress me. He seemed as attracted to me as I was to him. I also liked that he didn't seem to be particularly interested in other girls when he was with me.

Chris had his own car, which was a bonus in a number of ways. My mother had been teaching me to drive but that hadn't always worked out well. She would sometimes not be as patient as I might have wished. There were times when my leg would sting from the slaps that I got during my lessons. Chris was a kinder teacher.

I recall sharing with Chris that my parents weren't always happy together. It worried me that that could also be my fate. Chris told me that our relationship would be different, and he made me want to believe him. He didn't make any other promises. That might have been why I soon became convinced that we could have a happy life together.

Our courtship had its challenges. I think that's one of the reasons why it lasted such a short time.

It was obvious that Chris's parents didn't like me. I was told by people who knew them that how they felt about me had something to do with the colour of my skin. I defiantly told those people that I was a gift. Ironically, Chris and I looked alike enough that shortly after we met, one of his co-workers asked him if he could take his sister, me, out. Years later I would, accidentally I think, see a photograph of Chris's mother's family with an older, stately looking, obviously Black woman seated in the centre of the group. I learned that she was a great-grandmother. Genetics don't lie. Chris and I are still told that we resemble each other.

Chris was an only child. I wondered if that could also have made it difficult for his parents to be comfortable with the idea that they might be losing him. Perhaps they wished for someone other than me for their son. Perhaps they would have preferred to have more time to get to know me.

It was, and still is, quite normal for Jamaicans to want to make connections when they first meet others, whether in personal or professional settings. There were no such connections between Chris's family and mine, nothing that either his parents or mine could hold onto for comfort or peace of mind.

My mother would stay awake until I got home from our dates and would insist that I get out of Chris's car right away. That was usually shortly after midnight because the live entertainment at the night clubs that we went to usually started at around ten o'clock. As soon as Chris's car got to the top of the long driveway up to my parents' house, Mommy would leave her bedroom and stand on one of the balconies overlooking the parking area. The light on that second-floor balcony would be turned on. She would next appear on the landing of the outside stairs that led from the second-floor entrance to the house to the parking level. Knowing that she wouldn't stop there, and wanting to avoid further embarrassment, I would usually emerge from the car at that point. My mother's message was both stern and simple: "You are not married yet." That ritual continued until the night before our wedding day.

I would learn, several years after the fact, that Mommy had told Chris I wouldn't be able to do housework. She said that I had a strong mind and a strong heart but, physically, I was weak. She was right, but I am happy that revelation by my precious mother did not scare Chris away. In fact, he took the warning to heart, never expecting me to clean our home or do the laundry.

Mommy also blamed Chris for "distracting" me from pursuing medicine as a career. In reality, Chris had nothing to do with that decision. I had already decided, before I met him, that I needed to be able to support myself, sooner rather than later. A career in information technology would provide me with the opportunity to achieve that objective.

Chris and I got engaged on Christmas Day, just four short months after we had met. The following June, on a warm Saturday morning, in the presence of around sixty guests, Chris and I said "I do" at Stella Maris Church, a short distance from my high school. My long-sleeved dress was made of Swiss lace and stopped about six inches above my knees. Miniskirts were the fashion in those days and a morning wedding allowed for that, being both fashionable and practical. Father Glavin, who had seen me grow up from my years at St. Theresa's Prep School, was the celebrant. Guests included close relatives and friends and a few nuns, all of whom I actually knew and all of whom knew me. I had asked my parents not to invite anyone who would say things like, "My goodness, you have grown," or "I haven't seen you since you were so high," or "It's been too long since I have seen you."

The wedding reception was held at my parents' home. My parents went all out in the preparations, Mommy even flying to Miami for a day of shopping for the event.

When I was a young wife adjusting to my new life, Chris reminded me that "for better or worse" were the vows we had made. I am sure I was in shock when I repeated what Father Glavin had told me to say. So when Chris threatened to type them up and stick them on the door of our refrigerator, I guess he was trying to be sure that I knew what I had promised.

Every year on our wedding anniversary and sometimes on other occasions when I am feeling mellow, I marvel at how wise we were. Chris disagrees. He says we had no idea what we were doing. I know I chose well, my companion for life, even as I have heard that a famous Hollywood actress has said that when the "'til death do us part" bit was written into marriage vows, people weren't living as long. "For better or worse, in sickness and in health," Chris continues to be my constant, my companion for life, and my best friend.

Getting married at such a young age was a remarkable thing for me, because unlike many of the other girls in my year in high school, I had not had a boyfriend before I met Chris. I was nineteen when we each said "I do." Chris was twenty-two. It's no wonder my parents were traumatized. Fortunately, they loved Chris, a lot.

My mother was of the opinion that I would get married when the time was right, but there had been no indication as to when the time would be right for me to have a boyfriend. That line of thinking seemed to go hand in hand with her belief that there was no need for sex education. When the time was right, all would be miraculously revealed. I have thought of my mother's philosophy on that subject whenever I have heard it suggested that sex education should be left to parents and not be included in the school curriculum.

As head girl at my high school, attending the graduation prom meant my mother asking a friend if her son could be my escort. Joe Rhoden was handsome and a perfect gentleman, but the embarrassment I felt about the situation caused me to not ever want to see him again. I would later learn from Chris that he and Joe were in high school together. Two decades later, then a mother myself, my opinion was quite different when other mothers asked my son Nick to escort their daughters to their high-school proms. I felt proud that they knew my handsome son was also a perfect gentleman and could be trusted to take good care of their daughters. It's funny how these things work.

Waiting a few years before having children seemed wise, so Chris and I rented a nice, fully furnished one-bedroom apartment and settled in for a long honeymoon, or so we thought.

Not many months later, when the doctor told me the news, I came to realize that I was the stronger one. Chris wondered how this could have happened. How would we manage? I went on the defensive, or perhaps the offensive, and declared we would be just fine. That was that strong mind at work, of course, the one my mother had told him about. Deep down, actually just below the surface, I was as nervous as Chris was, but I knew it had to work. We would make it work.

The one-bedroom apartment we had rented when we got married was perfectly fine for us as a couple but, in our view, would not be suitable for raising a family. Chris and I went house hunting. My parents bought a rocking chair and a crib, absolute necessities for every grandparent's home.

When I sat across from the manager at the New Kingston branch of the Royal Bank of Canada as we sought his help in securing a mortgage to purchase our first home, my pregnancy was obvious. In those days, that meant my income would soon be a thing of the past. When we ruled out Chris's father as an unwilling guarantor and my father because he wanted us to forget about the bank and allow him to finance the purchase, our bank manager became creative. Obviously believing that he could rely on us to honour our commitment and recognizing that I was too young to legally be granted a mortgage, he offered to place the mortgage in Chris's name with me as guarantor. The balance in the bank account that held my high-school scholarship funds became the deposit on our new home.

Appliances for our kitchen and laundry were purchased from the slightly damaged section of a store owned by one of my father's friends. Once installed, any damage would be well concealed by an adjacent wall or cupboard. We did very well. Furniture for other rooms was purchased on store credit plans, and each month I would take the little card into Courts, the furniture store, to make a payment on the account.

When our son, Nicholas Andrew, was born, I felt like I had died and gone to heaven. My mother made a point of telling everyone she considered important that eleven months had gone by since the wedding. That obviously really mattered in those days.

I was able to get computer programming work on contract while I was on maternity leave, and when I returned to work, I joined Chris's routine of brown-bagging sandwiches for lunch most days. We were very proud of how successful we were at managing our finances.

Three years and two months after Nicky was born, his brother, Stefan Wayne, arrived. Nicky came to the hospital to meet his baby brother, all excited, even more so when he realized that his brother's little fist held, tightly, a candy that Stefan had brought as a gift for his big brother. Nicky had been looking forward to the arrival of the baby. He would rest his head on my tummy to feel the baby's movements and to listen for sounds that he might make. The love affair between Nicky and his baby brother was sealed in the hospital that day. He declared that Stef would be his best friend.

Just months later, as Stefan held onto the railing of his playpen, his mouth wide open but not making a sound and with a look of extreme distress on his face as the complexion of his skin changed, it was Nicky who yelled, "Stefan can't breathe." Chris and I came running. We held Stefan upside down and slapped his back, to no avail. Our little boy was obviously suffocating. Chris reached into his mouth and discovered a leaf. As soon as he removed the leaf, Stefan screamed and the four of us sat on the couch in our living room, crying and hugging each other. This all happened shortly after arriving home with the boys that evening. I had picked them up from child care after work, as usual. As I carried Stefan inside from the car, he must have picked the fading leaf from one of the rose plants by our house and he must have held onto it for a bit before putting it in his mouth. Once inside, I put him in his playpen and went to the kitchen to start preparing dinner. I would not have heard his silent cry for help. Fortunately, Nicky was playing close to his brother's playpen. He saved the life of his best friend.

Chris and I have only ever wanted our sons to be good people and we have always believed that if they could feel well loved by the people they care for, their happiness would be assured. Our job was to ensure they would always know that we loved them, to tell them that they were wonderful and that we believed in them, and to show them how to respect and care for others.

I love our sons unconditionally. I love them more than I love myself.

Chapter 4

My Ways Are Not Your Ways[1]

CHRIS AND I HAD FULL-TIME jobs. As a young wife and mother, I needed help juggling my job with my responsibilities for raising a family and looking after our home. My mother had made it clear to me that I would have difficulty accomplishing all of this. Being a mother, she said, should mean staying home to care for my children. Contrary to her own experience and the path she had taken, or perhaps as a result of both, Mommy had always encouraged me to have a career that would provide me with financial independence. That was not the path she had taken, and I knew she had not always been comfortable with having to depend on Daddy for financial support.

I hired Ida as a part-time helper in our home. As was common practice for domestic workers, she had knocked at the gate at the end of our driveway one Saturday morning, looking for "days work," the term commonly used to describe part-time work done

---

1 Isaiah 55:8.

by household helpers who sometimes had more than one employer. "Days work" could be one day or maybe more like employment each week, depending on the needs of the particular employer and the availability of the helper. Ida worked with us two days each week. She kept our home clean and did the laundry. Apart from doing their laundry, I didn't need Ida to take care of our little boys. On my way to work every day, I would take them to the home of someone who provided child care. I did the cooking, having learned that skill from my mother while I was growing up. Our home was not far from my parents' home and from time to time, Mommy would send Daddy over with a dish of something delicious.

Ida was different to Vera, who had worked with my parents until Chris and I got married. Ida was pleasant and reliable but always very serious. She didn't talk much. I can't recall her ever laughing. There was less of the personal relationship that Vera and I had enjoyed. Ida's focus was on getting the work done. She never complained about anything. She carried herself in a manner that was simultaneously purposeful, humble, and composed.

Ida had two daughters; twins, I think. On a couple of occasions, they had come to our home to meet their mother at the end of her workday and to accompany her home on the bus. They were teenagers, lovely young ladies, always neatly dressed and polite. Their hair was combed back away from their faces, showing its natural texture, tidy and unprocessed. Their faces revealed perfect, unblemished skin, absent the acne that some teenagers wished would go away. I could tell that they loved and respected their mother but that their future was destined to be different from hers. It was obvious that their mother's primary, perhaps even sole, purpose in life was to provide for their well-being, regardless of the sacrifices that might require her to make. I had no sense that there was a father involved in the girls' lives.

———

Shopping for food meant living within the budget Chris and I had established for ourselves. We weren't alone in paying close attention to our finances. In the early 1970s, Jamaica was experiencing a balance of payment deficit from more money leaving the country for imported goods and services than was coming in from exports. This economic situation led to government-imposed restrictions on foreign exchange used to import goods and some basic food items being in short supply. To deal with this, some grocery stores rationed the items that were in limited supply, giving preference to select customers.

As I would enter the supermarket and pick up my shopping cart in full view of the people in the management office located on an upper level overlooking the action below, unmarked brown bags would be deposited in my cart. It didn't seem to matter that my family of two adults and two young children had no need for large amounts of corn meal, rice, or other imported food items that had limited availability. No one even thought to ask me if I needed them.

I would get a hint of what was going on as I pushed my cart close to the back where customers banged on locked doors to the storerooms, shouting their protests. They knew that items in short supply had been delivered to the supermarket but had not been placed in the display areas. They knew, intuitively, that those items were being made available to select customers and they knew they were not among the preferred customers. They had the money to purchase those basic food items, but even so, that would not give them access to what they needed for their families. How maddening that must have been for those people. I would learn, in the weeks ahead, that people were grabbing shopping bags from customers as they loaded them into their cars. Desperate times were demanding desperate actions.

Rather than declining the bags that were placed in my shopping cart, I would take them home to give to Ida. She would likely not be considered a preferred customer at my supermarket, and she had herself and two teenage daughters to feed.

What moral justification could there possibly be for a practice of giving preference to who should have access to food, based on management's perception of the value of the customer? It wasn't as if the price was negotiable, with the items going to the highest bidder. Whoever was able to get them would have to pay the posted price. The management and staff at the supermarket had no knowledge of my family's needs. They didn't even know me. Their actions were unethical and discriminatory yet accepted in that environment. The supermarket had sole discretion in determining who would have the privilege of purchasing what they were selling. The customers who were given special treatment probably didn't give a second thought to what was happening. If they did, I wonder if they felt they were entitled to preferential treatment, given the amount of money they regularly spent there. Or perhaps they were all going to do what I was planning to do. Somehow, I didn't think so. It seemed the best I could do under the circumstances was to recognize my privilege and try to share its benefits with Ida. That seemed to be the extent to which I could realistically and practically apply some semblance of moral authority.

On one occasion, the brown bags that I gave to Ida were so large and heavy that I knew they would be difficult for her to take home, travelling, as she always did, on the bus. I told her I would drive her home. My offer was received with a combination of appreciation and apprehension. I thought Ida did not want to inconvenience me so I insisted that it would not be a problem. We headed out, with Ida giving me directions along the way. I realized getting to work at my home required Ida to change buses a few times. Eventually, we got to an area quite different from where my family lived, and soon Ida told me that I would not be able to go much farther. "Why not?" I asked. Her response was that, as a stranger, I would not be safe leaving her area on my own. Still thinking about the load that she would have to carry on her own, walking the rest of the way, I insisted that I drive her all the way in and we reached an agreement that after unloading the bags at her home, she would drive back out with me to the main road.

That was the day I got to see the small zinc shack where Ida lived with her two daughters. I also noticed, not far from her shack, a standpipe, which was shared by others in the large yard for water. I would come to learn that Ida's daughters had their minds set on attending the University of the West Indies and that their exam results from high school were outstanding, certainly better than I had achieved not many years before. All of this despite the cramped, substandard physical conditions in which they lived.

Ida's daughters knew their mother would not be able to support them while they furthered their education. Their decision to work for a year before starting university was an obvious one. That meant securing jobs, hardly a difficulty in the 1970s when a high-school diploma accompanied by outstanding marks was viewed the way we now view a bachelor's degree from a reputable university or college. Ida's daughters applied to almost every well-known private-sector corporation in Jamaica without success or, to be more specific, without even the acknowledgement of their applications. After weeks of this, I became suspicious of what might be happening. I apologized to Ida for the ignorance of these corporations and held my breath while I wondered out loud if it might make a difference if her daughters resubmitted their applications using my home address. Ida welcomed the idea with grace, quite unlike the embarrassment I was feeling as I proposed the idea. My mailbox filled up with responses addressed to Ida's daughters. And as Ida's gratitude became even more evident, my stomach boiled with anger. I felt sickened by the reality that these and, no doubt, other bright young people overflowing with the desire, ability, and potential to contribute to the well-being and success not only of themselves and their families but also to that of their country would be prevented from having the opportunity to do so simply because of where they lived. How could they ever change their circumstances if they were always to be branded as high risk or unworthy?

My mother and my younger sister, Pat, emigrated to Canada while I was pregnant with Stefan. It was either late 1973 or early 1974. Pat, who was single, was looking for a change and invited Mommy to join her. Mommy and Pat were close and saw a move together as a workable plan. The timing, coinciding with me being pregnant, made my mother's departure from Jamaica a particularly emotional experience for me. I cried myself to sleep the night after hearing their plans. Although I had not often had to call upon Mommy to help with Nick, our first son, I always knew she was there for us should the need arise. I wondered how well I would manage having a second child without Mommy nearby. I knew I would miss Mommy immensely, for every reason I could imagine.

The thought of them leaving my father in Jamaica was also difficult for me. I had intentionally assumed the role of mediator for my parents for what I knew would be a character-building experience that would also serve to develop my skills in diplomacy. I learned to listen and I learned when it might be best to keep my opinions to myself. I loved both my parents dearly and I knew they loved me.

Vera, who had worked for my parents until Chris and I got married, had not forgotten about me. Instead, she continued to try to run my life from her new home in Toronto. Vera would send acquaintances who were visiting Jamaica to me with letters asking or, to be more accurate, telling me to give them specified amounts of money to be distributed to her many "adopted" children in Jamaica. Vera had no children of her own but had always generously provided support for at least a few children and youth who resided in Jamaica.

Chris and I had purchased our first home less than a year after we got married and we were living from one payday to the next while expecting our first child. What on earth was Vera thinking, and why did it have to involve me? Vera should have known that we were having to manage our cash flow very tightly. I guess she must have believed the good Lord would provide. And somehow, the people she sent with her letters and instructions never went away without their mission having been fulfilled. Even as I questioned, in my own mind, whether Vera had lost hers, I would somehow find the cash that she had requested I provide.

A few years later, in either late 1974 or early 1975, Vera embarked on another mission. She was convinced that we should leave Jamaica, preferably to live in Canada. As was always the case, she did not or could not explain why, and by that time we were living more comfortably and raising our two young sons without difficulty. Stefan, our second son, was born in July 1974. Our family was exactly what we had wished for. We were content. Chris and I had jobs that we enjoyed and also paid well. We often spent weekends in Ocho Rios, on the north coast of Jamaica, and we visited Disney World in Florida. We saw no need to do as Vera had suggested but we eventually concluded that applying for Canadian visas would not commit us to moving to Canada. Neither did it mean that we would have to make any hasty decisions. Canadian visa applications took a very long time for approval at the best of times.

As the months went by, Chris and I began to see the wisdom in Vera's belief that we should leave Jamaica. Things were changing in Jamaica politically and the economy was weakening. Although the prime minister, Michael Manley, told Jamaicans that if we were unhappy there were five flights to Miami every day, leaving Jamaica at that time was viewed by many as unpatriotic. I started checking in with someone I knew at the Canadian High Commission, anxious to get word about the status of our visa applications. I wasn't seeking special treatment. We were simply becoming increasingly concerned about the situation in Jamaica. People were starting to leave the country, quietly. It was best not to share such plans beyond relatives, friends, or work colleagues who absolutely needed to know. Those who weren't yet ready to leave were moving their money out to the United States and to Canada. In those days the Jamaican dollar was worth more than the Canadian dollar.

For us, moving to the United States of America wasn't an option. With the U.S. having been at war in Vietnam since 1965 and a draft system in place to keep America's armed forces resourced and replenished, taking two sons to that country, even as young as ours were, was out of the question. By the time the U.S. left Vietnam in 1975, more than fifty-eight thousand American soldiers had died. Over the years, as I have learned about the deep-rooted curse of anti-Black racism that permeates life to this day in many parts of the United States of America, I believe it would have been a huge mistake to have chosen that country as home for our sons. In Canada, our sons have had experiences that I have found troubling, but I believe their stories should be theirs to tell.

Our Canadian visas were issued on July 18, 1976, one year after we had submitted our applications. By then, we were eager to make the big move. Chris and I were among the lucky ones because the Canadian government had identified labour market needs that placed domestic workers and people with computer skills at the head of the line.

The government of Jamaica had let IBM know they were aware that IBM staff were leaving Jamaica for positions with the company in its operations in North America. IBM pulled back in response, which meant that Chris could not expect that a transfer to the company's operations in Toronto would be an option available to him.

Shortly after accepting an executive position with the Bank of Nova Scotia in Jamaica, Bill Phillips, who had been my boss before he moved to the bank, encouraged me to consider joining him there. He wasn't concerned that I was pregnant with our first child at the time. That pleased me and had me thinking that the bank must be a progressive employer. Having invited me to meet with him, Bill had pulled out a manual on the company's benefits to share with me the details of staff loans and mortgages. It was then that we both learned those benefits were available only to male employees. That was the early 1970s. I thanked Bill for thinking I would be good for the bank, but I didn't think the bank would be a good fit for me. The bank had just set up a data centre for its operations in Jamaica and was in the process of automating its retail banking systems. While I was on maternity leave, the bank contracted me to do computer programming for them. I was grateful for that.

A few years later, when I spoke with Bill Phillips in confidence about our application for Canadian visas, he kindly offered to introduce me to a member of the bank's management team from Toronto who would shortly be visiting Jamaica. A meeting was arranged, as promised, with Don McLean, the man from Toronto. As I look back at that meeting, I am thinking that so much has changed since the mid-1970s. I arrived at the hotel in New Kingston not realizing that the meeting would be taking place in Don's guest room. This was someone, a man, I had not met before. I was a young woman, twenty-five years of age. I cannot imagine myself feeling comfortable about that kind of arrangement now, but the meeting went well. I do recall that the door between the hallway and the guest room was left ajar. Don was very professional, and I spoke freely with him about my family's plans to move to Canada.

"What about your husband?" he asked. "Will he be joining IBM in Canada?"

"We hope so, but he will have to apply when we get to Canada," I said.

Don suggested that we make my employment his priority, but if Chris experienced any difficulty in securing employment with IBM Canada, I should let him know and he would see what opportunities might be arranged at the bank.

I don't recall us discussing anything about my technical skills. I assumed Don and Bill would have had that conversation when Bill suggested that we meet. As our meeting wrapped up, Don said, "Good luck with your visas. Call me when you get to Toronto."

The meeting had seemed more like a conversation than an interview. No promises were made but I felt good that it had taken place.

The tightening of foreign currency regulations in Jamaica made us realize that we would not be able to take much money out of the country. With what we had, we began shopping for furniture, beautiful Jamaican-made mahogany furniture. The empty spare bedroom in our home was brought into service. A living room coffee table and matching end tables, bedside tables, a chest of drawers, a vanity with a large mirror, and a headboard for a king-size bed were stored there in their protective warehouse packaging, ready to be loaded on to a container for shipping. Our home sold quickly, and we made door-to-door moving arrangements.

On the day of the move out of our home, we took a break for lunch. As we ate beef patties and drank sodas on our front patio, an older member of the moving crew, a soft-spoken and thoughtful man who obviously loved his country and cared about its future, asked us what would happen to Jamaica when young professionals like us left the country. The tone of his voice reflected genuine concern. My heart ached. I felt a sense of guilt, like I was abandoning a people for whom and a place for which I could have been of value.

There are some who think that Jamaica has never fully recovered from the wave of emigration that took place in the seventies. The so-called brain drain would be replaced by the benefit of remittances being sent home by members of the Jamaican diaspora in countries like the United States of America, the United Kingdom, and Canada, providing needed financial assistance to those experiencing economic hardship in Jamaica.

I would also miss year-round summer. Poinsettias grew wild and bloomed every year just in time to make the place beautiful for Christmas. We had some in our garden; they grew so well that we would have to cut the plants back shortly after Christmas each year. Poinciana trees and bougainvillea plants bloomed in several different colours and flourished whether or not it rained. The blossoms on the ackee trees and on the breadfruit trees with their large, beautifully shaped leaves meant we could look forward to harvesting these delights in their season. There were several varieties of fruit trees. Mango trees laden with blossoms also signalled sweet, juicy fruits to come; even when it was not mango season, the shade from the large, leafy trees would provide relief from the hot sun. There was the smell of the sea and the comforting breeze courtesy of the mountains and so much more I would miss.

We left Jamaica on August 27, 1976, a little more than a month after our visas were issued, feeling a bit anxious about what the future would hold but at the same time filled with optimism.

Canada was going to be good for us and we were going to be good for Canada. Chris and I often reflect on adopting Canada as our home as one of the best decisions we have ever made.

Vera came to visit us shortly after our arrival in Toronto. We were shocked when she handed us a passbook from the Bank of Nova Scotia, where she had opened an account in my name and deposited the Canadian dollar equivalent of the money that I had given her messengers for delivery to her adopted children in

Jamaica. It was almost as much as the amount we had legally been allowed to take with us from Jamaica. It helped us to purchase our first home less than a few weeks after arriving in Canada, a comfortable three-bedroom townhouse in a new real estate development that was ready for occupancy and ready to receive the furniture that we had shipped from Jamaica.

When Chris and I got married and Vera left my parents' home and, shortly after that, left Jamaica for Canada, she had said that we didn't need her anymore. She was wrong. I think she must have known that.

———

On our first visit to Jamaica, seven years after we had left to start our new life in Canada, my father met us at the airport in Kingston. By then, he was no longer able to drive his car himself. We greeted each other warmly and as I was about to head to the foreign currency exchange counter, Daddy told his driver to hand him the brown envelope he had brought for us. When I opened the envelope, I found four smaller envelopes, each one bearing the name of a member of my family, each containing Jamaican dollars to spend on our vacation. I had always refrained from asking my father for money, but this time I graciously accepted, knowing that it would have broken his heart not to have allowed him this act of generosity and genuine show of affection toward his daughter and her family. It was a celebratory visit. My father even ignored his doctor's orders and had champagne served when we had dinner with him.

"Are you sure you should be drinking alcohol, Daddy?" I asked, given his health condition.

"If I can't have a drink with my daughter ..." was his response.

My father died at Nuttall Hospital in Jamaica on August 12, 1985, nine years less fifteen days after Chris, our sons, and I had left

Jamaica to start our new life in Canada. His death registration form shows his cause of death as bronchopneumonia. He was seventy-six years old. For a few years prior to his death, Daddy had also been suffering from Parkinson's disease and diabetes mellitus.

At the time of his death, my father had a wife, my mother, albeit estranged; an adult son; three adult daughters; and two grandsons. We were all thousands of miles away in other parts of the world. With the passage of time, our family had evolved from my childhood memories of togetherness and happier times. That was difficult for me to reconcile. As if in a reminder of those times, there were large mango trees in the yard at the nursing home that could be seen from the window in Daddy's room. Daddy had sometimes talked about mangoes in a less-than-coherent way when I was able to speak with him on the phone from my home in Toronto.

With the news of Daddy's passing, I sought comfort in the fact that Chris, Nicholas, Stefan, and I had visited him just a few weeks earlier. That visit was not without its own reckoning as I observed the stark difference between the luxury and expansiveness of our parents' home and the sparsely furnished bedroom of the small nursing home where my father spent the final years of his life. I recall I had left the nursing home with a sense that we had just said our final goodbyes.

Chapter 5

O Canada

SCOTIABANK FELT LIKE A NATURAL fit for me because of its connections to Jamaica. Fortuitously, the timing of my arrival in Canada and the experience I had gained from working in consulting in Jamaica on various models of computer hardware and software comprised my ticket to success in securing employment.

Having had what seemed to be a positive and encouraging meeting with Don McLean, the senior member of Scotiabank's management team, while he was travelling through the Caribbean, I called him on the first business day after our family arrived in Canada. I had not known then that Don's tour of the Caribbean had included a request from an associated bank in Bermuda that would require the computer skills I happened to have. Being unemployed with two children to care for made finding jobs our number one priority, so I was very happy to be invited for an interview with him and two people from human resources, the very next day.

I recall Don asking me two questions during the interview. "Why do you want to work at the bank?"

"I want to be able to change jobs without changing employers," I said, "and I think I should be able to do that at the bank."

Don seemed to think that was a good answer. "How do you feel about travelling on business?" was his second question.

"I enjoy travelling with my family on vacation, but I'm not interested in travelling on business because I do not want to be away from my little boys," was my response.

"You will learn to like it," he said, and proceeded to offer me a job in international systems.

I was hired with a start date of September 13, 1976, "at an initial salary of $16,350 per annum as a programmer." The day after my interview, in the business section of the *Globe and Mail* newspaper, I saw an ad for Scotiabank's international systems department. Willingness to travel was stated as a condition of employment. In hindsight, I realized it was fortunate that Don, who was head of international systems, didn't really care how I felt about travelling on business, because had he considered my concern, he might not have given me the job.

There was also another lesson to be learned, which is the importance of being well prepared and informed when you are hoping to impress someone who can help you be successful. I had done no research at all in preparing for my interview. I didn't know what Don McLean's area of responsibility was. Given that his visit to Jamaica was part of a tour of the Caribbean, I guess I should have concluded that he had an interest in the bank's operations in that region. Had I thought about that, I would not have been so quick to reveal that I had no interest in travelling on business. It appeared Don had known enough about my skills, the fact that they were needed in Bermuda, and also that this was an area of weakness among the staff at the bank. Those factors were worth the risk of me needing to adjust to the requirement for business travel.

One of the people from human resources whom I met on the day of my interview at the bank was Shirley Giles. Shirley was a bundle of energy, an absolute pleasure to meet. She told me she was known as the "loan arranger" and she was obviously eager to tell me about the staff loan and mortgage benefits the bank offered. Shirley was also proud of the fact that, in 1961, she was the first female at Scotiabank to be appointed a branch manager. Timing is everything, as the saying goes. Scotiabank had addressed that weakness in their staff benefits since Bill Phillips and I had seen them in the manuals only a few years before. Fortunately for us, mortgages and loans at preferred rates were now available to both male and female staff. Chris and I would be needing financing for the home that we were about to purchase.

Chris noticed that people in Canada spoke about the weather a lot. He wondered if that meant they preferred to keep conversations impersonal. We arrived in Canada in the last week of August. Within a month after we arrived, we were checking the weather reports every night, so that we would know how to dress the boys the following day. We quickly realized that, unlike Jamaica, where the weather varied little from one day to another, it was now important to pay attention to the forecasts. We also learned to make the best of the good days and to avoid putting off outings the way we had nonchalantly done in Jamaica.

Vera told us that many trees seemed to die during the winter. I could certainly understand how she had come to that conclusion. But what was obvious was that before the trees played dead, the fall would bring out their spectacular splendour in leaves that turned yellow, orange, and red. Whether on their own or along with the green that remained yearround, the magnificent display of colours was nature at its most glorious. Then would come winter with its own glory — like the snow angels the children would make as they lay flat on their backs and moved their outstretched arms up and down on the pure white, freshly fallen, fluffy snow — and also its danger.

My car hit a snowbank piled against the median going east on Highway 401 that first winter. The strong wind and heavy snowfall had combined to create poor visibility and periodic whiteouts. I had left my office at around midday to collect Nick from kindergarten at St. Edmund Campion School and take him to Mini Skool, the child-care centre where he would spend the afternoon with Stef until I picked them both up at the end of my workday. It was likely my inexperience driving in those conditions that caused me to lose control after hitting the snowbank on the north side of the highway. My car swerved ninety degrees and slid across three lanes of highway until it stopped by the snowbank against the guardrail on the south side of the highway. I sat in shock, my heart pounding in my chest as I realized that miraculously, I had not been hit by any other vehicles. As I readied myself to back out from the snowbank, I questioned my judgment in voluntarily leaving behind a climate of year-round summer.

While my colleagues at work seemed to have little difficulty understanding the challenges that sometimes arose from the need to juggle being a mother with children in child care with the expectations of my job, my mother often reminded me of her opinion that staying home with my young children should be my priority. For me, this would be a dilemma that would often arise in a variety of forms to challenge my choice to pursue a career, an ever-present doubt seeking to find root in my psyche, one to which I was determined not to succumb.

The scare on the highway taught me to respect other winter conditions like freezing rain and black ice. One evening, as I exited the parking garage attached to my office building, I realized my car's braking system was no longer taking its orders from me — a terrifying feeling, to say the least. I managed to get to Don Mills Road, where I struggled to turn north. Fighting to keep the car in the curb lane, I got to a shopping plaza nearby, where I turned into the parking lot, got out of the car, locked the door, and shuffled on foot to the closest bus shelter. It was dark, snowy, and, worst of all, icy. At that point, it hardly mattered where the next bus was going. I only knew that I would be on it. When it was time to get off that bus and transfer to the York Mills/Ellesmere bus that would take me east for the rest of the ride home, I realized that the bus had stopped right next to a pile of snow where I would once again have to test the tread on my winter boots as I ventured out. I had no idea how to do that gracefully. I got to the eastbound bus without incident and was happy that I had no difficulty getting a seat. As if I had not already experienced enough for the evening, we got to a "hill," hardly what we would refer to as a hill in Jamaica, causing the bus driver to send all the passengers to the rear of the bus, where we were told to jump up and down to give the bus enough traction to enable it to move forward. Seriously! Miraculously, it seemed, I made it home safely that night.

We were determined that with winter now part of our new reality, it would be best to find ways to enjoy the season. Chris and the boys learned to skate. I made a half-hearted attempt and decided it was best not to risk injuring my back. It was after we came to Canada that a doctor had diagnosed the source of the sometimes-debilitating pain in my lower back as scoliosis. Bert, one of my colleagues at Scotiabank, had once asked me why I was walking like I had polio. I had thought I was doing a good job of disguising the pain that happened to be acute that day. The ice rink where our sons had their skating lessons was also a practice rink for some junior hockey teams. I heard a mother complain to a hockey coach that she was concerned that her son was a wimp. Her son's coach told her not to worry because by the time he was finished with him, he would be an animal. That was my signal that hockey would not have a place on our sons' list of sporting activities.

———

We were very interested in getting to know Canada, its vast and varied landscape, its cities, its people, and its cultures.

In early spring our family went to the sugar bush for the tapping of sap from the sugar maple trees. In June we picked strawberries on a farm outside Toronto. In September we went apple picking at Chudleigh's Apple Farm. The day would end with delicious freshly baked apple pie with cheddar cheese from the bakery on the property. The russet apple, in appearance the least attractive of all the varieties, would become one of our favourites.

Our sons played T-ball, soccer, and basketball, and took swimming lessons. Chris was one of their soccer coaches. They were also introduced to volunteering at an early age. We played bingo with the senior residents at a nursing home in our neighbourhood. The residents loved having the boys around, in part I think because the boys never corrected them when they cheated or made mistakes, unless the mistakes were not in their favour. We also painted ceramic items made in the kiln at a home for unwed teenage mothers in the months before and after the birth of their babies. In those years, the home was run by a French Canadian order of Catholic nuns. Proceeds from the sale of the ceramic items went toward the services offered by the home. That was also an opportunity for the boys to meet members of the Toronto chapter of my high school's alumni association who had chosen to support the project.

When we vacationed on beautiful Vancouver Island with its mild weather, we wondered why so many retired Ontarians spent winters in Florida. We then realized that Florida is much closer to Toronto than Vancouver Island is to Toronto.

While visiting Montreal, the boys needed to use the washroom. It was a Saturday, and we were downtown in the heart of the business centre. We decided to try our luck in Place Ville Marie. We used the ground-floor entrance to the main forty-seven-storey tower, where we saw a security guard on duty at his station.

"My little boys need to go to the washroom," I said as we approached the guard. "Would it be possible for them to use a washroom here?"

The security guard rose from his chair, contacted a colleague by radio to let him know he would be leaving his station, picked up a bunch of keys, and walked us to a hallway beyond the lobby area where he unlocked the door to the men's room. Not needing to use the ladies' room, I waited with the guard in the hallway. I expressed my appreciation for his kindness, and he told me it was his pleasure. He went on to say, "When the anglos ask to use the washrooms, I send them to the metro," he said. "There are washroom facilities for the public there."

The metro is Montreal's underground transit system. The security guard had a French accent and he was white. I realized there might be more to the issue than race or ethnicity. That was my introduction to the tension that existed between anglophones and francophones at that time, a tension that included language rights, but also more that I would come to learn about as time went by, not only regarding historic tensions in Quebec but also in other parts of Canada.

Relatively oblivious to Nova Scotia's history of anti-Black racism, Chris and I vacationed close to the waterfront in Halifax and made our way through coastal towns like Lunenburg, soaking in the salt water–flavoured air and the abundance of fresh seafood. There and in Prince Edward Island, we donned our bibs and had our fill of traditional lobster suppers. The waterfalls and heavily wooded mountains on Nova Scotia's Cape Breton Island were well worth the drive from Halifax. Halifax, the capital city of the province of Nova Scotia, was the destination of more than 1.5 million immigrants from Europe between 1928 and 1971. People from the Netherlands, including the family of my daughter-in-law's mother, were the fifth largest ethnic group to arrive at Pier 21. The Canadian Museum of Immigration is located on the site of Pier 21.

On my first Scotiabank-related visit to Halifax for a single day of meetings, I asked the taxi driver how long it would take me to get back to the airport. I knew the traffic would be heavier at that time of day and I didn't want to miss my flight. He told me the time I should leave the office. I asked him how difficult it would be for me to get a taxi from the office. He told me not to worry, he would return to pick me up for the drive to the airport. Concerned that he might not do as he had promised, I asked him how I could be sure that he would be there as he said he would. He told me not to pay him for the trip from the airport until he had driven me back to the airport. He did exactly as he had promised, and I tipped him generously. I suspected I would never have an experience like that in Toronto.

On another trip to the East Coast, the man sitting next to me on the airplane told me that he had actually been scheduled for a flight the day before, but the high winds at the airport in St. John's, the capital of the province of Newfoundland and Labrador, had caused the cancellation of that flight. We landed in rain and some wind and, while Chris and I waited for our turn at the car-rental counter, we overheard the complaints of another man who had arrived on the flight with us from Toronto. Responding to the man's comments about the weather, the young woman working at the car-rental agency summed things up really well.

"People don't come to Newfoundland for the weather," she said, "they come for the hospitality."

We fell in love with the warm hospitality of the people, their obvious love of life and their industriousness, the stunning rock formations in shades of blue, grey, and purple, the large "ponds" at all elevations, and, of course, the lobster and other fresh seafood.

There is both humour and irony in the fact that Jamaica's national dish is salt fish and ackee, given that while ackees grow profusely in Jamaica, it is trade that brought salted cod fish to Jamaica and rum back to Newfoundland. Jamaicans refer to their island as "The Rock." Newfoundlanders refer to Newfoundland as "The Rock." One morning at breakfast, while on a family vacation in Jamaica, Nick asked each of us what it would take to make our day perfect. In true Newfoundlander style, Nick's partner, Katrina, responded, "It's already perfect."

———

West Hill, in the east end of Scarborough, would be our home for twenty-eight years.

Our family physician was from Jamaica. Dr. Forde's office was located in his home, and he had operating privileges at Centenary Hospital, close to where we lived. He was single and he seemed to be available for appointments whenever we needed to see him. Best of all, he did house calls, absolutely a blessing for a family with young children, especially during those winters that seemed to be so much harsher in our early years in Canada. I don't think that was a common practice. We certainly considered ourselves fortunate to have Dr. Forde as our family doctor. It would also take me a while to get accustomed to not having to make a payment for each appointment with the doctor, as we would do in Jamaica, thanks to universal health care in Canada.

Four years after arriving here and purchasing our first home, we were able to upsize to a larger, four-bedroom detached house, about ten minutes east of our townhome. The proximity of our first and second homes to each other meant that very little had to change in our lives. In our garden, we planted two apple trees, a russet and another variety for cross-pollination, and two purple plum fruit trees. Along with junipers and spruces that we could enjoy year-round, we also planted an ornamental red maple tree, a tribute to Canada, in our backyard.

Eileen and her husband, Doug, had moved into their home in this new residential development before we moved into ours. Our property backed onto the side of theirs. Eileen had moved to Canada from the state of Massachusetts when she married Doug. Her pregnancy was obvious but did not deter her from walking up the steep grade at the side of our house to bring us a cake that she had made to welcome our family to the neighbourhood. Eileen worked as a nurse at Scarborough General Hospital. She was a committed gardener. In the midst of a wide variety of perennials in her garden was a small sign that declared "A weed is but an unloved plant." A bumper sticker on the rear of her sports car read "Pushing forty is exercise enough," but Eileen was clearly fit and had an abundance of energy. By any measure, Eileen and Doug were great neighbours. We also enjoyed Don and Louise, our neighbours on our east side; Christine and Ken on the west side; and Don, directly across the street from us.

We really liked our neighbourhood. There was a wonderful bakery owned and operated by a Chinese-Jamaican family, located halfway between our doctor's office and our home. They made hard dough bread, a Jamaican favourite.

We were happy with our sons' elementary and high schools, Chris was involved in activities at St. Joseph's Church in the quaint village of Highland Creek, and I sang in the choir.

Our sons' Catholic elementary school was just a fruit orchard away, a short walk from our home. In Nick's class, there was a student from a Jamaican family of Lebanese ancestry. His father worked at Scotiabank, and his mother and I attended the same high school in Jamaica. In Stef's class, there was a student whose family were Jamaicans of Chinese ancestry. Her parents owned a popular hardware store in the neighbourhood. Her mother had also attended the high school I had in Jamaica. At that time, as far as we were aware, there were only three families, other than ours, with Jamaican roots whose children attended the same school as our sons. While on duty as a crossing guard at his elementary school, Stefan challenged a fellow crossing guard, a student whose family hailed from Jamaica, to sing the Jamaican national anthem before he would give her back her winter gloves. In grade 4, testing conducted by the Toronto Catholic School Board resulted in him being referred to the board's program for gifted kids.

Stefan joined the Royal Canadian Air Cadets, a program offered by Canada's Department of National Defence and the Air Cadet League of Canada, when he was thirteen years old. He excelled and rose to the position of chief warrant officer of his squadron. His summers included various courses offered by the program and, through their flying scholarship program, he earned his glider pilot's licence at the age of sixteen. At seventeen, he earned his wings in the power flying program. Stef's choice of atmospheric science for his university major was entirely logical. At nineteen, the mandated retirement age for cadets, he joined the cadet instructor cadre, a section of the Canadian Forces Reserve, where he continues to serve, currently as commander of the Borden Cadet Flying Site, the largest air cadet flying site in Canada. On weekends in the spring and fall of each year, he leads a team of instructors and cadets in providing flying-familiarization opportunities on four Schweizer 2-33A gliders and two Bellanca Scout airplanes, to approximately 2,500 air cadets from twenty-four air cadet squadrons.

As a governor with the Ontario provincial committee of the Air Cadet League of Canada, each year I had the pleasure of participating in graduation ceremonies for the glider scholarship program at the Mountain View facility not far from Canadian Forces Base Trenton. This was always an exciting time for the cadets, sixteen- and seventeen-year-olds who, over almost two months during their summer school break, would do classroom instruction and flying training exercises to earn their glider pilot's wings. While most teenagers were eager to learn to drive, some of these new pilots did not even have their driver's licence. That had also been the case with Stef when he earned his pilot's wings years earlier. Flying seemed to be their first love. Learning to drive could wait.

Ahead of the graduation ceremony, the cadets would march onto the parade square in their squadrons and assemble in front of a hangar where parents and special guests were seated. Instructors and other staff members typically stood behind the guests by the entrance to the hangar where they had full view of the cadets. Parked in a special formation behind where the squadrons of cadets assembled were gliders and tow planes that were used for the training program. The scene never failed to cause goosebumps to surface on my arms, so I could easily imagine how proud the cadets and their instructors must have felt. But as was the case with these kinds of ceremonies, the cadets maintained a professional, disciplined posture.

It was through the air cadet program that Stefan would meet his future wife, Minka. One summer, I had the extra-special pleasure of presenting a particular cadet with her wings. I had not met Cadet Roersma prior to that day. Minka, a tall, slender, pretty girl who looked me in the eyes somewhat shyly, couldn't hide the most beautiful dimples I have ever seen, even with the very slight smile that I was able to initially get from her

"Congratulations," I said as I presented her with her wings. "I love your dimples."

"Thank you," Minka replied, as, for just a brief moment, her smile became more obvious and her dimples deepened.

I later learned that my son, Stefan, was observing the encounter between his mother and Cadet Roersma from his spot by the hangar. He had been the commander for her squadron that summer. Following the graduation ceremony, I gather he asked Minka to tell him what I had said to her as I was presenting her with her wings.

Beyond air cadets, Stef helped Minka with her homework while she completed high school and encouraged her as she pursued degrees in kinesiology and education at York University. They got married at St. Vincent de Paul Church in beautiful Niagara-on-the-Lake in June 2001, while Minka was still attending university.

Nick was selected as president of his high school's student council. While in high school and then during his years in university, he spent his summer vacations working in what was then the City of Scarborough's special needs recreational programs for young people with physical and intellectual disabilities.

Nick also worked with an Ontario group home for disabled adults and a life-skills and independence-building program for teenagers. He invited me to his workplaces to meet his clients. I was always touched by his gentle but non-patronizing manner. I was struck that he would take the adults in the group home to the library, where he would read to them from a wide variety of books. He took them to see art exhibits and he took them to church. He held open houses and garden sales in the hope of building relationships between the adults he was supporting and curious but hesitant neighbours. As the neighbours became more familiar with the residents of the group home, they would contribute baked goods for the garden sales. Nick spoke to the residents as though they were perfectly capable of understanding him, regardless of the fact that they didn't speak back. He told me that while he could not observe their response, neither could he be certain that they were not understanding him.

Many years later, while serving as Ontario's minister of children and youth services, I would find inspiration in those memories.

Nick had taught me how to move beyond simply being sympathetic to recognizing that people with disabilities were capable of living full and rewarding lives.

———

Our family had lived in a beautiful area with heavily wooded parks and walking trails that weave through gentle hills and valleys and tributaries of the Rouge River leading to nearby Lake Ontario. It was a great area for raising a family. After our sons grew up and had homes of their own, taking our little granddaughter on one of those walks took a lot longer than when Chris and I walked on our own. As we pushed the empty stroller, Alexa would stop to pick the dandelions that we considered to be weeds. She discovered that if she blew on the fading flower, the tiny petals would all fly away. She gave us a different appreciation for what we had previously taken for granted.

We have remained connected to the West Hill area of Scarborough East, even after moving our "empty nest" to a more practical condominium apartment about twenty-five minutes west of there. Our family physician and dentist are there, as are other medical specialists who take good care of us. Our hospital is there. The UTSC, my alma mater, is there.

Vera, who had left Jamaica when Chris and I got married, did very well in Canada. It might have been more than twenty-five years after we moved to Canada that she invited me to her home. It was a large, older, multi-storey house in the Oakwood – Vaughan – St. Clair area of Toronto, not far from popular Jamaican eateries, barber shops, hair salons, and remittance agents for sending money abroad. Vera was caring for several seniors in her home. I wasn't surprised. This was entrepreneurial, caring Vera at her best. She took me to one of the upper floors of the house, which had large windows and afforded a wide view of the houses on the other side of her street. There was a purpose, of course. Vera wanted my advice and I felt proud and ready to share my wisdom generously.

"Miss Mary Anne, you see that house across the road?" Vera was pointing toward a house even larger than the one we were in, which appeared well maintained, at least on the outside.

"Yes, Vera."

"I am thinking of buying it. What do you think?"

"Do you think you can get enough for your house to enable you to purchase that one, Vera?"

"I'm not planning to sell this one, Miss Mary Anne. I am thinking of having both."

I was speechless and felt inadequate. Vera had succeeded well beyond my capacity to offer advice. I smiled and gave her a hug.

Whenever I think about Vera, as I often do, I always remember, with gratitude, how much she obviously cared about me and how fortunate I was to have had her in my life.

Chapter 6

A Delicate Balance

TAKEN BY SURPRISE WHEN NICK told me that, among his friends, I was the only mother who worked full time, I asked him how he felt about that. I instantly felt numb and held my breath waiting for his response. He was sixteen at the time. Stefan was thirteen. Having managed to get through all those years without having a crisis we couldn't survive, I had thought I wouldn't have to face a conversation with my sons about the pros and cons of being a working mom. I began to fear that I might have let my sons down, that Nick might have felt I had neglected him. But wasn't it too late to be able to do anything about that now? I wondered how Stefan felt. What had I done to my sons? What could I do at this stage? I started to breathe again and swallowed hard when, to my immense relief, my darling Nick said, "If working makes you happy, Mom, I am happy." I hugged my son as tightly as I could.

When our sons were in elementary school, my mother would come to our home to be with them when they got home from school. She would remain until either Chris or I got home from work. I was very grateful for this arrangement but it wasn't without its challenges. From time to time, especially when I mentioned that I had been speaking with Daddy on the telephone, Mommy would remind me that my ability to work depended on her being present to take care of the boys in my absence. That wasn't just an idle threat.

I still feel guilty, some forty years or so after the fact, about arranging for Chris to get chicken pox from Nick, so that he would be home with Stef when he got it. Mommy had not yet had chicken pox. At her age, we couldn't risk having her exposed. We told her to stay away from our home until it was safe for her to return. I had been staying home with Nick and it was obvious that Stef would be next because as soon as he got home from school, each day, he would head for Nick's bed to have fun with his brother. Realizing my dilemma as a working mother, I needed help so that I could return to the office. I saw a solution in the fact that Chris had not yet had chicken pox, so I encouraged Nick to be as affectionate as he normally was toward his dad. My plan worked. Chris and Stef both came down with chicken pox at the same time and that was when I realized that adults really should not get chicken pox. Unlike Stef, who had a very mild case of the chicken pox, Chris became very sick. His rash was everywhere; absolutely everywhere. Chris was home with Stef, but it was Stef who was caring for his dad while I returned to work and Nick returned to school.

———

As the telephone call that Debra had made to me seeking my advice on a possible career move was coming to an end, she asked what was for her perhaps the most important question of our forty-five-minute conversation. "Mary Anne," this highly competent and well-respected head of internal audit for a successful multinational group of companies asked, "How did you balance the demands of your career and your family?"

Somehow, I must have given the impression that I had figured out how to do that. I really hadn't. That whole superwoman persona is a myth, as far as I am concerned.

I found myself, yet again, reflecting on the fact that while I have been asked that question by dozens of women, no man had ever suggested to me that it might be a factor in his consideration of a career opportunity. To be fair, that is not to say that I have never heard men allude to the impact of being away from their families while on special assignments. I have been told, "My wife looks after things."

I have also heard, "My wife is really the brain in our family, but she put me through my MBA and then gave up her career so that I could pursue mine."

Infrequently, I have met women in high-profile positions whose husbands have accepted the very important but lower-profile role of minister of home affairs, as a former High Commissioner to Canada described it. Having more often found women in these very senior high-profile positions to be single, I use every opportunity that I have to thank the husbands who hold the positions of ministers of home affairs or in other ways sacrifice their own career opportunities in support of their wives' career aspirations.

And there is no doubt whatsoever, in my mind, that men who have families might also regret not being able to achieve work–life balance. When a former colleague chose to retire from the bank after a very successful career, he told me that for thirty-five years, the bank had been his life. He also told me that as a grandfather, he wanted to try to make up for the time that he had not spent with his two sons by spending more time with his two grandsons.

While employment equity percentages or absolute numbers can help to tell a story, what speaks best for progress in providing access to opportunities is the culture of an organization. This can be difficult to define but is the kind of thing we know or can sense — especially where it does not exist. Perhaps that's why role models and mentorship can be so effective and perhaps that's why I am often asked how I achieved whatever it is others think I have achieved. Sometimes organizations need to more fully appreciate the subtle and systemic barriers that prevent women and, in more recent times, progressive men from having the opportunity to contribute to the fullest extent of their abilities.

I once received a standing ovation when I advised a group of more than three hundred professional women to choose their partners well. But when I went on to tell them that I also gave that advice to men, I saw heads bow in agreement.

I believe both women and men need the understanding and selfless support of their partners in order to balance the demands of their personal lives and the demands of their careers. I was fortunate to have that kind of understanding and support from my husband.

———

Scotiabankers were very much a part of my mother's life. In her early eighties, Mommy purchased a one-bedroom apartment in a new condominium property. She made full use of the apartment's large sunroom for her year-round indoor garden and spent hours caring for the many plants she grew there. The apartment overlooked a beautifully landscaped courtyard, which also gave her pleasure. My office was located just a short drive away, and some of my Scotiabank colleagues, dear friends, would sometimes join me for lunch with her. Margaret Brathwaite, Shelley-Ann Barlow, Georgia Geropoulos, and Carol Simpson enjoyed being with Mommy as much as she enjoyed having them in her home.

Mommy no longer had a car, but she got around quite well using public transit. The trip to her Scotiabank branch required two buses each way. One day, during a snowstorm, Gigi Coelho, her branch manager, spotted Mommy as she was leaving the bank, stopped what she was working on and drove my mother home. It had not been wise for Mommy to have left home in that snowstorm. I sent the staff at the branch a large, heart-shaped chocolate chip cookiegram to thank them for taking good care of their customer, my mom. When I was invited to speak at a Toronto Scotiabankers' association dinner a few months after that incident, I called Gigi to the stage to recognize her exemplary service in the presence of a few hundred other Scotiabankers. Gigi and I had not met each other prior to that occasion. A few years later, she was transferred to the Scotiabank branch where I did my banking. I very much enjoyed having her as my branch manager.

On her way home from a subsequent trip to her Scotiabank branch, Mommy found herself confused about the bus route and which bus she should take. I had also started to suspect that she wasn't taking her medication as prescribed, so I got her a pill container with labelled sections for each day. Every weekend when I visited, I put the pills that she should be taking during the following week, in each day's section. My suspicion was confirmed as I would see that she would sometimes skip days and at other times, she would take more than one day's pills in a single day. My worry escalated when I saw that one of the heating elements on her electric stove had melted. I took it home with me and showed it to Chris. He told me that the burner had obviously been left on high for an extended period of time. It was becoming obvious that, for her own safety, my mom's living arrangements would have to change.

As Mommy's ability to take care of herself as well as she had done in the past started to deteriorate, there were times when I would have to listen for subtle clues, like the tone of her voice when

I called to say that I was about to leave for Ottawa for one of my United Way of Canada board meetings.

"How are you, Mommy?"

"Fine."

But there was a weakness in her voice that indicated distress and caused me to question her further. With a bit of prodding from me, Mommy revealed that she had just bought a vacuum cleaner from a salesman she had let into her apartment. I left my office immediately and instead of driving to the airport to get my flight to Ottawa, I headed to Mommy's building. What I discovered was that my mother had purchased a vacuum cleaner for $2,500, causing me to remark that at that price it should also be able to prepare her meals. While obviously unsure of what was happening, Mommy had given the salesman her chequebook so that he could fill in all the details, leaving only her signature for her to add. It was after he left her with the huge box containing the vacuum cleaner that she had just purchased, a contraption that I had difficulty lifting myself and she would have found impossible to operate, that Mommy realized she had made a mistake.

The vacuum-cleaner salesman had apparently been let into the building by another resident and, while there, had used the opportunity to visit other apartments. When I questioned the concierge who would normally screen visitors, he seemed unaware of the man's presence in the building. Tracking down the unscrupulous salesman became my priority. Getting to Ottawa would have to happen later. I needed to act quickly. It was a Friday afternoon and I needed to get the cheque back before the salesman took it to the bank. I used the purchase documents he had left behind to track him down and I threatened him with every legal action I could imagine. I insisted he return to Mommy's building immediately with the cheque. He did. Accompanied by the concierge, he came to the apartment to collect the vacuum cleaner. I asked him how he would feel about some other salesman doing to his mother what he had done to my mother. Perhaps I shouldn't have been surprised when he told me that his mother had already purchased one of his vacuum cleaners.

Scotiabank hosted some fraud-against-seniors information sessions. I took Mommy to one that was held at the Royal Ontario Museum. By then, she seemed to have no recollection of what had happened to her. It was simply an outing with her daughter, something she always enjoyed.

The concierge at Mommy's building kept an eye on her as well as he could. When, one day, she fell on the icy sidewalk on her way back from a trip to the fruit market a short walk away, he did as much as she would allow him to do when he realized she had badly bruised one of her knees. That incident happened while I was in Ottawa for another one of my United Way board meetings. I learned about the fall when I visited Mommy after returning to Toronto. I could see that the wound had not been cleaned thoroughly. I could see that there were still grains of sand in the wound. A few days later, she called me to say she could not put any weight on that knee. Mommy would have to be admitted to hospital.

During a meeting with my management team at the bank, they could tell that I was distracted and questioned me as to what was going on. I cried as I told them what had happened to Mommy. I also told them how guilty and hypocritical I felt that I was away working on caring for people across the country whom I didn't even know, while my own mother had fallen on the sidewalk with no one to give her the care she had needed.

My friends Margaret, Georgia, and Carol, who would visit her at her apartment, visited Mommy in the hospital. I placed my favourite photos of my parents, my handsome father and my beautiful mother, taken when my mother was pregnant with me, on the table by her bed. The result was remarkable. Her nurses, her geriatrician, and even the young Jamaican fellow who mopped the floor of her room started spending more time with her and asking her about her life. It was as though they were seeing her as a younger person who was there to get better rather than an old person who had little life left in her or someone who was incapable of communicating with them. There was, in fact, a lot of life left in my mom and a lot of joy that she would continue to give to those who loved her.

———

While Mommy and I sat in the waiting area of the neurologist's office, I asked her, "What's most important to you, Mommy?"

"My privacy and my independence," she responded without a moment's hesitation.

A feeling of tenderness came over my head, like the beginning of a headache. Somehow, I had known that was exactly what she would say and, sadly, I knew she was about to lose her privacy and her independence.

It felt like I was sending my mom off to boarding school as I signed the required documents. It was impossible for me to conceal my tears. Mommy reached out and rested her hand on mine in an attempt to soothe me. I don't think she really knew what was happening.

My support group of friends from Scotiabank helped me to move the television and lounge chair from her apartment into her private room in the long-term care home where she would spend the last few years of her life. I placed my favourite photograph of her in the large frame next to the door to her room so everyone who came by would want to get to know my mom.

Chapter 7

Being a Scotiabanker

IN *THE SCOTIABANK STORY: A History of the Bank of Nova Scotia, 1832–1982*, it is written that in 1889, Thomas Fyshe, who ran the bank for almost the entire last quarter of the nineteenth century, had stated in response to a letter from a former colleague, "We have been repeatedly urged to open a Branch in Jamaica but we have always resisted — principally because we had the impression the Island was unprogressive...." To Mr. Fyshe's credit, he visited Jamaica the very next month and found that his former impression of the island was out of date. According to *The Scotiabank Story*, Mr. Fyshe attributed improved economic conditions in Jamaica to "a number of political and social reforms ... advances in agriculture ... improvement in shipping service" and "greatly improved output of the island's traditional products, sugar, rum, and coffee and a new crop, bananas, now being grown for the United States market." Scotiabank opened its first branch in Jamaica that year, 1889, making it the first Canadian bank to have a branch beyond the United States and the United Kingdom.

It wasn't until 1897, eight years later, that the bank opened its first branch in Toronto.

When, not long after I started as a computer programmer at Scotiabank, my colleague, a blond Canadian-born woman who was a business analyst, observed that I was competent and conscientious, so probably also ambitious, I was surprised that she saw my prospects at the bank as being limited. My parents had always told me that I was wonderful. When I knew I wasn't being particularly wonderful, I took their unequivocal confidence in me as a not-too-subtle message that they expected me to be wonderful. So, that night, before falling asleep, I thought about what my co-worker had said and decided that I had two choices. I could either roll over and play dead, or I could ignore her. I chose the latter. Some years later, when she was leaving the bank, she was still a business analyst and I was a senior manager, well on my way toward being appointed a senior vice president. I was convinced that my colleague wasn't trying to be hurtful. I believed, reflecting on her own realities, she was trying to help me to manage my expectations so that I wouldn't be disappointed if my realities fell short of my ambitions.

New to the banking industry and armed with only a background in information technology when my family arrived in Canada in 1976, I thought it would be wise to pursue courses that would help me to acquire an understanding of the world of banking. I attended evening and weekend classes at the University of Toronto and York University and earned the accreditation of Fellow of the Institute of Canadian Bankers with honours. I then pursued part-time undergraduate studies at the University of Toronto and, after seven years of attending classes in the evenings, earned a bachelor of arts degree, majoring in commerce. Within months of completing my degree, I was appointed vice president for executive offices and international systems development at Scotiabank. The year was 1989 and I was thirty-eight years old. None of this would have been possible without the incredible support I received from Chris. He would ensure that he was home with the boys while I was out at my classes. He became an expert at preparing a selection of dishes for dinner when I would be late coming home. He would also turn me away when I tried to watch television with the rest of the family before I had completed the course assignment I was working on.

———

Three weeks after joining the bank in 1976, I was sent to Bermuda, to the envy of my colleagues in international systems who had never had the opportunity to travel outside of Canada on business. Scotiabank had an agreement with a commercial bank in Bermuda for the provision of computer-systems support, along with some other administrative services. The hardware and associated software used by the bank in Bermuda was not familiar to Scotiabank's team in Canada. When I arrived in Bermuda, the bank's management asked me why it had taken me so long to respond to their request for support. I made three trips to Bermuda in my first year at Scotiabank. I would work until midnight each night so that I could return home more quickly. One night, during my second trip, I decided to walk back to my hotel rather than using a taxi. I was exhausted and I needed to clear my head. As I walked up the steep hill on a poorly lit road, I heard footsteps approaching me. I immediately started to regret my decision to walk by myself so late at night. As the footsteps got closer, I mouthed a silent prayer. "Good night, Miss," was what I heard the young man say as we passed each other. The following morning, as I walked to work, a fellow sweeping the street close to where the bank was located stopped as I passed by him and smiled as he said, "Good morning, Miss." When I arrived at the office, the head of human resources was waiting to inform me that the bank's senior management had become aware of the hours I had been working and had directed her to send me back to my hotel to rest. I protested and she sympathized, but she had orders she had been given and was required to follow. Instead of taking me directly to my hotel, she first gave me a tour of beautiful Bermuda.

I never felt sufficiently qualified to call myself a banker. My responsibilities at the bank involved using technology, computer systems, to make functions and processes more efficient and reliable. These systems were developed for use in both international and Canadian operations. Most were for banking applications but some were for corporate functions such as human resources and finance. Although I did not consider myself a banker, the work that I did required me to acquire a good understanding of the various functions I supported. I loved learning about various aspects of the bank's business and was always open to accepting assignments that increased my knowledge of financial services.

Armed with a healthy awareness of my abilities and areas where I needed further development, a commitment to lifelong learning, and a genuine respect for what I could learn from others who were specialists in their fields, I never hesitated to embrace new challenges. I felt there was little I could not accomplish. And, unlike some of my colleagues, who were more focused on their next promotion or their career goals, I was simply determined to do my job exceptionally well. A satisfactory or above-average performance rating would not be good enough for me. I was satisfied only with outstanding. I worked hard to achieve that.

As a relatively junior Scotiabanker, I ventured into dangerous places like senior management steering committee meetings. I would leave fairly unscathed and with the approvals and support I needed. I once had the dubious honour of presenting a case for a huge project to the president of the bank and his executive vice presidents, a presentation that lasted more than an hour. The project would involve using technology to achieve much greater efficiency in key areas of the bank's operation and enable increased functionality and additional product features. I didn't realize I was supposed to be nervous. The project was approved, and I managed it through to its successful completion. The exposure was good for me, because the project was a success. Had it not been a success, the consequences would no doubt have been detrimental to my career at the bank.

Sometimes we need to take risks in order to achieve success. My colleagues at the bank who were unwilling to offer to take the lead on the more challenging assignments did not have access to the kinds of opportunities that I had. I often use the example of turtles, who must stick their necks out from under their protective shells in order to move forward. Exposing themselves might result in them becoming turtle soup, but without taking that risk, they can go nowhere. At times, we must step outside environments we find comfortable and accommodating in order to grow.

———

My early years at Scotiabank also involved a few trips to the Bahamas. Those were interesting times. Trust businesses in tax havens such as the Cayman Islands and the Bahamas were getting a lot of scrutiny from the American government, which was eager to get access to information on the financial holdings of residents who had chosen to domicile their accounts outside of the U.S.A. I discovered it was in my best interest not to route my air travel through Miami, but instead to secure direct flights between Canada and the Bahamas. I also discovered that the Bahamian immigration authorities had little appetite for someone travelling on a Jamaican passport for the purpose of doing work or conducting business in the Bahamas. I would be questioned extensively and my luggage would be searched.

Chris and I had every intention of applying for Canadian citizenship for our family as soon as we were eligible. My experiences with the immigration authorities in the Bahamas reinforced the wisdom of our intentions. We submitted our applications for citizenship as soon as we met the three-year permanent residency requirement. The thorough citizenship court judge saw from the entries in my passport that I had been out of the country for weeks that he quickly determined would have reduced my time since landing in Canada to less than three years. Chris and the boys, not having travelled out of the country with me on those occasions, were in the clear. The judge told me I had not satisfied the three-year requirement. I appealed his assessment politely but firmly and he accepted my argument. In 1979, Chris and I rejoiced when our family was sworn in as Canadian citizens. As we prepared to take the oath of citizenship, our Stefan protested when he was handed the Bible, saying "I can't read," and opted instead to place his hand over his heart. I remembered the promise I had made when we were leaving Jamaica. Canada was going to be good for us and we were going to be good for Canada.

The documentation of our Canadian citizenship included a certificate declaring that each of us was "a Canadian citizen under the provisions of the Citizenship Act and, as such, is entitled to all the rights, powers and privileges and is subject to all the obligations, duties and liabilities of a Canadian citizen."

The certificates were accompanied by a letter from the secretary of state of Canada, which read:

> Now that you have received your certificate of Canadian citizenship, it is with a great deal of pleasure that I convey to you my personal congratulations and on behalf of your government — warmest best wishes.
>
> This is an important step you have taken — important for you and important for Canada. For you it means an

opportunity to share fully in the blessings of this land and, equally important, a responsibility to play your part to pre-serve and strengthen the ideals upon which our country rests. For Canada it means that you have chosen this among all the nations of the world as the one which you want to call "home." We are honoured by your choice.

With the rights and privileges you have acquired as well as the obligations which your citizenship carries, you share with all Canadians the ancient liberties of a free people living together in harmony under a democratic government which recognizes the rights of all of its citizens.

Again my congratulations. May the future hold for you a measure of the happiness which is Canada.

Yours sincerely,

David MacDonald

Some years later, Chris and I attended a citizenship court cere-mony at the invitation of presiding citizenship court judge Pamela Appelt. It was an opportunity to take in the proceedings without the distraction of being personally involved.

Later still, while a member of provincial parliament (MPP), I was invited to speak to new Canadians at their swearing-in. As I looked out at the hundreds of people present, a gathering that included women and men of every race, individuals there on their own, and families spanning two and three generations, what I saw in each of them was the smile on their face and the hope in their eyes. I asked them to recognize that as Canadian citizens, they were entitled to rights enshrined in our country's Charter of Rights and Freedoms, but along with those rights came responsibilities that were equally important. I asked them not to forget how excited they obviously were to now be citizens of Canada. I also challenged them not to become complacent or to be too quick to complain when things didn't go exactly as they would like, but to do their part to help to preserve the good that had made them want to be Canadians and to make life better for themselves and for others.

As my sons got older, I started to enjoy my travels on Scotiabank business. Scotiabank was the largest single shareholder in Maduro & Curiel's Bank (MCB) in the Netherlands Antilles. The relationship also involved the provision, by Scotiabank, of certain management services such as internal audits. In those years, our bank's internal audit function was known as the inspection department, and its reputation was as intimidating as its name. I was sent to MCB's head office in Curaçao with the inspection department's blessing, apparently to "help the medicine go down." I returned on subsequent occasions to facilitate carriage of some of Scotiabank's responsibilities and to provide project-management and systems-design assistance where needed. At my introductory meeting with Lionel Capriles, MCB's managing director, a man highly regarded as an outstanding business leader and a generous banker in local circles, I was welcomed with a small arrangement of flowers. Members of my team would always receive the fullest cooperation and support of MCB's management team.

I also visited Ireland on a few occasions. The first two occasions involved the acquisition of banking software to support our bank's opening of its first branch in India. At that time, India was not allowing IBM hardware into the country. The bank acquired computer hardware from a large British manufacturer, International Computers Ltd. (ICL), through its distributor in India and, with the assistance of staff in the bank's Pacific regional office, software from Triple A Systems, a developer in Ireland, was selected.

On one of my visits to Dublin, I accompanied a few of the fellows from the software company to a shop around the corner from their office to get sandwiches for lunch. I noticed a large church across from the shop where we had placed our orders. It had seemed to me that pubs and churches were equally prominent in Dublin but while I had been taken to several pubs, I had not been into a church. I saw the opportunity to make a quick visit to the church while we waited for the sandwiches to be made. This, however, would entail crossing a busy city street and I had already complained that Dubliners drove like Jamaicans. I headed to the curb by the pedestrian crossing and, to my surprise, the cars going in both directions immediately screeched to a halt. I waved to the drivers in appreciation and crossed as quickly as I could walk. I had the same experience on my return from the church to the sandwich shop. I told the fellows what had happened and apologized for my earlier criticism of the driving in Dublin. One of the fellows said the drivers could obviously tell I was a foreigner. I naively asked him how they would have been able to figure that out. The fellows all blushed with embarrassment. It was only then that it occurred to me that apart from the large billboards advertising Guinness Stout with the caption "Black is Beautiful," I had not seen any evidence of racial diversity in that city.

Tony Kilduff, owner of Triple A Systems, and his lovely wife were warm and gracious hosts. They invited me and my Scotiabank colleague to dinner at their home, and at one of Ireland's historic castles just outside of Dublin.

———

The automation of the bank's operations in India was not without its challenges. We had a firm deadline for getting the system fully installed. Staff in the bank's Pacific regional office, located in the Philippines, were having difficulty securing the cooperation of government officials in order that we could have an accurate and full understanding of India's statutory reporting requirements. Without detailed knowledge of those requirements, we were in trouble. I reached out to Abhilash Bhachech, a senior business analyst on the international systems team in Toronto. Abhilash held an MBA in management information systems and international finance from an American university and a bachelor of commerce degree, having majored in accounting and auditing, from the University of Bombay. He also held a postgraduate certification in public accounting and auditing from the Institute of Chartered Accountants in India.

Abhilash had joined Scotiabank in 1982, after arriving in Canada from India. His parents still lived in India. His wife had recently given birth to their first son. I asked Abhilash if he would be willing to go to India for four weeks. I had already secured approval for his wife and young son to accompany him. His assignment would be to work with the Indian government to determine their reporting requirements and to define those requirements for development within the new system. I told Abhilash that the bank would pay all travel and living expenses for his wife, their son, and himself even if they chose to stay with his parents in India. He discussed the request with his wife and she agreed.

The mission was a success. Abhilash completed his assignment ahead of schedule and stayed on to participate in the official opening ceremony of the bank's fully automated branch operation in India by Scotiabank's chairman, Cedric Ritchie. The ceremony included a symbolic but very important activation of the new computer system.

With a presence in some fifty countries, Scotiabank took great pride in promoting itself as the most international of Canada's banks. I was even prouder of the diversity of the bank's staff. In the 1980s, years before the value of diversity was embraced by Canada's business sector as a competitive advantage, Abhilash Bhachech was a vivid example of that. A brilliant man with what appeared to be limitless potential, Abhilash left Scotiabank in 1993 for the Office of the Superintendent of Financial Institutions, an independent agency of the government of Canada, where his several roles included that of managing director for risk measurement and analytics assessment services. In 2012, Abhilash was appointed inspector of banks and trust companies for the Central Bank of The Bahamas.

———

Like many of my colleagues, I referred to myself as a Scotiabanker. I was warmly welcomed when I joined the bank and it seemed I was given opportunities that few of my colleagues were as fortunate to have. One such opportunity was an invitation to attend the bank's annual general meeting in Halifax, Nova Scotia. I was a member of the international systems management team, albeit not at a very senior level, at the time. None of my international systems colleagues had ever attended the annual general meeting. Apart from the itinerary that had been sent to me, I had little knowledge of what to expect.

Scotiabank's annual general meeting was more than just a meeting. It was a grand experience. Local bank staff greeted guests and other staff visiting from Toronto when we arrived at the airport and drove us to the hotel where the meeting would take place. I heard that the local staff liked being able to introduce themselves to staff from the bank's head office and saw it as an occasion for networking.

Beyond the required formal business proceedings, it was an opportunity for me to meet long-standing elderly shareholders who wanted me to know that they had owned shares of the bank since before I was born. It didn't seem to matter whether their holdings were large or small, they were all welcomed guests and they obviously all felt proud to be there, valued and important. Some told me that dividends from their Bank of Nova Scotia shares had long been an important and reliable source of income for them. I met ladies for whom the occasion appeared to be one of their favourite outings of the year. They helped themselves to the delicious lobster sandwiches, and whatever they could not consume during the lunchtime reception could be stowed in their large handbags and enjoyed later at home. These shareholders were everyday Nova Scotians and there were many of them. I was struck by their loyalty to the bank.

The formal dinner event was an assembly of Nova Scotia's elite, a grand affair. Some of the men wore plaid Scottish kilts. The others wore dark tuxedos. I wore a simple but attractive full-length black dress that fitted perfectly. I have always preferred to feel comfortable in the clothes I wear. I wanted to look gracious but I had no interest in standing out in any crowd.

I arrived at the pre-dinner reception after many of the guests had already arrived and were enjoying liqueurs. That turned out to be a mistake. The men all looked older than I was and they seemed to all know each other. It might have been my imagination playing tricks on me, but I felt like the conversations came to an abrupt halt and all eyes turned toward the doorway where I stood motionless and numb, wishing I had stayed in my hotel room. My reaction must have been obvious. Frank Polanksi, the senior vice president of international banking, came to my rescue. He left the group he was with, walked toward me with his arm extended, and very kindly escorted me into the room. As the conversations resumed, some of the guests came over to greet me. Some asked me where I worked in the Caribbean. Others asked me when I had arrived in Canada, how long I would be staying, and had I come only to attend the annual meeting.

As soon as I saw an opening, I left the reception room and headed to the ballroom where dinner would be served. I thought it best to see where I was seated and to familiarize myself with the names of others who would be at the same table. I would then wait there to greet my guests, a preferred approach to making an entrance like I had inadvertently done for the reception. Just before I located my table, I heard a voice, a high-spirited female voice, coming from the entrance to the ballroom. I don't remember her name but she introduced herself as being a politician in Nova Scotia. What I do remember is what she said when she called out to me as she entered the ballroom: "A woman!" We hugged each other warmly.

———

At the bank, I served on a task force for the advancement of women in the workplace. I was a vice president at the time and, while 75 percent of the bank's employees were women, I didn't need more than my ten fingers to count the number of women at Scotiabank who held positions at my level or above.

We conducted a bank-wide survey to help us understand how Scotiabank's staff perceived accessibility to promotional opportunities at the bank. The results of the survey revealed that men and women shared similar concerns. The primary concern was that if you were not a member of the "old boys' club," you would have less access to opportunities at the bank. The survey results also revealed the old boys' club did not necessarily consist of old boys, but of anyone who had access that others did not have. I could relate to that. I believe I had benefited from that.

It had felt good to know that my opinion was appreciated but when I received calls from human resources from time to time, asking me to recommend people for appointment to senior positions, I would realize there were people I didn't know who were also qualified but might not be considered because there was no one putting their names forward.

We renamed the task force with the scope being broadened to encompass equity in the workplace, even as we maintained the focus on improving the representation of women in senior management roles. The decision was also made to post senior-level vacancies so that interested individuals with the required qualifications could put their own names forward for consideration.

———

I didn't always have bosses I admired, but I always did my part to contribute to the success of the bank. In so doing, I also made my bosses look good and I had no problem with that. The alternative would have been unacceptable to the conscientious professional I considered myself to be. I also realized that I could learn from everyone, even if what I learned was how not to deal with certain situations.

Twice, the tables were turned, resulting in individuals to whom I had previously reported now reporting to me. In one case, a former boss asked me for a job in my area while acknowledging that there was "water under the bridge." During the time that I had reported to him, I had mentioned something about a Jamaican newspaper, to which he had responded, "You had newspapers in Jamaica?" His silly comments to an Asian colleague of mine had caused her to leave the bank for a job elsewhere. I told him that as long as that water remained under the bridge, we should be fine. In the other case, I was promoted to a role where someone to whom I had previously reported would become a member of my team, one of my direct reports. In a meeting with me, when I had reported to him, he had started a sentence with "What you need to get through your thick skull is ..." When the reorganization that would have him reporting to me was announced, I initiated the conversation with him, asking him to tell me how he felt about the new situation. His response was that he would have had a problem with the change in the reporting relationship if it had been someone other than me.

I had another boss who arrived in a department where I was already a member of the management team. He went through the files of each member of the management team and reduced the last performance assessment that we had each had to a C rating. That act was symbolic only, as the ratings we already had would continue to stand. However, my colleagues and I interpreted it as a warning, or perhaps a threat, the message being that there was a new sheriff in town. When the next round of annual performance assessments was done, the fellow proudly proclaimed to all of us that he had given his first A rating, ever. I was the person who had received the A. One of my colleagues asked me how I had managed to change our boss's impression of me. I told my colleague that I certainly had not done anything differently, so obviously our boss had simply smartened up.

In "Anthem," one of his many beautiful songs, Leonard Cohen, an exceptionally talented Canadian poet, songwriter, and singer, gives good advice about appreciating that cracks let light in. Notwithstanding my inevitable share of unpleasant "personal development" experiences, thanks to a few of the people I worked with throughout my time at the bank, I felt like I belonged at Scotiabank.

I reported to Marty Schulmeister from May 1988 to February 1989, while he was vice president for the bank's projects and programs management office. I was then a senior program manager. He was a brilliant man, an American aeronautical engineer who had previously been employed by TRW, an automotive and aerospace company, and had worked with the U.S.A.'s National Aeronautics and Space Administration (NASA), managing the launches of unmanned spacecraft. Marty had a no-nonsense reputation and I know some of my male colleagues trod very carefully in their interactions with him. He was my favourite of all the bosses I had in my twenty-six years at Scotiabank. What I liked most about Marty was that he didn't ever seem to be intimidated by me. That allowed us to have frank exchanges with each other and I knew I could always count on his support. I really appreciated that.

It was while I reported to Marty that I was promoted to the vice president level. The position was vice president of executive offices and international systems development. As a vice president, I would subsequently be given responsibility for the projects and programs management office, retail services in the domestic customer service centres, and corporate and commercial services, also in the domestic customer service centres. In November 1998, I was promoted to senior vice president for electronic banking business services.

I earned a reputation for taking on special assignments and cleaning up functions that were in trouble. These would be added to my regular responsibilities until they were in a condition to be restored to a more permanent place in the organizational structure. Because of the nature and variety of these special assignments and the business functions for which I had responsibility, I had access to several executives other than those to whom I reported directly.

The senior positions I held at the bank also contributed to my profile in Toronto's Caribbean community. I sometimes found it difficult to determine whether I had been invited to speak at community events as a private individual or as a Scotiabanker. I would always ensure that my remarks could be viewed favourably in either context.

Sometime around 1994, when Tropicana Community Services was moving from its basement office in a strip plaza to a larger, better-appointed location, I called the head of the bank's real estate department and asked him if there might be a conference-room table that he could donate to the organization. He promised he would see what he had in storage. The beautiful table Tropicana received was a very pleasant surprise to its management team and its board members and continues to hold a place of prominence in the organization's boardroom.

I don't recall the precise year in the 1990s, but when Lloyd McKell, the equity officer for the Toronto District School Board, needed support for a large group of young steel-pan players from Trinidad, he reached out to me and I knew I could pick up the telephone and ask Calum Johnston, the executive vice president of international banking, for help. I had done a bit of research on the group and learned that they were from Laventille, a significantly challenged community. The steel band had won the top prize in the junior category in that year's carnival; however, the prize, a trip to Canada, came with insufficient funds to cover their expenses. Calum willingly agreed to sponsor the group generously. The timing of their visit to Toronto coincided with a celebration for long-service Scotiabankers, which was held in a ballroom at the Harbour Castle Hilton on Toronto's waterfront. The steel band from Laventille provided the main entertainment that evening, stealing the show from the moment they opened the event with the anthems of Canada and Trinidad and Tobago, proving that calypso is only one of the genres of music that can be performed expertly on the pans. They were truly impressive, not only because of their musical talent but also because of their delightful personalities. The girls and boys were also a sight to behold, sharply dressed in well-tailored black pants, white dress shirts, and red blazers — Scotiabank red, no less. Throughout the dinner, guests were leaving their tables to get closer to the young people. I heard about conversations with Scotiabankers and their partners that revealed the challenges the young people faced, as well as the appreciation and joy they expressed at being able to have the experience that the bank had provided. I felt so good that the bank was able to give these young people an opportunity that I knew they would not soon forget.

In September 1998, the *Toronto Star* newspaper ran a full-page feature article along with photographs of me and my family in its

"Life" section. The article was entitled "Banker with heart profits community." Based on my own observations of the bank's involvement in a wide variety of community initiatives, there had been no reason for me to think that bankers did not have a positive reputation, or that whatever I was doing was viewed as exceptional.

My senior volunteer involvement on boards of not-for-profit organizations was well supported by the bank. The bank responded generously when I asked for financial support and there was never any issue regarding the time that I spent in carrying out the responsibilities related to the positions. Of course, I still had to deliver on my responsibilities at Scotiabank, and my performance assessments always reflected my outstanding commitment and contribution to the company, as well as the competence of my very capable, conscientious, and loyal team.

When technical issues arose with the electronic services my area provided to a very large corporate customer, I knew it was important to inform Peter Godsoe, Scotiabank's chief executive officer. One of the members of the family who owned the company was also a member of Scotiabank's board of directors. I told Mr. Godsoe a bit about the nature of the problem and I assured him that we were doing everything possible to solve it. He expressed confidence in my team's ability to get the job done. I breathed a deep sigh of relief when my team's efforts were successful.

Mr. Godsoe was also very supportive of the work that I did with the University of Toronto, the United Way of Greater Toronto, and the Canadian Club of Toronto. He and his father were among four or five fathers and sons who had served as presidents in the more than 120-year history of the club. He saw my volunteer activities as good for the bank's image and he shared with me that he missed being able to spend more time on those kinds of activities. My son Nick and I have so far been the only mother and son to serve as presidents of the Canadian Club of Toronto.

Peter Godsoe invited Chris and me to accompany the Scotiabank board of directors on their visit to Jamaica. It was a very special few days and marked the first time that the board of the Scotiabank Group had ever met in Jamaica. On the flight from Toronto to Montego Bay, I saw Denham Jolly. I will say more about Denny later. We chatted just long enough for me to tell him the reason why Chris and I were on our way to Jamaica. The following night, the group from Scotiabank had dinner together at the clubhouse on the beautiful Rose Hall golf course. We were treated to entertainment by Karen Smith. No one was more surprised than I was, when Karen dedicated one of her songs "to Mary Anne Chambers on behalf of my uncle, Mr. Denham Jolly." A deeply thoughtful and generous man, Denny has always had a unique way of sending messages. I believe his message that night was meant to convey that in the midst of, but yet different from, this exclusive group of notable and influential Canadians was a special daughter of Jamaica.

I made a good living working at the bank but my life was about a lot more than that. I enjoyed my work in the not-for-profit sector very much and, as my eligibility for early retirement from Scotiabank approached, I made it known within the bank and in the broader community, recognizing how tightly the community connected me with the bank, that I would likely retire as soon as I was eligible. Being debt free, financially sound, and with both our sons having graduated from university, there was nothing preventing me from doing that. After years of combining my volunteer work with my employment, I had developed a life plan and knew the direction I wanted my life to take when the time was right. My life plan included early retirement from the bank and more time dedicated to the not-for-profit sector.

The man who would be my last boss at the bank would from time to time ask me what I needed from him. I asked for his support in providing access to performance incentives for members of my management team. I also asked for help in securing more office space so that we could locate staff in less-cramped facilities. He always found a way to deliver.

I took my responsibility for ensuring the well-being of the hundreds of staff who reported either directly or indirectly to me very seriously. I believed that providing a positive, supportive working environment, where all members of my team would see themselves as valued and essential to the achievement of our ambitious objectives, would serve us all very well. Members of my team appreciated that. They knew that I was there for them.

I had been reporting directly to Albert for four years. Prior to that, I had reported to him indirectly as a member of his management team for around ten years. Albert had played an instrumental role in my progress through senior management positions over the years. We sometimes had disagreements that would cause me to feel frustrated and distressed. Chris would remind me that on previous occasions when that had happened, I would always find the energy I needed to persevere and to accomplish what was expected of me, and more. My performance assessments consistently reflected that.

My response to Albert's question about what I needed from him had always included an over-arching request, which was that I be involved in discussions where decisions were being made that would have an impact on my team and my areas of responsibility. How else could I lead my team with confidence? How else would members of my team know that they could always depend on me to be honest with them? I decided it was time to take the early retirement step when Albert did not live up to what I had said I absolutely needed from him in order to carry out my responsibilities effectively. The time had come when I no longer felt like I had the energy or the drive to fight for what I absolutely believed I needed in order to do my job. I felt like I could no longer trust the environment in which

I worked. I was unhappy enough that I discreetly sought the advice of an employment lawyer. That turned out to be unnecessary.

I received a phone call from Peter Godsoe, who was clearly not happy about the situation. He told me that I had always done what was right for the bank and the bank would honour my wishes and take good care of me. They did and they have.

I will always have a special place in my heart for Scotiabank. The bank helped to provide a soft landing when I arrived with my husband and our young sons in Canada and, in many ways, would serve as a launching pad for much of what I have been able to achieve and the quality of life that my family has been able to enjoy. There are feelings of pride and comfort in knowing that, as a retiree, I will always be a Scotiabanker.

Chapter 8

Governance

WHILE SERVING ON A FUNDRAISING campaign committee for the United Way of Greater Toronto, a fellow volunteer told me that someone in the Office of the Premier of Ontario had sought his help in identifying members of the Black community for appointment to boards of organizations associated with the government of Ontario. Grace-Edward Galabuzi, who is now an associate professor in the department of politics and public administration at Ryerson University, was the person in the premier's office. The New Democratic Party (NDP), under the leadership of the Honourable Bob Rae, governed the province of Ontario from 1990 to 1995. Grace-Edward asked me to consider serving either on the board of the Metro Toronto Convention Centre or the governing council of the University of Toronto. I believed serving on the governing council of the University of Toronto would be more challenging than being on the board of the convention centre, so I chose the university, and an interview with the chair of the university's governing council was arranged.

The fifty members of the governing council included University of Toronto administrative staff, faculty, students and alumni elected by their constituencies, senior officers in the administration appointed by the president, and sixteen lieutenant governor in council (government) appointees. I was one of the government appointees. The University of Toronto's unique-in-Canada, unicameral system of governance meant that there was no separate senate for academic matters. The academic board, one of three boards of the governing council, dealt with academic matters.

Being a government appointee did not mean that the government had influence over my contributions. It was only during the appointment process that I had contact with the government in relation to my role on the governing council. When my first three-year term ended, I was reappointed by the Conservative government led by the Honourable Mike Harris. That was also the government that reappointed me for my third three-year term. My reappointments involved only paperwork.

Student governors, on the other hand, seemed to walk a fine line between representing the concerns of their fellow students who had elected them and the interests of the institution. They focused on issues they considered to be of vital importance and often challenged proposals more forcefully than other members of the governing council. However, the commitment that I observed in each of my fellow governors, whether they were students, staff, faculty, alumni, administration, or government appointees, would serve as a model for wherever I would happen to serve. The absolutely outstanding professionalism and competence of the governing council secretariat also led me to establish an expectation that I have since maintained of what is necessary to support good corporate governance.

It took me at least a few cycles of meetings to grasp the workings of governance in such a complex environment but I soon became comfortable as a governor and started to really enjoy the experience. I served as a member of the business board and chaired the university affairs board, which provided me with greater opportunities to connect with students and to understand their issues. The student governors kept other governors and the senior administration accountable and focused on issues of vital importance to them.

At the time of year when governors deliberated the administration's proposals on tuition fees, we could expect to have dozens of students with placards in the governing council chambers, registering their protests. As an executive of a major bank, I knew students were referring to me when placards would be positioned in the area where I was seated, denouncing the presence of bankers on the governing council and the influence students perceived large corporate donors as having over the university administration. I was in good company. Tony Comper, then president and chief executive officer for the Bank of Montreal, was chair of the governing council for some of my term. It was he who asked me to serve as vice chair. Under Tony's leadership, Bank of Montreal had acquired an impressive reputation for its promotion of women to senior leadership positions.

I got to know some of the more dedicated student activists well. Ironically, those experiences taught me to look beyond the somewhat offensive approaches to ensure that I could gain an understanding of the issues that were of concern. There were a number of occasions while I served in the Ontario government when I was happy that I had acquired that ability. But I would caution against assuming that my willingness to separate the approach from the issue is the norm. More often than not, inappropriate approaches distract attention from the issues that we want people in positions of influence to understand, and when that happens there is the risk that something of value might be lost.

Years later, when I attended an awards event hosted by the Urban Alliance on Race Relations, one of the award recipients spotted me in the audience and, while delivering his remarks, shared with everyone in the room that "Minister Chambers respected us and we respected her."

As a student in the law school, that young man had been declared persona non grata on the university campus at one point but had gone on to be very successful, with a practice in human rights, criminal, constitutional, and social justice law. It was a pleasure to see Selwyn Pieters in attendance, along with other invited guests, at an event held in the Jackman Law Building at the University of Toronto's law school in honour of Supreme Court Justice Rosalie Abella, the 2019 recipient of the Rose Wolfe Distinguished Alumni Award. Selwyn Pieters is now licensed to practice law in three countries, including Canada.

———

Rose Wolfe served as chancellor of the University of Toronto from 1991 to 1997. President Robert Prichard aptly described her as "the perfect chancellor." Rose was succeeded by the Honourable Hal Jackman, whose time as Ontario's twenty-fifth lieutenant governor also spanned 1991 to 1997. He served as the university's chancellor from 1997 to 2003. Rose Wolfe applauded me for agreeing to serve on the board of my local hospital. She told me that she was happy that residents of Scarborough, Pickering, and Ajax would be the beneficiaries. Hal Jackman was one of the first people to donate to my campaign for political office. A Conservative himself, he told me that politics needed people like me.

Others who served with me as government appointees in my final term as a governor included the Honourable William Davis, a Conservative who served as premier from 1971 to 1985 and created Ontario's community college system; the Honourable David Peterson, a Liberal who served as Ontario's premier from 1985 to

1990; and the Honourable Bob Rae, the NDP premier under whose government I had first been appointed to the university's governing council.

I was saddened by the passing of Dr. Claude Davis, who lost his fight against cancer in 2011 after serving three terms as a governor. He had been an environmental consultant and former lecturer in chemistry at the University of the West Indies, and a man I had long admired for his patient, unintimidating brilliance; I had recommended Claude for appointment to the governing council, confident that he would serve with distinction. He was a highly respected and admired governor.

I have many fond memories of my time as a member of the university's governing council. One of those memories is being chosen to "hood" the Most Reverend Desmond Tutu, Archbishop Emeritus of Cape Town and Nobel Peace Prize recipient, when the university conferred upon him an honorary doctorate at a special convocation on February 15, 2000. "No future without forgiveness" was the clear message he delivered in his convocation address. The Right Honourable Adrienne Clarkson, governor general of Canada, and the Honourable Hilary M. Weston, lieutenant governor of Ontario, participated in the ceremony, which also included a performance by the Nathaniel Dett Chorale. It was definitely a special occasion.

I also had the opportunity to serve on a University of Toronto task force on tuition and student financial assistance. Through that work, I was introduced to financial-aid mechanisms such as the Ontario Student Assistance Program (OSAP) and other funds that post-secondary institutions might have the ability to offer in grants, whether based on academic performance or financial need. Recommendations from that task force led to the implementation of a policy that no student would be denied access to the university because of insufficient financial resources. What I learned from my involvement on that task force would be very helpful to me as minister of training, colleges, and universities in working to make post-secondary education more accessible and affordable for students.

Serving as chair of a committee that conducted a review of the office of the university's ombudsman introduced me to how organizations can utilize an independent function to provide another avenue for resolving issues that arise from time to time when the paths through regular operational and management structures have been tried without success. That review also led to an increased presence of the office of the ombudsman on campuses beyond the main campus. Having studied at the Scarborough campus, I had developed an interest in ensuring that students at all campuses could have fair and convenient access to the valuable services that the university provided.

When a long-serving and revered head of the university's governing council secretariat retired, I was tasked with chairing a committee for the review of the secretariat and subsequent advisory committee on the appointment of a new secretary. That work would expose me to another reality and serve to provide another kind of lesson. We invited input from the university community and I recall a young man writing to the committee about his experience applying for jobs and taking care to not include anything in his resumé, even volunteer activities, that might suggest he was gay. He had learned from experience that such information could be detrimental to his success. As it happened, the person the advisory committee proposed for appointment was gay. When his appointment was announced, the tone of the sentiments expressed by members of the university community could best be described as celebratory. There seemed to be a sense that such a thing would never have been possible at the University of Toronto. In the years that followed, I would see an increased presence of Pride symbols on the university's campuses. It felt good that I had been involved in an appointment that recognized that a person's qualifications, not their gender, race, or sexual orientation, should be all that mattered. The wisdom of that appointment would also be reinforced, in subsequent years, by feedback I would receive from other university secretaries, who recognized Louis Charpentier not only as an exemplary university secretary but also as one who was always available to guide and advise others.

Having attended the University of Toronto in the 1980s as a part-time mature student, my relationship with the university during those years had been somewhat distant. I didn't even attend my own convocation. I would later participate in several convocations as a governor of the University of Toronto. And of course, I attended Nick's, Stef's, and my daughter-in-law Minka's convocations at their universities. At Nick's convocation, tears trickled down my cheeks when I heard a male voice in the audience shout, "Way to go, Mom," as his mother approached the chancellor. I regretted that I had missed the opportunity to have my family celebrate a significant milestone that I could not have achieved without their understanding, accommodation, encouragement, and support. At the time, it had not seemed that important.

Serving as a member of the governing council of the University of Toronto from 1993 to 2002 gave me a chance to significantly strengthen my relationship with the university and provided me with countless experiences that have greatly enriched my life.

In 2010, when I was informed by the University of Toronto that I would be awarded the degree of doctor of laws, *honoris causa*, my tears flowed freely. The university was giving me another chance to attend my own convocation and to celebrate that honour with my family.

Chapter 9

Answering the Call

I HAD ABSOLUTELY NO INTEREST in being involved in the political arena. When my siblings and I were growing up in Jamaica in the 1950s and '60s, my parents cautioned us not to speak about anything that we might have heard them say about politicians or political parties. No one was to know which party they supported. I had the sense that politics in Jamaica was taken very seriously.

I recall, as a young girl, attending a political meeting with my parents. We had walked to the meeting, a short distance away from our home. A large crowd had gathered for what seemed to be more than just a meeting. It was really an event. It didn't matter where you were standing. Huge speakers positioned by the specially installed stage amplified everything, making it easy to hear what was being said in between the music that was played intermittently. Some people danced to the music. I think we would have heard everything from where we lived, but that would have deprived us from experiencing the feeling of excitement and the drama.

We weren't actually there just because there was a meeting happening. My mother's brother, Morris Parkin, was one of the candidates in the upcoming elections and he would be speaking along with other representatives of the Jamaica Labour Party. As we stood in the crowd, we were approached by a man my parents recognized as one of the paid workers on my uncle's campaign team. He was handing out campaign pamphlets that we assumed were for my Uncle Morris, but our assumption turned out to be incorrect. The materials he gave us were for a candidate who was running against my uncle. That was the kind of experience that contributed to my impression of the world of politics — at least how politics worked in Jamaica.

A year or so after I migrated to Canada, I happened to be on Bay Street in the financial district in downtown Toronto when I saw that a supportive crowd had gathered around a man who was speaking. The man was Prime Minister Pierre Elliott Trudeau. Pierre Trudeau was viewed by many immigrants as the leader of the Liberal Party who had made it possible for them to come to Canada. What I remember most, from seeing him in person, was that he was quite a bit shorter than his reputation had somehow caused me to imagine him to be. Provincially and federally, I had always voted Liberal, but I had never been a card-carrying member of a political party.

Over the years, when colleagues and friends suggested that political office was something I should consider pursuing, I would tell them that they were confusing me with someone else. Politics in Canada seemed quite different to what I had known of politics in Jamaica, but I still had no interest in that level of involvement.

I was completely taken by surprise, actually speechless, when in early 2003, the Honourable John McKay, a political veteran and federal member of parliament (MP) for the riding of Scarborough East, was the person who called me to say that he and someone else in the party thought I should run for the provincial Liberals in the election that was expected to be called at any time. They had apparently already suggested me to the provincial Liberals as a potential candidate for the Scarborough East seat.

It had been only a few months since I had taken early retirement from the bank. My plan for my retirement had long been to focus on my not-for-profit governance work. I had had a rewarding career at the bank but had been finding my volunteer work in the not-for-profit sector increasingly more fulfilling.

I had never discussed the possibility of political office with Chris because I had never seen it as something I wanted to pursue. Chris wondered why I hadn't immediately dismissed the proposition. I also wondered why I hadn't said "no" right away when John McKay had called. I had always voted in federal, provincial, and municipal elections. I saw voting as an important civic duty. I had also made donations in support of candidates I admired and the party I favoured, but that was usually as far as I went.

Entirely coincidentally, I was only a few months away from completing a major in political science at the UTSC. I had no interest in holding political office but I had enjoyed the subjects that I had been taking in that discipline over the years. After taking a third-year course on the politics of Canada's health policy following my appointment to the board of the Rouge Valley Health System, I realized I needed only two more credits to complete the major.

I had not even given any thought to the fact that 2003 would very likely be an election year in Ontario. Had the ask come before my decision to retire from Scotiabank, I would have found it easy to graciously decline the "opportunity." I might have questioned why anyone would expect me to give up the rewarding career that I had at the bank in order to pursue this new and very different direction. Deep down, I might have been wondering if early retirement from the world of business, followed by entry into the world of politics, could possibly be part of some kind of master plan. Referring to my not-for-profit interests, a former bank colleague suggested that I probably couldn't make a more not-for-profit choice than government.

Faced with having to respond to the request that I represent the Liberals in the upcoming elections, I consulted a number of people with whom I had developed a relationship, primarily through my volunteer work. The most profound response was from Dan, the president of the undergraduate students' association at the UTSC. A position such as the one Dan held required him to do a certain amount of campaigning, asking other students to trust him to do right by them. Dan and I were on a selection committee for a new principal at UTSC. I would pick him up in Scarborough and we would drive together to the meetings of the committee, which were being held at the St. George campus in downtown Toronto. I admired Dan for the thoughtful contributions he made to the discussions that we had at those meetings. He was a very serious young man, obviously very mature. That and the position he held as president of the undergraduate students' association were the primary reasons why I had consulted him about being asked to run for political office. My question obviously took Dan by surprise, to the extent that he seemed troubled by it. He told me that I did not fit the profile of the typical politician, which was why he thought I should say yes. But that was not all that Dan said. He told me that I should not allow anyone to change me. I wasn't certain that I understood Dan's reference to "the profile of the typical politician" but were I to guess at what he might have meant, I would think he was referring to the sense that politicians weren't generally known to be among the most respected or trustworthy people in society. Dan's comment also caused me to recall the *Toronto Star* headline "Banker with heart profits community" on the very positive article about me and my family, which the newspaper had published in

1998. It seemed bankers were not widely viewed as being caring or having hearts.

I was still wrestling with how to respond to the party some three weeks after they had reached out to me when Chris called me upstairs. He was seated in front of the computer at one of the workstations that we had built into the fourth bedroom of our home, which we used as a study and home office. My husband announced that he had created a file for "the people's work." Looking over his shoulder, I saw there was a new file called "Mary Anne Chambers MPP." I realized that this was Chris's way of telling me that he was giving me his "blessing." As if to ensure that I didn't get too carried away with my expectations of him, he told me that he would support me in every way that he could but he would not canvas door to door. A few weeks before election day, Chris would drop even that reservation and become one of my most influential canvassers.

But before I actually agreed to run, I asked for a meeting with Dalton McGuinty, the leader of the Ontario Liberal Party and leader of the official opposition. We met, just the two of us, in his Queen's Park office. I shared with him my reservations. My first reservation was that while I had always raised money for worthy causes, I felt that raising money for my campaign would be different. I would feel like I was raising money for myself. My second reservation was that I had always resisted presenting myself as better than others, which would certainly factor into how I campaigned. The third and perhaps most significant reservation that I shared was that, rather than blindly toeing the so-called party line, I had always believed and would continue to believe that good ideas were not the exclusive domain of any one political party. The leader seemed to understand my reservations. He didn't try to downplay any of them. Instead, he asked me to work with him to change politics.

While at Queen's Park for my meeting with Dalton McGuinty, I surveyed the photographs of the members of provincial parliament who had served the people of Ontario through its thirty-seven previous legislative sessions. It was obvious to me that their collective lack of diversity was not reflective of twenty-first-century Ontario.

I dropped by Alvin Curling's office, which was just down the hall. During our light conversation, I facetiously asked him how difficult it was to convene the Black caucus. Alvin was the only Black MPP at the time. A very popular and astute politician, he was first elected in 1985. After our party won the election in 2003, Alvin was elected speaker of the house. In 2005 he resigned from political office to accept an appointment as Canada's ambassador to the Dominican Republic.

The party had taken what I, a political neophyte, would learn is almost always a highly controversial step in asking me to run, overriding the riding association's wish to run an experienced but previously unsuccessful candidate. Apparently, the party believed that the two-term Conservative incumbent would be a formidable opponent. My cooperation in agreeing to let my name stand for nomination as the candidate for Scarborough East upset members of the riding association executive as much as the party's decision not to accept the candidate they had been planning to run. Although I didn't see myself as responsible for the decision, the tension it created was inevitable and I knew the situation would be primarily mine to resolve. I asked Greg Sorbara to help me make peace with these women and men who, for many years, had worked so hard on behalf of the party. Greg played a lead role in the party's campaign strategy. A phone call from him would go a long way in soothing the hurt. Riding association stalwarts deserved the party's respect and appreciation.

Present at my nomination meeting on the evening of Wednesday, April 2, 2003, were Ontario Liberal Party veterans Greg Sorbara, Alvin Curling, and Sandra Pupatello, and Barbara Hall, former mayor of Toronto. Members of the riding association helped organize the meeting. In attendance were teachers and fire-fighters whose unions would later endorse my candidacy. There were also dozens of other supporters who cheered me on and were among the first to sign up as volunteers. My remarks served as an introduction of Mary Anne Chambers, the Ontario Liberal candidate for Scarborough East, and included the following:

So why am I running as a Liberal, and why do I believe that you should all vote Liberal?

I value fiscal responsibility. I worry that some policy-makers believe that fiscal responsibility should be achieved on the backs of those least able to care for themselves.

I value accountability. I worry that some leaders believe that they are not accountable to all the people ... that parliamentary procedures are just suggestions that can be followed selectively.

I value an education system that enables all students to achieve their full potential to be contributing members of society. I worry that the promise of a crisis in education has become a reality. I worry that our children and youth are being short-changed. I worry about what this will mean for the future of Ontario.

I value safe and accessible health care for all. I worry about long wait times for critical care. I worry about the impact on the delivery of safe care, when excessive demands are placed on health care providers while jobs are being cut in the sector.

I value affordable housing for all. I worry that market forces do not usually benefit those who are financially disadvantaged. I worry about what will happen if rent controls are lifted for all levels of housing.

And I value a climate that encourages investment ... business investment that creates jobs and economic growth, and

investment in research and post-secondary education that will
position Ontario well for the future.

Getting to this point was not without its challenges. Some members of the riding association who were particularly upset about the party not accepting the individual they had been supporting remained suspicious that I had known there was a candidate-in-waiting who had invested a lot of time and energy since the last elections to improve his likelihood of success in 2003. I was the Liberal Party's choice and, while I had no interest in running against anyone else for the candidacy, I did not like being the person who had unwittingly intercepted someone else's dream. The party did not support the previous candidate or anyone else. The man who had been hoping to represent the party withdrew and with there being no other candidates vying for the nomination, my candidacy was an acclamation. The nomination meeting was really a required formality.

Chapter 10

My Political Campaign

AS A FORMER SENIOR VICE president of one of Canada's top banks and someone recognized for extensive contributions as a volunteer in the not-for-profit sector, I was considered what was referred to as a "star candidate" and publicly declared as such by the media. The party's next step was to privately inform me of where I really stood. I was paid a visit at my home by a senior member of the party's central campaign team, who wasted no time getting to the point. While I had been a senior vice president at Scotiabank, that would no longer matter. He wanted me to know that. I would need to understand that that was then and this was now. Now, I would be taking directions from him. I did not receive that very well. The meeting ended quickly as he became the only person I have ever told to leave my home.

At the time of my nomination, in April 2003, as the Liberal candidate for the riding of Scarborough East, the Ontario Liberal Party had no idea when the provincial election would actually take place. There was no fixed election date at that time, leaving it to the governing party to make that determination.

I asked my neighbour, Doug, a consultant who had been a successful marketing executive in the private sector, to be my campaign manager. We started to build a campaign team, initially drawing upon experienced people who had loyally worked on John McKay's campaigns for years and a few others, including my husband, Chris, whose professional and administrative skills would prove essential to the proper running of what would be a substantial undertaking. Without knowledge of when the election would be called, and given my lack of experience in the political arena, we felt it important to start working on getting my name known as the Liberal candidate for Scarborough East. We rented a ground-level storefront space in the same plaza where John McKay's constituency office was located. The candidate for the NDP also had his campaign office in that plaza.

The Conservatives, being the party in power, called the election in September 2003, officially launching my campaign for political office. Three hundred people came out to volunteer. Most were people who had worked with me at the bank or in other settings. Financial contributions came in without me having to beg for support, enough to fund my campaign completely. When I received a cheque for the full amount allowed from a corporate donor, accompanied by a letter stating that the donor was expecting me to support a particular bill that would soon be coming before the legislature, I returned the cheque along with my own letter stating that I would not be willing to commit to what the donor was asking of me.

Reactions varied among two very significant institutions in the riding of Scarborough East where I had established relationships before my candidacy for political office became known.

In the case of the Rouge Valley Health System, I made it known that I would be seeking political office and would take a leave of absence from the board when the election was called. The institution soon heard from supporters of the Conservative incumbent, who complained that, as a member of the board, I had an unfair advantage in the hospital environment. Responding to that pressure, as well as advice provided by their government relations consultant that suggested the Conservatives would be re-elected, the Rouge Valley Health System's leadership began to see me as a liability. Chris and I discussed the situation and we came to the conclusion that my time on that board would soon be ending. If I was elected, I would need to resign from the board in order to focus entirely on my responsibilities as an MPP. If I was not elected, I would not want to remain on the board. After all, as a board member, I had served competently and conscientiously. Over the years, I had also been a generous donor. But the institution was now making me feel that, regardless of the various ways in which I had supported them, my political affiliation would be how my value would be determined. I was made to feel unwelcome.

The reaction at UTSC was different from that of the Rouge Valley Health System. I took my mother with me to an event hosted by the university. The occasion was the announcement of major funding from the Ontario government for a new capital project. The principal introduced the Conservative incumbent in a way that caused me to say that he sounded like he was campaigning for the incumbent. Acknowledging my concern, the principal apologized and informed me that the government had provided him with a script to use in the introduction. The principal promised me his support, and he honoured that commitment when asked to remove the "Great Mind" banners that featured me and hung on the university campus and along major roads in the area around the university. The banners celebrated notable alumni and others in the University of Toronto community and formed part of the promotion of the university's fundraising campaign. My banner carried a large photograph of me along with my name and a bit of information about me ("Senior VP, Bank of Nova Scotia, and Graduate, University of Toronto at Scarborough"). Similar to my presence on the board of the Rouge Valley Health System, the banners were viewed by supporters of the Conservative incumbent as giving me an unfair advantage. Unlike the hospital, the university stood firm. My banners remained in place.

My six-month campaign, having begun very shortly after my nomination, was an opportunity to introduce myself and my party's platform to voters in the riding, but it was also the beginning of an immersion process for helping me to understand how people felt government policies affected and should improve the quality of their lives.

Consistent with policy areas that I had highlighted in my nomination meeting remarks, my campaign team organized four town hall meetings on education, health care, affordable housing, and the environment. While I moderated the meetings, we invited four or five people who held positions of leadership in each of those fields to form the panels on the topics. They spoke about successes and challenges in their particular fields and responded to questions posed by residents of the riding who were in attendance. Each panel also included a member of the Liberal Party who had served as a member of the opposition in Ontario. I learned a lot from those town hall meetings.

The acts of kindness I experienced are too numerous to share in their entirety. I quickly saw and very much appreciated how hard people were willing to work to help their preferred candidate or preferred party to win. Six months of campaigning was perhaps more intense and more tiring than anything else I had ever done. On days when I felt weary or wondered if I had made a mistake when I agreed to let my name stand, it was those people who pushed me along.

One morning, before the sun had fully risen, I sat in the parking lot at one of two GO Transit stations in the riding, waiting for the train carrying Velma, a volunteer, to arrive. Thousands of commuters used the GO trains to get to and from work every day, making the early morning rush at the stations an efficient way to greet people and to hand out our campaign materials. Velma and I were going to be doing exactly that at the Guildwood GO Transit station that morning. I was fortunate to have two GO stations in my riding, Guildwood and Rouge Hill. As I sat in my car thinking that I could easily have used another hour of sleep that morning, it occurred to me that Velma would have had to leave her home at least an hour before she arrived at the Guildwood station and would likely have had to be awake another hour or so before that. Velma had taken a leave of absence from her job as an elementary school teacher in order to volunteer with the campaign. I knew the classroom was where she belonged when we visited a school together. Some of her former students recognized their beloved teacher and greeted her with big smiles and warm hugs.

One morning, on my short drive from home to the campaign office, a police officer pulled me over for exceeding the speed limit. He asked me where I was going and where I was coming from. I think he was trying to determine whether or not I should have been familiar with the reduced speed limit in that area. The officer asked me why I was going to that plaza. I told him that I was a candidate in the upcoming provincial election and my campaign office was located there. To my surprise, he told me to observe the speed limit and sent me on my way. He said he knew I didn't need this kind of attention.

Gary Anandasangaree, then a law student, now a federal MP and parliamentary secretary to the minister of Crown–Indigenous relations, brought university students from his community, the Tamil community, to volunteer for me. They enabled me to access residents in buildings in the riding, responding in their language when we knocked at doors that remained closed until the occupants felt comfortable with who they said I was. A member of the team I had led at the bank had reached out to me to offer to translate my candidate's card into the Tamil language. I was able to hand those cards to the residents whom these students allowed me to meet. The students also took me to their community radio station and served as translators so that I could deliver my message to their listeners and respond to their questions.

Community activist, businessman, philanthropist, and son of Jamaica, Denham Jolly, who lived several ridings away from mine, arrived at the campaign office one day, bearing dozens of Jamaican beef patties for anyone who happened to be there. Many years later, on November 1, 2019, a day so cold that it was difficult for me to speak clearly, I happily braved the weather along with dozens of others to witness and celebrate the dedication of Jolly Way, a street running through a new community of beautiful homes in Scarborough. I could think of no better way to recognize the contributions of Denham Jolly, a man I admire and am proud to call my friend, a man whose huge heart and commitment to humankind has led to a better quality of life for so many. Many know of Denham Jolly, the man who has fought long and hard for social justice and never gave up on his quest to launch the first Black-focused radio station in Canada. Relatively few know about Industry Cove Basic School in Jamaica, located not far from Negril's world-famous seven-mile stretch of beautiful white-sand beach. Industry Cove Basic School was founded by Denham's mother, Ina Euphemia Jolly, in 1962. Thousands of children from the ages of three to six have since had their first exposure to formal education at Industry Cove in an environment that would be the envy of many other early childhood institutions, thanks to the ongoing support of Denham Jolly, himself a former high-school teacher.

When students from UTSC who had been in the classes I took in the months just prior to the launch of my campaign came to my campaign office to volunteer, Audrey, my campaign office manager, a seasoned and dedicated Liberal organizer, thought they had confused me with someone else. Given the difference in our ages, how could we have attended university together? The students insisted and Audrey signed them up for volunteer duties.

One day during the campaign, I received a phone call from a man who identified himself as a janitor at my former office building at Scotiabank. He had seen one of my candidate cards on someone's desk. He said I was the only executive who would always say hello and ask how he and his fellow janitors were doing when I would walk by where they were working. He brought his crew out to campaign for me.

I had no interest in paying any attention to the candidates from the other parties and I asked my team to avoid any negative references to them. When I tried to ignore the tactics of one of the other candidates, residents in the riding who found such tactics offensive stepped forward to speak out against them at an all-candidates meeting. That was a very powerful moment.

Mike, a recently retired executive and former colleague at Scotiabank, told me I would need someone like him to manage my campaign signs. At the bank, Mike was known to be brilliant, well respected, fearless, and feared. I was one of perhaps only a few people at the bank who knew that he had a huge heart. On more than one occasion, in the room where the signs were kept at the campaign office, I would hear his no-nonsense response to whomever had mistakenly thought he was running a self-serve operation. Mike led a team of carpenters and firefighters who ensured that signs were delivered promptly to homes that had agreed to take them. He also roped in his son, a university student who lived in the United Kingdom and was visiting him that summer. Thanks to Mike and his team, I was one of the candidates who didn't have to pay a fine for failing to collect signs within the designated period following election day.

Early on the morning of the first official day of the campaign, I looked out my bedroom window and there on my front lawn was one of my huge campaign signs, hammered in by Doug, our neighbour and my campaign manager. I felt numb. That was probably when I knew there was no turning back. I paid a visit to my parish priest before going to the campaign office that day.

Chris provided technical support in the campaign office. He had said he would do anything to help my campaign, except knocking on doors. But in the last weeks of the campaign, when he had a change of heart, people in the riding told me that they had met my husband and my sons while they canvassed door to door for me. They told me they were impressed by them. People also told me they were impressed by what volunteers who had worked with me at the bank had to say about me. My good friends and former Scotiabank colleagues, Tony and Christine, kept the campaign's financial books in perfect order. Doris from my church helped keep the various databases up to date. My dear friend Margaret, the most capable and caring human resources manager with whom I had the pleasure of working at Scotiabank and a mentor to more people than she realizes, helped soothe my nerves and keep me sane.

My volunteers and I knocked on thousands of doors. Absolutely no one gave me reason to feel unsafe. More than a thousand residents agreed to let my team place my campaign signs on their lawns. The riding was diverse in the income levels and ethnic origins of its residents. Some were first-time voters new to Canadian citizenship, but many had lived in the riding for generations.

My candidate card included my name, photograph, website, riding name, the official Liberal Ontario election logo, an invitation to join my team, contact information for my campaign office, and the following brief biography:

Mary Anne Chambers, former senior vice president of Scotiabank, brings a wealth of corporate experience and community service knowledge to the political arena.

"I've lived in Scarborough East for twenty-six years. I want to create an environment where people can comfortably bring their concerns to me and I will do my best to get them resolved."

She is a strong advocate for education, health care, affordable housing, and the rights of women, seniors, and minorities.

A former vice chair of the Governing Council of the University of Toronto, she contributed to the policy that guarantees no student will be unable to complete studies because of inadequate financial resources.

She is currently the vice chair of the board of the Rouge Valley Health System, the immediate past chair of the board of the United Way, and a past president of the Canadian Club of Toronto.

Mary Anne is married and has two sons.

I came to realize how important it was to people in my riding that I had balanced my business career with years of volunteer activities in the not-for-profit sector. I could never have imagined that, in so many ways, I had long been preparing for this time and the role that I was asking people to trust me to play.

In my view, there is neither glory nor glamour in campaigning for political office. I have always been respectful toward others but I called women "ma'am" and men "sir" more often than I had ever done before, and I said "thank you" a lot.

I steeled myself against the degrading "you're a politician" comment and its various manifestations that seemed to come with a common message that positioned its target as less than honourable. I found it hurtful that people would say things that seemed insensitive, things that had never been said to me before. I heard myself tell someone that I was still the same person I was before I made the decision to run for political office. It was as though I felt the need to explain that or to defend myself. Difficult as this was to process myself, it was even more difficult to share with others.

Someone told me about a book entitled *Why Politicians Lie.* I didn't think I needed to read that book to understand what its title likely meant. The author's message was that politicians tell people what they want to hear in order to get their support. I was determined not to do that. Instead, I found ways to avoid making commitments I might not be able to keep. Sometimes that meant saying I didn't yet know enough about the issue to speak confidently about it. I don't think my campaign team felt totally comfortable when I would take that kind of position in all-candidates meetings, providing the incumbent and his supporters with an opportunity to laugh at me, but I think my team understood and respected my ethical approach.

I was most impressed by the candidate from the Green Party because what he had to say always seemed to comprise evidence-based, researched, and interesting facts that were thoughtful and enlightening rather than political and designed to score points. His party's platform was rather limited, being primarily focused on the environment, but I believed that there might come a time when, with a more comprehensive platform, the Green Party could become a more prominent player in the world of Canadian politics.

I never really got accustomed to the short notice I would receive and the feeling of being summoned to attend campaign rallies and platform announcements that were being made by the leader of the party. Candidates were positioned like wallpaper behind and beside the featured speakers and served as cheering sections for those kinds of events.

One morning, as I hurried out of the Bay-Adelaide parking garage to attend a campaign announcement that was to be made by the leader, I tripped on the uneven pavement just outside the door of the garage and landed on the lower sidewalk, face first. It was early enough in the morning that the usually busy downtown Toronto area was relatively quiet. I recall a woman handing me my purse, which had been thrown out of my hand as I flew several feet through the air above the walkway and the steps that led to the sidewalk. A man, who I think was with a movie-production crew that had their vehicles parked by the sidewalk where I had landed, helped me to my feet. The woman offered to call an ambulance. She told me my face was bleeding. I thanked them and told them I was fine. I imagine they must have been very concerned when I declined their help and walked away.

It seemed I didn't have any difficulty remembering that my destination was the Sheraton Centre. Somehow, I managed to cross the normally busy Bay and Richmond intersection, south to north and east to west, or maybe I crossed east to west and then south to north. I have no idea how I managed to do that safely. Neither do I know which entrance I used to get into the Sheraton Centre. I became aware of where I was when I saw my face in the mirror of the ladies' washroom on the lower concourse level of the complex. That area is not close to any of the entrances I would have used to get into the centre from the street. I have absolutely no recollection of how I had gotten there. I recall wetting some paper towels with water from the tap at one of the basins and using them to wipe the blood from my face. One of my knees felt sore but, at first, I didn't see that the pants of my suit were torn. I left the ladies' wash-room and was surprised but relieved to see Stephen Cheng from the party's central campaign team standing in the lobby just outside the ladies' washroom. I remember saying "Stephen, I fell." He told me he knew and that he had been waiting for me so he could get me the help I needed. We went up the escalator together to the busy ground level of the Sheraton Centre.

Stephen had called Chris, who was working on an information technology project at the Canadian Depository for Securities, which, fortunately, was located a very short walk to the Sheraton Centre. I have no recollection of how Stephen had known how to reach Chris. I can only conclude that I must have been moving in and out of consciousness during the entire ordeal. Chris arrived while a lady from the hotel's human resources area was dressing the bruise on my knee as I sat in a hallway off to the side of the lobby on the main level of the Sheraton Centre, under Stephen's supervision.

Chris accompanied me in an ambulance that took us to St. Michael's Hospital. A scan revealed that I had suffered a mild concussion. Hours later, with a couple of stitches in my upper lip and a bruised nose and forehead, I thought the fresh air would be good and I ignored the curious stares as we walked to the garage where I had parked the car that morning. Chris and I stopped to look at the uneven pavement outside the parking garage and wondered if others had also tripped there.

There are two other things that I remember from that day. Sometime, either weeks or months later, when our government learned the size of the deficit we had inherited, the premier told me he wished he had tripped that day and missed the event at the Sheraton Centre where he had signed the promise not to raise taxes. I also remember telling Stephen Cheng that I would be forever grateful to him.

Chris and I voted in the advance polls. I was starting to realize that there was no opportunity to turn things back to where this had all started, the day when I had said "yes" to allowing my name to be on the ballot. I was absolutely exhausted, ready for all of this to end. I would willingly accept whatever the results would be on election day. Never before had I worked so hard for a job, and it wasn't even a job I was convinced I wanted.

On October 2, 2003, residents of Scarborough East elected me with 51.5 percent of the votes cast, leaving the four other candidates to share the remaining 48.5 percent of the votes. The Ontario Liberal Party formed the new government, having won a majority of the 103 seats in the thirty-eighth Legislative Assembly of the Province of Ontario.

The real work had only just begun.

John McKay had been the federal MP for that riding, which is now known as Scarborough Guildwood, since 1997. He knew the landscape and the landmines well and was extremely generous with his time and wisdom in introducing me to how things worked and to those who helped make things work. After I was elected, the wonderful staff in John's constituency office were also very helpful in guiding my team, all of whom were new to the operations of a constituency office. For the first few years, our offices were located close to each other in a plaza on Kingston Road. John McKay has held several key roles and currently serves as the parliamentary secretary to the minister of national defence.

Chapter 11

Training, Colleges, and Universities

ON THE HEELS OF THE Liberal Party's successful provincial election in 2003, there was speculation in the media about who might be appointed to which cabinet positions. The word was that I would become a minister, but I knew it was best to ignore the rumours. When the time came, some of us were told to be available for a call between certain hours on a particular day. My telephone call from the leader of the party came at the scheduled time, informing me of my appointment to cabinet as minister of training, colleges, and universities. It was a short conversation. The leader also promised I would receive a mandate letter with details of what he expected of me. I told him that I appreciated his confidence in me.

I suspect the experience I had gained while serving for nine years on the governing council of the University of Toronto, including three years as vice chair, had contributed to my appointment by Premier Dalton McGuinty as minister of training, colleges, and universities in the government of Ontario. I was very happy to have been assigned that portfolio.

Swearing-in ceremonies for the premier, members of provincial parliament, and cabinet ministers took place over the following few days.

The minister's office is associated with the premier's office and staffed by individuals known as political staff. Their roles include stakeholder relations, communications, policy analysis, legislative assistance, scheduling, and transportation. The team in my minister's office was headed by my extremely competent chief of staff, Meg Connell. Meg was with me from the beginning and stayed with me until I left Queen's Park. That was not typical.

As soon as I was informed by the leader that he was appointing me to cabinet, I called Meg. I had met her when I joined the board of directors of the Canadian Club of Toronto in 1995. Meg was the club's executive director. I was impressed by the way she held the club together while a new president would take the reins each year. When I was appointed president for the 1998 to 1999 season, Meg introduced me to the concept of sober second thought. That was her way of getting me to slow down and think twice about what I wanted to do. Meg had important institutional memory. She knew what had worked in the past and what had led to disappointing results. I relied heavily on her calm demeanour, her attention to detail, her appreciation of proper protocols, her professionalism, and her ability to work well with others.

With Meg by my side, my year as president of the club had been a great success. We hosted thirty-four events, each with an average of 306 attendees. Through corporate sponsorships we were able to welcome over eight hundred students, more than double that of any previous year, to the club's luncheons. The club received extensive media coverage for its events, which featured national and international speakers from business, government, the arts, education, and social services. The Canadian Club had had a long-standing reputation for being a venue for Toronto's business community.

American business tycoon Michael Bloomberg of Bloomberg News fit right in as one of the speakers we hosted while I served as president. And perhaps that was why when we hosted Howard Hampton, then leader of Ontario's NDP, only seventy-five people attended. Since 1999 was an election year in Ontario, there was absolutely no doubt in my mind that hosting Mike Harris, leader of Ontario's Progressive Conservatives, and Dalton McGuinty, leader of the Ontario Liberals, meant we would also have to host the leader of the NDP while hoping that attendance numbers would not embarrass any of the leaders, or for that matter, the club. In the report I delivered at the club's annual general meeting at the end of my season as president, I highlighted how proud I was about the audiences that we had attracted. The following is an excerpt from my report:

> *The Canadian Club of Toronto continues to be a platform of choice for high-profile speakers and topics. I am convinced that we have an important role to play in facilitating the delivery of important messages and as long as we continue to feature timely and topical programs, the club will continue to enjoy a positive, prestigious, and strong reputation. And while we sought ways to market our events to a broad, inclusive Toronto population, it seems the way to achieve the greatest success is to feature speakers and topics that are of interest to a broad and inclusive population. One need only look to the 577 people who came to hear Marguerite Jackson, Director of the Toronto District School Board. The* Toronto Star *described this and the Anne Golden event on homelessness as unusual events for the Canadian Club of Toronto. Many of the people in attendance at these events were first-time guests of our club. So while table sales were down slightly from the 1997/1998 season, individual ticket sales were significantly higher this season.*

My term as a director of the Canadian Club of Toronto had ended in 2001. In hindsight, it would seem that Meg and I were destined to work with each other again. She had proven that she could cope with my habit of pushing the boundaries. I knew there must have been days when she would have needed to exhale when she got home from work, but she would always return, apparently undaunted, with her full commitment to the club's success.

So, when I telephoned Meg that night in October 2003, I had my fingers tightly crossed. She wasn't on my shortlist. She was the one. I was thrilled when she told me that she and her husband, Kevin, had actually had a conversation about the exact thing I was asking her to do. Coincidentally, Kevin was a senior public servant in Ontario's Ministry of Training, Colleges, and Universities at the time. Meg wondered if that might be of concern to me. There was no sober second thought required, as far as I was concerned. I knew without a doubt that with Meg and Kevin, consummate professionals that they are, no conflicts would ever arise. I was correct.

David Rajpaulsingh also worked with me for my entire four years as a cabinet minister. He was a highly respected member of the team in my minister's office. His responsibilities involved logistics and transportation, which included the coordination of my activities with my chief of staff and scheduler to ensure that I could be relied upon to meet my demanding commitments. David's training in security and personal protection had also earned the confidence of members of my security detail of Ontario Provincial Police (OPP) officers.

David's professionalism, strong work ethic, consistently sound judgment, and refreshing interpersonal skills all combined to make him an outstanding member of my team. Those impressive personal attributes also gave my family the confidence that they would never need to be concerned about my safety and well-being when David was with me.

Beyond his responsibilities in my office, David volunteered as a big brother with the Big Brothers Big Sisters of Ontario organization. I sometimes overheard conversations between him and his little brother and between him and his little brother's mother. David's genuine and caring commitment, through mentorship and academic tutoring, was admirable and it is my understanding that they have remained good friends and his former little brother has developed into a successful young man.

David had previously worked with other cabinet ministers, members of the Conservative Party. I had met with him for a relaxed interview before deciding that he would be a good fit for my minister's office team and knew, instinctively, that I would not need to be concerned that, for several years, he had been close to ministers who were members of the opposition party. I wasn't at all disappointed. David was loyal, absolutely trustworthy, and an excellent driver.

More often than not, I was unaware of the route we would be using and I usually didn't know exactly where we were at any particular point in our travel. When we were out at night, I would sometimes lean back and take short naps. During the day, I took great pride in being able to accomplish copious amounts of reading and writing. My head would be down, sometimes for almost an hour at a time, focused on the binders that I had on my lap. My neck and my back would suffer the consequences. David seemed to know that. Every morning, as soon as we parked in the garage in the building where my minister's office was located, David would quickly come to my door and take away the heavy binder I had been working on. I would then slowly emerge and survey the garage, stretching my neck and my back as discreetly as I could, before walking away from the car. In the months after I left Queen's Park, when people would ask me what I missed most, without hesitation, I would say, "David."

"I so miss David," I kept mumbling to myself while breathing heavily during my brisk walk past the Chinatown shops with their large, overstocked bins of every fruit imaginable, imported from all over the world, encroaching on the sidewalk area meant for pedestrians.

I must have driven on every side street north of the Art Gallery of Ontario. Most were single-lane, one-way streets, complicating and frustrating my attempts to find parking. I had started my search for parking on Dundas Street West, where the gallery is located. After all, Chris has always said I am lucky with finding parking close to where I am going. That was certainly not my experience that day.

Ever since our departure together from the world of government, Meg had been working at the St. George campus at the University of Toronto, an easy walk shaded by large, leafy trees on a perfect summer day. I had circled the area more than once, wishing I could just abandon my car as I searched for a place to park, finally finding a spot three blocks west of the gallery.

Meg and I hugged each other. "You must really miss David," she said, accurately reading my mind as I apologized for arriving late for our lunch at the restaurant at the gallery.

My security detail, the team of officers from the OPP that were assigned to me, also took very good care of me. We sometimes travelled together and they accompanied me to events based on their assessment of the potential risk. We had great conversations on all kinds of topics. They provided advice on how I could protect myself and my home and they visited my constituency office and made recommendations on how it should be laid out.

There was someone in my riding who had made a habit of harassing a member of my constituency office staff who was Black. The man even tried to convince a white female staff member that she should not be working with her Black colleague. I sent a message to the offensive constituent, inviting him to be brave enough to come to my office while I was there. My OPP security detail did not think that the challenge I had issued was wise and told my staff that they would want to be at the office if ever I expected the man to meet with me.

I am still amused when I think of the time when a female member of my security detail met me when I arrived in Ottawa on a flight from Toronto very late one night. The officer drove me to the hotel where we would both spend that night. When she stopped in front of the entrance to the hotel lobby where I was to get out of her vehicle, I remembered that I did not like that hotel's underground parking garage. The officer would be parking there after delivering me safely to the lobby on the ground level. I remembered the garage as being not well lit and having a driveway that weaved crookedly through unevenly laid out parking spots and dark, recessed areas, the kind of layout that caused me to think that the decision to use the area for parking was an opportunistic afterthought rather than an intentional part of the original architectural design of the building. I guess it was my natural protective instinct on display when I told the female officer I wanted to accompany her into the parking garage. The officer, a tall, attractive, young, obviously fit, blond woman, responded firmly, "Minister, I have a gun."

"Right," I said, as I got out of her vehicle, knowing that I had no reason to be concerned about her ability to take care of herself, that I would not likely have been particularly helpful were there to be a threat to our safety, and that I would not have made the same offer to one of the male members of my security detail.

As I think about my introduction to student protests while I was a member of the governing council at the University of Toronto, I recall that it was shortly after my appointment as minister of training, colleges, and universities, when thousands of college and university students gathered on the front lawn of Queen's Park to protest high tuition fees.

"I want to join them," I told my staff.

They were my stakeholders, after all. As their minister, I should not be afraid to be with them, as uncomfortable as the setting might be. I needed the students to know not only that I respected their right to protest, but also that I believed their voices were important for me to hear. I realize, now that I look back to that day, that the intention I expressed is exactly the kind of thing staff would prefer not to hear. Of course, my OPP security detail was informed of my decision and they accompanied me and helped me to climb onto the flat-bed truck where the leaders of the protest and the sound system were positioned. As they helped me up onto the truck, the officers informed me that they had recognized "professional" activists in the crowd, who were known to create disturbances at events such as these. They warned me that if they saw any sign of that starting to happen, such as items being thrown at me, they would immediately remove me from the scene and I should not try to resist their actions.

The organizers were surprised to see me. They allowed me to speak and I was well received. I left feeling proud of "my" students and grateful that all had gone well.

In one particular week while I was serving as minister, I visited two Toronto schools located not more than ten minutes' drive away from each other. The profile for one of the schools referred to the support the school received from parents and their community. This support had enabled them to equip their school with personal computers for the students.

I knew the other school would be quite different. Its profile revealed that the overwhelming majority of its students had been in Canada for less than five years, and English was not the first language for most.

Daddy.

Mommy.

Me as an infant.

At five years old.

LEFT: In my teenage years.

BELOW: My parents' home in Jamaica.

Wedding day for Chris and me.

With Chris and our sons just before coming to Canada.

ABOVE: Wedding day for Stefan and Minka in Niagara-on-the-Lake.

LEFT: Stefan and Minka as pilots in the air cadet instructor cadre, Royal Canadian Air Force Reserve.

Hope for the future: granddaughters Ashley (left) and Alexa with their dad, Nick.

Katrina and Nick on "The Rock," Newfoundland.

Family time at Christmas in Jamaica.

LEFT: Chris and me.

BELOW: As president of the Canadian Club of Toronto.

Honorary doctorate from the University of Toronto for Reverend Desmond Tutu. Pictured with Professor John Polanyi (left) and Chancellor Hal Jackman.

TOP: Provincial election candidate card (front). BOTTOM: Provincial election candidate card (back).

Swearing-in at Queen's Park with Lieutenant Governor James Bartleman (left) and Ontario Premier Dalton McGuinty.

Early learning and child care announcement as minister of children and youth services.

Celebrating the Centenary Hospital birthing centre.

Hosting a youth conference on mental health with Canada's Governor General Michaëlle Jean.

With the Honourable Roy McMurtry for the dedication of Roy McMurtry Youth Centre.

With Ontario Premier Dalton McGuinty.

ABOVE: Delivering a computer for Wait-A-Bit Basic School in Trelawny, Jamaica.

LEFT: With former prime minister of Jamaica P.J. Patterson.

Receiving an honorary doctorate at the University of Toronto from Louis Charpentier (left) and Chancellor David Peterson.

Celebrating the Order of Ontario with Chris.

As PACE president, presenting a cheque for All Saints Basic School to Jamaica's Education Minister Andrew Holness in 2010.

With Denham Jolly (left), acknowledging PACE fundraising brunch keynote speaker Armand La Barge in 2011.

With Ontario's Transportation Minister Kathleen Wynne and Michael Coteau at the launch of his campaign for the Don Valley East riding in 2011.

Receiving the University of the West Indies Vice-Chancellor's Award from Professor Nigel Harris in 2013.

Congratulating Toronto Youth in Policing Initiative graduates Zubair Abdelur (centre) and Travis Williams in 2015.

With Nana Frimpong (left), Ariel Brown, Janessa Bagwandeen, and Waris Amis at the Imani Academic Mentorship Program event in 2016.

Participating in the University of Guelph convocation for Dr. Rashelle Litchmore (second from right), with Saba Safdar, professor of psychology, and President Dr. Franco Vaccarino.

I encouraged the students at both schools to dream big and to keep working toward the achievement of their dreams. Then I asked them to share their dreams with me. The students at the school that enjoyed strong support from their parents and their community needed no encouragement at all to tell me what they wanted to achieve. At the other school, I had to resort to bribery in the form of movie passes before the students would respond. But I was pleased to discover that they also had big dreams — biologist, veterinarian, scientist, physician — and one boy wanted to be a professional basketball player. I was shocked when, as I was leaving the school, the principal took me aside and with the most solemn facial expression told me it broke his heart to know that most of his students would not complete high school, although they were smart enough to compete successfully against students their age who attended a well-known elite private school in Toronto. He believed that few, if any at all, would go on to college or university. I asked him why he felt that way. He told me that the reason was that 67 percent of his students were from families living below the poverty line, and the others were from families that were just scraping by.

That experience served to inspire our government's commitment to provide income-based, non-repayable tuition grants for post-secondary students so that their interest and their academic ability, not their financial ability, would determine whether or not they could pursue college or university studies.

When our government was able to make some progress on regulating tuition fee increases, I made the announcement at the University of Waterloo. A student leader who spoke after I did brought tears to my eyes when she said, "Minister, we won't disappoint you."

Early in my mandate as minister, the consul general for the People's Republic of China came to meet with me. She needed me to know that her government would stop granting permits for their citizens to come to Canada to pursue their studies through private career colleges in Ontario. She told me students were arriving to find that the programs they had registered for were not being offered or the descriptions used in the marketing of the courses were inconsistent with what they were experiencing. When they complained to the college, there was either no action taken or the college's response was unsatisfactory.

Shortly before my arrival at Queen's Park, I had read about some of those issues in the newspapers. With those reports still fresh in my mind, I asked for a briefing on private career colleges as soon as I was appointed minister. We concluded that the Private Career Colleges Act 1990 was due for a review, and enforcement of the existing act had not been consistently carried out by the ministry. I didn't need to convince my ministry officials that the situation required their attention.

We invited the board of Career Colleges Ontario, an organization that represents more than two hundred of the colleges, to meet with us to discuss how they could work with the government to improve their sector. They knew the reputation of their own colleges was at risk because of the practices of the poorly run colleges. We worked very effectively together, believing that the weak colleges would have to pull up their socks or, failing that, would not survive.

When I was able to tell the consul general that our government had already started to take appropriate steps to address the problem she had come to tell me about, the tone of the meeting changed completely. The consul general invited me and my family to join her at her official residence for dinner. She emphasized that the invitation extended to my granddaughters. I accepted the invitation and we were treated to a menu that included dishes from different provinces in China. It was an impressive spread but when my granddaughters, who were quite young at that time and not at all adventurous, declined everything on the menu, the consul general asked a member of her staff to order pizza for them. The girls were happy with that.

What I loved most about this portfolio was the breadth of opportunities it offered, including training and apprenticeships in several skilled trades, both publicly assisted community colleges and private career colleges, and universities. The dimensions of the portfolio allowed me to apply my natural inclination to help people to achieve personal success.

Very late one night, a lawyer called a plumber to his home to repair his toilet. With the job successfully completed, the plumber presented his bill. The lawyer was shocked.

"I am a lawyer and I don't make that kind of money," he said.

"I know. I used to be a lawyer," the plumber replied.

I told that fabricated story at least a few times to make the point that the skilled trades provide lucrative career opportunities. My audiences would always find the story amusing. Teachers and guidance counsellors in high schools sometimes expressed surprise when I revealed what a carpenter could earn for an hour's work. In those years, the average age of an apprentice in Ontario was twenty-nine. I asked young men in the plumbing program at George Brown College what they had been doing prior to studying to become plumbers. One fellow said, "Nothing much, Miss." The others nodded their heads in agreement. I thought of the many years that had been lost, years in which they might have been able to start and provide for a family, or might otherwise have enjoyed the fruits of a rewarding career.

I also tried to debunk gender stereotypes. A teacher at a Scarborough high school introduced me to the top student in his auto mechanics class. The student was a blond girl who was wearing blue eyeshadow. I was very pleased. I recalled that when my son Stefan was in elementary school, his teacher had told his class that the girls would be taking home economics and the boys would be doing woodworking. Stef insisted that I speak with his teacher about her plan. He wanted to do home economics. My intervention was successful. Stefan enjoyed his home economics course and brought home recipes, some of which I still have. In high school he took a woodworking course, with impressive results. I know from later experiences that Stefan was simply protesting the assumption or stereotype that girls, not boys, should learn home economics and boys, not girls, should learn woodworking. I smile whenever I think of the stand my son took at such a young age.

The skilled trades were a new and exciting experience for me. I saw that many trades had evolved from being labour intensive through the application of technology. That evolution made trades in construction, for example, more accessible to people with physical disabilities. It also meant that high-school mathematics was important. During a visit to the state-of-the-art Local 27 Carpenters' Training Centre, I observed a small group of young men huddled around a few computers, doing computer-assisted design. I asked them if they had always been interested in math. They shook their heads and told me that it was only when they had learned that grade 12 math was a requirement for training in carpentry that they had begun to take it seriously. For some, that had meant returning to school to earn credits in mathematics.

There were parents who had worked in some skilled trades who were not aware of the developments that had occurred in more recent years. Some of those parents were less encouraging of their daughters' and sons' interests in pursuing careers in the skilled trades. For those parents, the experience had been about a lot of hard work without the equivalent rewards and respect for the work they did. When I saw school buses delivering high-school students to competitions and exhibitions organized by Skills Canada and Skills Ontario, and how excited the kids were as they headed toward the exhibits, I wished their parents had accompanied them.

I heard that some presidents of community colleges were wary of my lack of experience with their sector. They were concerned I would not fully appreciate the value a college education offered. It was true that the sector was new to me, but that just meant I had to get up to speed quickly. I visited all twenty-four community colleges in Ontario. I would sometimes hear that I was the first minister with responsibility for their sector to have visited.

At St. Clair College in Windsor, I observed students in the dental hygiene program as they provided free care for members of the community in their on-campus dental clinic. In addition to providing this valuable service, they were gaining practical experience in their field of study.

Students at Niagara College have program options that include horticulture, hospitality and tourism, and wine sommelier, areas of study of particular value to the area of the province where the college is located.

At Confederation College in Thunder Bay, I was introduced to their aviation program and given the opportunity to land an aircraft in a flight simulator.

At several of the colleges, I observed students doing in-school training in a wide variety of skilled trades, in preparation for the next level of on-the-job training. Apprentices earn wages while learning their trade and typically graduate without the burden of student loans.

It was the community colleges our government often turned to in order to provide bridging programs for internationally trained individuals who required additional training to become certified to work in their fields in Ontario. The flexibility they offered included the ability to quickly provide the kind of curriculum that was required. The course schedules offered by community colleges also provided more options for students eager to start and complete their programs of study as they sought to enter the workforce as quickly as possible.

I learned that some students graduating from high school but not feeling quite ready to commence university studies would do a year of studies at a community college. I also learned that after graduating from university, some students do a program of study at a community college to complement their qualifications with practical, employment-ready skills.

When I visited Northern College in Timmins, I was warmly met by a welcoming party made up of board members, staff, faculty, students, civic officials, and local businesspeople. My visit obviously meant a lot to them. As a city in northeastern Ontario, located approximately seven hundred kilometres by road from Toronto with a population of under forty-five thousand, I quickly grasped how important it was for them to be able to provide a high-quality college experience. In doing so, they could help ensure their city had the skills required to keep their economy strong. They would also reduce the risk of out-migration of their young people to more southern parts of the province, not only to study but possibly more permanently if they were able to find employment in a larger city. I also heard about this challenge from universities in northern Ontario.

Smaller student populations can threaten the financial viability of these institutions, but these colleges and universities are extremely important to their communities. These dynamics can cause a variety of inequities in the post-secondary sector, driving the need for innovations in student recruitment and fundraising for student assistance and capital initiatives. The search for other revenue opportunities contributed to the recruitment of international students being a strategic priority.

The establishment of additional campuses through partnerships with communities that see the value of providing those kinds of educational opportunities locally for their young people has also been seen as mutually beneficial. Larger colleges might look more like universities, but universities that offer professional programs like medicine, dentistry, law, business, and engineering will find it easier to secure donations from their alumni and from professional practices and businesses with corporate head offices located in their larger cities. Faculties such as social science and education, on the other hand, can find it more challenging to raise funds. These challenges called for a review of the government's funding formulas and how fundraising for student assistance was matched by government in light of the capacity of institutions to raise those kinds of funds. What I learned also led to improvements to OSAP. When I visited the ministry's student loan centre, a member of staff told me that he was happy that we were putting the *student* back into *student assistance*.

I met with student leaders in the College Student Alliance. The alliance represents students from some of Ontario's community colleges. Of the forty student leaders in the room, only a few raised their hands when I asked them to tell me who among them were receiving assistance from their parents in order to finance their studies.

Students also advocated on behalf of other students whose circumstances were different to theirs. At the University of Windsor, a large group of Canadian students met with me to ask for my help in changing the federal regulations that prevented their international counterparts from being able to work outside the university. They told me that contrary to what some people thought, many international students were not from wealthy families.

Colleges and universities, particularly those in northern Ontario, heard about my interest in knowing how Indigenous students were doing. When I visited, my itinerary would include the opportunity to meet with those students. I always had one question and one request. I would ask the students to tell me how they had succeeded in getting into the institution and I would ask them to share their stories with other youth when they were on their reserves.

There were reserves in Ontario where I got the sense that the young people would be fine. Six Nations of the Grand River, also home to Six Nations Polytechnic, and Chippewas of Rama First Nation, also home to the popular Casino Rama and Resort, were two of those reserves. Their leaders have invested in helping their young people understand the value of education, establishing partnerships with degree- and diploma-granting post-secondary institutions nearby, and providing their young people with enabling scholarships.

Visiting every college and every university in the province was an education in itself, time very well spent. My ministry's portfolio extended beyond post-secondary education. The portfolio also included responsibility for adult literacy. I recall attending a graduation ceremony for students of one of the literacy programs my ministry funded. Simple pleasures that I had long taken for granted were new experiences opening windows and doors to new realities for these students.

One of the graduates was a man in his mid to late forties from an Indigenous community. I was told he was one of the vendors at the Harbourfront Toronto open-air market. This man was on the evening's program to read a few of the short stories he had written about his life — quite the achievement. But when he got to the podium, he was so overcome by emotion that he could not speak. He wasn't able to read his stories to us.

There was a young Guyanese woman in her late twenties, who told me her goal was to become a chef. In Ontario, chef is a skilled trade that requires formal studies and apprenticeship. This young woman planned to pursue studies at George Brown College in Toronto. She told me that, for her, the most enjoyable and uplifting part of the literacy program was when the members of her class were taken to see the theatrical production of *Mamma Mia*. She said she had had no idea that love stories were performed live, on stage, in theatres. For a brief moment, I wondered how she could not have known about live theatre. But then I remembered that until recently, she couldn't read. Unless someone else had introduced her to live theatre, how would she have known it existed?

Then there was the older woman, a Jamaican woman, I guessed in her early eighties. She was dressed in her finest outfit, her Sunday best, as they say where I come from, complete with gloves and hat for this very special occasion in her life. As she got close enough to whisper to me, she told me with obvious pride and excitement that she could now read her Bible to herself every night before she fell asleep.

Helping to ensure that internationally trained professionals would be able to contribute their skills and experience for the benefit of the people of Ontario was also within the mandate of the ministry. In developing their campaign platform for the 2003 provincial election, the Liberals reflected what they were hearing about the challenges being faced by internationally trained individuals with credentials from their countries of origin. The campaign platform promised to address the waste of skills and experience.

I heard the frustrations expressed by individuals who had discovered it was just about impossible to acquire the Canadian work experience many employers were asking for, because they were not being given the opportunity to work in their fields of expertise. The results of industry surveys showed that when presented with applications from a Canadian-trained individual and an internationally trained individual, employers were more likely to choose the Canadian-trained individual. Yet when given the opportunity to have an internationally trained individual as an intern under the Ontario government–funded career-bridge program, most employers were so impressed that they were hiring their interns before the period of internship was even completed. I would also be telling only a portion of the story if I did not mention that individuals who had the good fortune of having a job offer from an employer in Canada, before arriving in the country, would find the process much more welcoming.

There were different considerations that surfaced among the approximately thirty-six regulatory bodies with which I met. The regulatory college for dental surgeons had been requiring all internationally trained dental surgeons to do a costly two-year university program. But to their credit, when they analyzed the results of the program, they realized that the majority of internationally trained dental surgeons had not needed to do the full program of study. The college made a simple yet very significant and effective change to their process. They tested the knowledge of the internationally trained dental surgeons to first determine what gaps existed in their skills in order to identify what, if any, particular areas of the study program they would need to complete to be certified to practise in Ontario. The Ontario college took their idea further. They invited me to join them at a meeting of their national body to support their pitch for the proposed change. The approach proposed by the Royal College of Dental Surgeons of Ontario was accepted by the national body for implementation across the country. At my first meeting with representatives of the Royal College of Dental Surgeons of Ontario, their president introduced himself to me as being the husband of Elizabeth Witmer, a Conservative MPP and former minister of health in the government of Ontario. Dr. Witmer told me he hoped that would not be a problem. I told him, sincerely, that Liz Witmer was one of my favourite MPPs. I would later learn from Liz that he shared our exchange with her.

I recall asking participants at a conference of settlement agencies, who had been working with me to improve access to accreditation by regulatory colleges, if they knew which profession had by far the highest number of newcomers to Ontario. They knew the answer to my question. So when I spoke about the challenges of integrating approximately seven thousand internationally trained engineers, annually, into an employment environment that was simultaneously receiving about five thousand new graduates from engineering programs in Ontario universities, it became obvious to me that they had already come to the same conclusions. I did not find it difficult to understand the challenges that the regulatory body for professional engineers faced in coming up with an expedited process for accrediting internationally trained engineers.

Medical doctors were in short supply in remote parts of the province, and if internationally trained physicians could be incentivized to accept placements in those areas, that would be acceptable to Canadians in that profession. I learned about differences in the experiences of family practitioners and specialists and how that sometimes influenced the choices made by medical students. The financial rewards, for example, varied by specialty, and being a family physician or a child psychiatrist, for example, was viewed as being less attractive as a career.

I heard from nurses that they were uncomfortable with government policies or actions that would make it easier for nurses to leave developing countries in desperate need of their skills in order to secure better opportunities in Canada.

Some industries complained we weren't paying enough attention to skilled trades where anticipated demand for workers exceeded supply.

By working with regulatory bodies and professional associations, we were able to identify and fund several programs to help internationally trained individuals become certified to work in their professions in Ontario. The programs included occupation-specific language training, career-related orientation and workplace internships, and mentoring.

I sometimes found myself having to clarify that internationally trained professionals weren't necessarily new immigrants, although this was very often the case. Canadians who have earned their professional qualifications in non–Canadian affiliated institutions outside of Canada, for professions that are regulated in this country, are also required to be certified to practise in their field by the relevant regulatory college here. Individuals who have earned their professional qualifications in Canada are also required to meet the certification requirements of their particular regulatory college. The process is more of a formality, however, as the qualifications required by the regulatory bodies will have already been built into the curriculum offered by our post-secondary institutions.

The challenges this file encountered included concerns that a few of my colleagues anticipated would arise from their stakeholders. I experienced how much more complicated things could get when more than one ministry was involved. The pushback I received caused me to take an even stronger stand in pushing for attention to the issue and support for what I was proposing, reminding my colleagues that the commitment to address the matter of internationally trained professionals was actually in our party's campaign platform. When the premier asked me to meet with him, I thought he was going to offer me advice on how to be more diplomatic when conveying my position on controversial matters. Instead, the premier asked me to help him to better understand what I was trying to accomplish. My spirits were lifted when he told me that colleagues who were not supportive were trying to protect the interests of their stakeholders while I was trying to protect the interests of the broader community. The premier gave me his approval to proceed. I breathed a sigh of relief as I left his office, feeling empowered and grateful for his support.

In September 2004, our government appointed the eminently qualified Justice George Thomson, then the executive director of the National Judicial Institute and a former deputy minister in the Ontario and federal governments, to conduct an in-depth review of regulatory processes and to provide the government with his conclusions and recommendations. George Thomson was respected by stakeholders of different perspectives for his inclusive and comprehensive approach to consultation and his thoughtful analysis of complex issues. The mandate for the assignment was based on specific principles:

1. Candidates should have access to an independent appeal of registration decisions based on established grounds.
2. Regulators are responsible for protecting the public interest by ensuring a high standard of professional practice.
3. Competence to practise a profession should be determined according to merit-based criteria.
4. Candidates should have access to clear and well-defined registration and appeal mechanisms.
5. Improving access to professions by internationally educated professionals requires collaboration among regulators and others while respecting their unique roles and mandates.

In May 2005, Mr. Thomson submitted a draft of his report to me. In June 2005, I was appointed minister of children and youth services, and the responsibility for access to the professions and trades for internationally trained individuals was moved from the Ministry of Training, Colleges, and Universities to the Ministry of Citizenship and Immigration. In November 2005, George Thomson's official *Review of Appeal Processes from Registration*

Decisions in Ontario's Regulated Professions was delivered to Ontario's minister of citizenship and immigration.

The report's recommendations were very well received by stakeholders representing new immigrants and regulators and served to guide subsequent steps taken by the Ontario government. The passage of Bill 124, the Fair Access to Regulated Professions Act, 2006, requiring Ontario regulators to have a quicker, fair, and open registration process, and the creation of the Office of the Fairness Commissioner to ensure fair, clear, and open licensing processes for regulated professions, were among the recommendations implemented.

The premier recalled that this work had been led by me as minister of training, colleges, and universities. David Caplan, one of my colleagues, reinforced the premier's recollection, saying, "Yes. Give credit where credit is due." We all lost a good human being, one who genuinely cared about serving others, when David Caplan passed away in 2019.

In 2003, applicants for visas to migrate to Canada were not being provided with labour market information. They did not know what qualifications were in demand, or what they would need to do to have their academic or professional credentials recognized when they got here. I received an invitation to appear before a committee of federal parliamentarians and public servants on the subject of immigration and settlement and used the opportunity to share the challenges that the Ontario government had identified and to outline recommendations such as the provision of labour market information and the accreditation requirements for regulated professions to individuals applying to immigrate to Canada. I stated my belief that prospective immigrants needed that kind of information in order to make informed choices, choices that could include any of the following:

- a decision to pursue or not pursue their application where the prospects for accreditation and employment in their chosen field would likely be too challenging, or
- a decision to pursue employment in a field other than their preferred field, or
- an alternative destination in Canada where employment prospects seemed more promising, or
- a decision to start the process of acquiring additional qualifications toward the requirements for accreditation and employment while awaiting the results of their visa application.

An express entry process, more recently introduced by the federal government, is now giving priority to applicants who have skills that are in demand, thereby improving their success at securing jobs in their particular fields of expertise. I think about the many people who told me they had resigned themselves to not being able to pursue their preferred careers and instead were focusing only on helping their children to be successful in the careers they had an interest in pursuing. Hopefully, with the new process in place, the sacrifices individuals like those were having to make, as well as the loss to society because their credentials were not being recognized, will occur less frequently.

Sometimes solutions are a lot simpler than the systems in place are designed for them to be. What is often needed is a greater will on the part of policy-makers to change the status quo.

I was given no time, really, to savour the 2005 Budget, which provided for the largest new investment in post-secondary education since former premier William G. Davis had created Ontario's community college system more than thirty years earlier. Shortly after the delivery of the Budget, there were rumours that a cabinet shuffle was likely.

The premier had branded himself as the education premier. I had experienced the benefit of being able to ride that wave. That was especially important to me as I would recall that, among the thousands of homes I had visited during the campaign, not one person I met had mentioned post-secondary education as a priority or a concern. Parents had told me that they wanted their children in school. They wanted the next government to resolve the tension that had existed between the government of the day and the teachers' unions.

Some of my MPP colleagues viewed post-secondary institutions, particularly the universities, as ungrateful and elitist. They told me that a matter of days following announcements of millions of dollars in government funding, the celebration would end and these institutions would be back asking for more, saying that what they had received was not enough. Some MPPs suggested that much smaller grants to organizations in their ridings would be received with much greater appreciation. This was viewed by some as better politics, the kind that got parties re-elected.

It was in June 2005 that I was called to a meeting with the premier. I sat outside his office, nervously awaiting word of my fate. Changes to cabinet ministers, or at least to their assigned portfolios, were anticipated following the Budget, according to reports in the media. The Queen's Park press gallery always seemed to know what was about to happen. I assumed I would be losing the Ministry of Training, Colleges, and Universities portfolio. Why else would the premier want to see me? It was not what I wanted to hear.

When I was finally called into his office, the premier informed me that I would be re-assigned as minister and moved to the Ministry of Children and Youth Services. The meeting with the premier lasted no more than a few minutes. I had no reason to believe there was room for negotiation. I thought of what my mother would sometimes say to me: "Go perform."

I would cringe every time she said it. It seemed fake, like I was to put on an act, pretend to be something I was not, play a role I might have been reluctant to play, but I knew it was her way of telling me to rise to the occasion.

Gerald Butts, the premier's principal secretary, met with me next. It was his job to provide an introduction to the priorities of my new portfolio. He told me about the Best Start program for early learning and child care, and did his utmost to make it sound exciting and very important.

I was disappointed that I would be giving up a portfolio I loved but, when I told my husband about the scope of my new responsibilities, he commented that perhaps the premier actually knew me better than I had thought he did.

In the days following my appointment as minister of children and youth services, I felt more anxious than excited. That weekend, while out shopping for my mom, I held my breath and stood perfectly still behind a rack of ladies' clothing, hoping to avoid being spotted when I heard the voices of what I assumed were a mother and child approaching in the nearby aisle. The child's voice revealed her disability. A week before that I might not have noticed, but now she would be mine to be concerned about.

I had always thought of myself as a compassionate person, but I knew my new responsibilities would require me to extend myself well beyond that. I prayed for wisdom and the strength I would need to do the work ahead of me.

Chapter 12

Children and Youth Services

THE LANDSCAPE THAT SUMMER, AS we approached for landing in Pikangikum, was beautiful, a forest of evergreen spruces stretching as far as my eyes could see, spotted with several small lakes. Pikangikum is a fly-in Ojibwe First Nation reserve with a population of under three thousand people. Only in the winter, when the lakes are frozen, forming ice roads, are trucks able to access the community to deliver supplies. A few Indigenous communities own Wasaya Airways. The aircraft was an older but obviously well-maintained model of the Pilatus that my son Stefan flies for the OPP. On some of the flights I have taken to visit Indigenous communities in northern Ontario, someone would ask my group from the Ministry of Children and Youth Services to allow them to hitch a ride with us. On one such occasion, our guest was a chief of one of the communities that own Wasaya. That caused us to chuckle, given that we were actually using his airplane, and there he was asking us for a ride. We landed on an airstrip at the beginning, or end, of a long, dusty road. That day, I took advantage of my position as minister to head to the cab of the pick-up truck that met us at the airstrip, for the seat next to the driver. That way, I would have to contend only with the dust already inside the truck.

What a different experience this would be from the fly-in trips that I had made to the Appleton sugar estate in Jamaica for one of my information technology consulting contracts. It was a smaller airplane in Jamaica, landing on an unpaved clearing between rows of sugar cane, a limousine waiting to whisk me off to the office and my son Nick to the nursery school at the country club. I would see him at lunch and then again at the end of the day, when we would be driven back among the seemingly endless fields of sugar cane, their long, leafy stalks blowing in the breeze. We would head home to Kingston, just my little boy and me, with our pilot and our airplane to ourselves.

I don't think the men in the second truck were coming to say goodbye as I left the community centre for the airstrip in Pikangikum. I think they wanted to be sure that I got on the plane. Earlier in the afternoon, I had told the residents on this desolate and depressed reserve that they would make no progress until they allowed their women to have a voice. According to the briefing notes prepared by the staff at my ministry, I wasn't to expect any of the women to speak to me, and I shouldn't make them uncomfortable by trying to engage them in conversation. The women of Pikangikum didn't speak to strangers. It seemed to me that they hardly spoke at all. But if it was the men who were in charge, they certainly had no reason to be proud of themselves. It was as though God had turned his back on this place. Could this really be Canada?

It was hardly surprising that a thirteen-year-old girl had hanged herself from a tree by the lake a few days before my arrival. Pikangikum is said to have one of the highest suicide rates in the world. They invited me to look at her body. It was in a room in her grandparents' house. The temperature in the house seemed even warmer than it had felt outside. I asked them to let me remember her as she was in the school photos that they had shown me. Then I left the house as gracefully as I could, trying not to show just how eager I was to get out of there.

My visit had included a tour through a forest led by a female OPP officer. It felt like the tour would never end. She wanted me to know that the older children spent the night in the forest sniffing from garbage bags that contained gas siphoned by the younger ones from trucks on the reserve and also drinking from cans of hairspray diluted with water. The officer told me that the kids wandering around with their hoods over their heads were also probably high from sniffing the liquid paper, white-out, that they had painted on their upper lips.

No one smiled. The residents of Pikangikum looked like they might have preferred life to have passed them by entirely, rather than forcing them to abide this terrible existence. I concluded this was what despair looked like.

That was my first encounter with the people of Pikangikum. My next encounter would be about two years later when I made my second visit to Kitchenuhmaykoosib Inninuwug First Nation (KI), Big Trout Lake.

I had asked Chief Donny Morris of KI to help the people of Pikangikum. It was as much my way of acknowledging that I had been impressed by what I saw of the leadership and facilities at KI as it was my cry for help for their brothers and sisters.

For sure, in KI's Co-op there were small quantities of exorbitantly priced vegetables and fruits and a few plastic-wrapped packages with discoloured and dried-out portions of chicken that supermarkets in Toronto would long have thrown out, but their standard of living was vastly better than what I had observed in Pikangikum. I had returned to KI to announce that our government had been successful in acquiring the beautiful, large log house on the reserve, no longer occupied by Bell Canada workers, for KI's residential mental-health program. Other northern Ontario reserves would find this centre closer and more accessible than off-reserve facilities, as well as more conducive to the well-being of those who needed this kind of support. The ways they would help youth who needed care would reflect their culture. It would be theirs, for their people, in ways that others had not understood to be necessary.

After my announcement, KI's Chief Donny Morris led me to a small room in the building. I had no idea what was in store for me behind the closed door. My heart raced as I entered the room and saw three people from Pikangikum, easily identifiable by their particular style of dress and their solemn facial expressions; two men and a woman. They spoke to me about their sense that theirs was a lost community. And they spoke about their concerns for their children. I was at a loss for words. It felt as though something had raised the temperature inside my chest, exactly where my heart was supposed to be.

I listened as my shock at seeing them there subsided and was replaced by relief. I knew they were there because Chief Donny Morris had embraced my request that he extend his hand to support others who seemed much less capable of helping themselves. And they had accepted his hand. And the woman from Pikangikum spoke to me. And the men revealed to me their despair. So much for my cautious, well-intentioned, and otherwise useful briefing notes. Hurrah for my heart.

After I left government, my son Stefan applied to be posted for three weeks in Pikangikum. I was very proud that he would want to do that. It was February, sometimes −30°C. He experienced far more than I had experienced and the stories he shared served to reinforce what I already knew, which is that my son is a wise and decent human being, a good man.

My first announcement as minister of children and youth services generated advice from my communications staff that it was time for me to move on. I, on the other hand, thought the event had gone quite well. It was about early learning and child care, the Best Start program, but as I surveyed the beautiful, energetic, and curious children at the child-care centre, I also saw apprentices in the skilled trades and college students and university graduates. I saw hope and opportunity and limitless potential in these little ones. It was the official start of my love affair with the children and youth services portfolio.

I would soon find myself being faced with the reality that for some children, the concept of limitless potential involved significant challenges. Those challenges ranged from socioeconomic to the need for protection, through physical, psychological, and neurological complexities. And when the other systems, or perhaps other aspects of life, failed some youth, I would have responsibility for those who found themselves in conflict with the law and calling the youth-justice system home for a while.

This could not have been brought home to me more starkly or in greater contrast than the day when I drove to Hamilton with an itinerary that included two stops. The first stop was at an elementary school that also housed an early learning centre where parents and grandparents could accompany their pre-kindergarten and kindergarten-age children and grandchildren for enriching learning and development activities. As soon as our car had come to a stop in the fenced parking lot outside the early learning centre, a little boy with a bright smile ran out of the building, followed by an obviously worried and perhaps embarrassed staff member. It felt wonderful to be able to put my arms around the little guy, this bundle of energy, stopping him as he ran toward us. After greeting the adults in the centre, I was led to the school's auditorium where students, staff, and school board officials were waiting to welcome me. They were all dressed in pyjamas for their celebration of "joy day." I left the school filled with hope, believing that the future belonged to those children.

Our next stop was the Hamilton-Wentworth Detention Centre. I can still hear the sound of the heavy turnstile gate closing behind me: metal banging against metal. I remember thinking, *so this is what it feels like to be in jail.* Before going through the gate, I was required to surrender my purse to the guard. I would be able to collect it on my way out at the end of my visit. Unlike what I had experienced at the first stop, no one smiled. No one seemed eager to greet me.

Children and youth services was entirely new ground for me. There was so much for me to learn. The portfolio was extremely challenging but it didn't take me long to fall in love with all that it entailed.

Having been more familiar with my previous portfolio of training, colleges, and universities, where it seemed I had several options and a variety of supports to offer every young person in Ontario who had an interest in continuing their education in pursuit of a fulfilling career, I found myself seeking divine intervention to enable me to serve the needs of children and youth in the child-protection system, and children and youth with complex special needs such as developmental disorders, mental-health challenges, autism spectrum disorder, and youth in the justice system.

I immersed myself in briefing documents prepared by ministry officials and made myself available for consultations with a variety of stakeholders and advocates. My ministry officials eventually overcame their nervousness about me wanting to meet real parents, to hear from them directly what it was like raising children with complex special needs or mental-health challenges or autism, a particularly delicate policy area as our government had inherited a court challenge that was still under way.

The dimensions that can often give government its slow-moving reputation include the need for consultation. In government, unlike in the world of business, where a healthy sense of urgency can contribute positively to the bottom line, the process is at least as important as the outcome. The fact that government also relies on a multitude of partnerships can also present some challenges in terms of who is really responsible for how services are delivered. A large portion of the ministry's annual operating budget was distributed through hundreds of transfer-payment agencies to deliver services to children and youth. The ministry itself was staffed by more than two thousand public servants. When necessary, I reminded service providers that I was not the minister of transfer-payment agencies but rather the minister of children and youth services. That meant I saw them as partners with government, and together we had a responsibility to make children and youth better off because we were involved in their lives.

I knew we were doing the right thing when parents, staff, and volunteers of children's treatment centres across the province cried in response to an announcement we made, in 2006, of the first significant increase in annualized funding in several years. As a result of additional investments in services for children with complex special needs, seven thousand children who had been languishing on wait-lists or receiving diluted services were able to receive the therapy and other interventions they needed to help them to achieve their best possible performance.

I realized the provision of services for children with autism beyond the age of six would result in a significant rise in the demand for services, and would require not only an increase in funding, but also greater service provider capacity through the training of more behaviour therapists, and the training of early childhood educators, teachers, and education assistants. We tripled funding and created a new college graduate–level program in autism and behavioural sciences, which, in only its first two years of being in place, had graduated 203 new therapists from nine Ontario colleges. Soon there would be twelve colleges offering the program with an annual enrolment of 220 students. We eliminated the age six cut-off, almost tripled the number of kids receiving intensive behaviour-intervention therapy, and provided funding for summer camps for eight hundred kids and respite services for more than three thousand families. And because we knew there is much more to learn about autism spectrum disorders, we established a research chair in autism at the University of Western Ontario.

The need for licensed child-care spaces was great. Parents were registering their children before they were born to secure a place in the queue. I didn't expect to find myself in a struggle for child-care funding because the new federal Conservative government had decided to cancel the early learning and child-care agreement I had signed with the previous Liberal government on behalf of families in Ontario. Despite that, we supported the creation of twenty-two thousand new child-care spaces in my last two years as minister. That represented unprecedented growth. Having made no progress with Minister Diane Finley, his predecessor, I was truly grateful to the Honourable Monte Solberg who responded positively to my personal appeal for his support, soon after his appointment as the federal minister of human resources and social development in January 2007. Minister Solberg demonstrated that it is possible for individuals from different political parties to work together in the interest of serving the public good.

Public policy in support of licensed child care was not without controversy. There were some who positioned government's initiatives as attempting to undermine or detract from parents' responsibility for raising their children. In the opinion of those voices, government's support for child care was akin to supporting the institutionalization of children, an unpleasant prospect at best. In some corners, child care was seen only as a social construct, discounting the breadth of its value. The proponents of that opinion, many of whom professed to be fiscal conservatives, failed to consider the economic aspects of child care, such as the reality that its unavailability was the primary barrier to parents being able to enter the workforce. Economists and child-care advocates estimated that for every dollar invested in child care, seven dollars were generated for the economy. The reality is that there are both social and economic imperatives to be considered.

Our government took several steps to improve the accessibility, affordability, and quality of early learning and child care. The creation of thousands of new child-care spaces helped to increase accessibility. On affordability, we changed the way eligibility for fee subsidies was determined, so that twenty-five thousand more families would qualify for subsidies. To improve quality we established a regulatory college for early childhood educators, the first ever in Canada.

Through the Early Childhood Educators Act 2007, the College of Early Childhood Educators was established with the following objectives:

- to regulate the practice of early childhood education and to govern its members;
- to develop, establish, and maintain qualifications for membership in the college;
- to accredit programs in early childhood education offered by post-secondary educational institutions and other bodies;
- to provide for the ongoing education of members of the college and to accredit ongoing education programs;

- to issue certificates of registration to members of the college and to renew, amend, suspend, cancel, revoke, and reinstate those certificates;
- to establish an appeal mechanism for registration decisions;
- to establish and enforce professional standards and ethical standards that are applicable to members of the college and that demonstrate a respect for diversity and a sensitivity to the multicultural character of the province;
- to receive and investigate complaints against members of the college and to deal with issues of discipline, professional misconduct, incompetency, and incapacity;
- to promote high standards and quality assurance with respect to early childhood educators and to communicate with the public on behalf of the members; and
- to perform the additional functions prescribed by a regulation.

I found it absolutely critical to hear, first-hand, from parents who had no idea how or where to access the support they required to help their children with their mental-health challenges. The children's mental-health sector had not received an increase in funding in twelve consecutive years, despite the high prevalence of mental illness among children and youth. There was also more to be done to better integrate the work of the more than 250 mental-health agencies funded by the ministry, so that access to services could be less fragmented. However, the sector was strengthened, and programs that had been threatened owing to funding challenges received substantial increases from our government.

A woman in a social service organization that was partnering with other organizations, including a school in her area, to provide a network of supports for children with mental-health challenges told me that it was important to be able to tell the difference between a disturbed child and a disturbing child. The response to the two situations would be different, she said. While some form of discipline might be required for the disturbing child, mental-health interventions were likely to be what the disturbed child might require.

I recall visiting a centre in London, which operated a Section 23 school for children who had been expelled from the regular public school system. Some of the children were only four or five years of age and they had already been expelled from school. To me, that seemed like a life sentence.

I visited a centre in York Region where the children in their Section 23 classes told me how they were learning to effectively manage the behaviours they wanted to change. I left there inspired and convinced that those young people would be fine. I also found myself thinking about adults, including myself, who could benefit from the kinds of interventions and life skills that centre was providing for those children.

I did not anticipate the experience, which I found to be either uninformed or political in character, that I would have when an agency that provided mental-health supports to children suddenly started experiencing wait-lists for service. My ministry officials and staff in my minister's office were in the midst of developing a proposal for a significant increase in funding for the mental-health sector. In addition to an increase in the regular payments made to agencies, the proposal included a special pool of emergency funds that could be accessed by agencies experiencing unusual demand for service due to crises they had not anticipated. An example of that might be a sudden and significant increase in suicides in a northern Ontario community. We had learned during our visits to some communities that situations like this existed, and when they occurred, agencies would be unable to increase their capacity to deal with the rise in demand for service. Some agencies had been experiencing growing wait-lists for their services. We knew the increase in funding would be helpful. One agency that had not previously experienced a wait-list for children and youth requiring its services had suddenly found itself in that position. It went public with its demand for an increase in funding and its MPP amplified its situation through one of the means available, this being question period in the Ontario legislature. Given that other agencies were already dealing with wait-lists, I believed it would be wrong to simply bring the agency that was new to that experience to the front of the line in an effort to silence the attacks I was receiving, in particular from the MPP for the riding where the agency was located. I needed to have a better understanding of what had caused the changes at the agency, so I asked my ministry officials to investigate. What they found was that the agency was located next to Canadian Forces Base Petawawa. This was the base from which military personnel were being deployed for duty in Afghanistan. Children of members of the military were experiencing anxiety and other challenges related to that new reality. We also discovered that while the federal government provided mental-health supports for servicemen and servicewomen, those supports were not extended to their children. I made the situation worse for myself when I shared the observation, publicly, that the federal government needed to understand the impact that those deployments had on families.

Contrary to a claim by the-then federal minister of health, my observation wasn't meant to be a political statement, but I guess the fact that I was a Liberal minister and the federal government of the day was Conservative clouded the reality of the situation. In an attempt to settle things down, the premier's office met with the-then Ontario ombudsman who had created a role for himself in the situation. I thought this was ironic — rich, as some would say — given that he had previously served as ombudsman for the Department of National Defence. Shouldn't he have been aware of the gap that existed in the support services for military families? As originally intended, the agency involved received its appropriate share of the new funding, as did the other agencies in the province, and my ministry officials worked with their counterparts in Ottawa to help with the development of policies to support military families.

I will never forget the youth from Ottawa who told me they could help me to help them. They knew what they needed to help them deal with their mental-health challenges. They just couldn't do what was needed without the help of others.

I will also always remember hearing the young man who said the prayer before dinner at a Variety Village event, asking for God's blessing for those who were not as fortunate as he was. This young man did not have the use of his arms or his legs and offered the prayer while seated in his specially designed motorized chair. Time and time again, I was struck by the positive attitudes of youth whom I met.

I had to face the realization that the solutions to these challenges would require much more than my very best intentions and the best efforts of the staff in my office and in my ministry, and more than success at convincing the custodians of the treasury that my ministry's proposal warranted the financial investment we had identified as necessary. Taking the solution from concept to delivery sometimes proved to be more easily said than done.

I sometimes found myself unhappy with the management of particular children's aid societies, but I always empathized with the staff who worked on the front lines in incredibly stressful situations day after day. It was not well understood that while all the children's aid societies were governed by the same provincial legislation, each society operated under its own board and management. Recognizing that there were weaknesses in the administration and inconsistencies in the approach to and quality of service delivery across the system, and given the substantial nature of government funding provided for child protection, our government had broadened the powers of the provincial auditor to include the children's aid societies. While the auditor's first report did not clearly link the findings to specified children's aid societies, my ministry had been made aware of those links. In response to some particularly troubling findings, a few board members of one of the largest children's aid societies contacted my minister's office to express their concern and to convey the message that they had not been aware of the situations and practices reflected in the findings. This was hardly consoling to me, and while some societies bristled under the increased attention they received from my ministry officials, it was I, as minister, who had to face the criticisms.

While working in the private sector, there were times when I had thought that the downside of being in senior management was having to take the heat for any failure on the part of even one member of my team. I recalled comparing my team to a theatrical production. Whether a team member's responsibility was managing the lighting, organizing costumes or stage sets, playing the roles of main or supporting actors, or directing, the success of the performance would always come down to how well we each did our part.

Ministries are staffed by public servants, also known as bureaucrats or ministry officials. In Ontario, ministries are headed by deputy ministers who report to the head of the Ontario public service, who also serves as secretary of the cabinet and clerk of the executive council. I valued and respected the experience of my ministry officials. I marvelled at their ability to be objective and professional when a change in government resulted in the need for them to adjust to changes in political ideologies. They respected the fact that I read everything carefully and thoughtfully. I knew I could rely on the support of my senior officials in the public service and they appreciated my emphasis on good policy over clever politics. They knew I would always have questions and they knew they would need to provide credible answers. They understood I would not always agree with their recommendations, but when we had arrived at an agreement on public policy or a particular course of action, they knew I would carry the ball forward with confidence. Because we worked hard to reach agreement on how to proceed on our various files, we accomplished a lot of good things together.

Responsibility for legislation, policy-making, and governance, not day-to-day implementation or operation, is the theoretical scope of the minister's power. But in reality, the minister is ultimately responsible for everything. Ministerial responsibility, in governments that follow the conventions of the Westminster system, means that the cabinet minister is responsible for the actions of her or his ministry. In the simplest terms, I, as minister, would be the person scrummed by the media and challenged during question period in the legislature, despite being told during my rookie orientation that it would be helpful to remember that it was question period, not answer period. In my view, the best approach was for the bureaucracy and the minister to work together to reach common ground. In that way, positions I felt I couldn't support would not be taken and positions I could support would be unequivocally defended by me even when it was staff in my ministry who were responsible for the actions taken.

The Honourable Lincoln Alexander had also given me a preview of what to expect during question period. Linc, a lawyer by profession, was the first Black MP and the first Black cabinet minister in the government of Canada. First elected in 1968, he served as an MP until 1980. His time as a cabinet minister was much shorter, serving as the minister of labour from 1979 to 1980. Having been encouraged to run for political office as a Progressive Conservative, Linc told me that when he won his seat but his party lost the election, he asked the leader of his party to help him understand his role in the House of Parliament. Linc shared with me that his leader, the leader of the opposition, told him that his role was to ask the government embarrassing questions. Linc said that his leader had told him he didn't need to have an interest in the subject or care about the response to the question. Being well aware of Linc's sharp wit, I had thought he was joking. My own experience in the Ontario legislature would make me realize that my friend had not been joking about question period at all. The Honourable Lincoln Alexander was appointed lieutenant governor of Ontario in 1985 and served in that capacity until 1991. A tall, gracious, warm, and charming gentleman with an encouraging word for everyone he encountered, Linc would always cause me to smile as I observed first-hand on many occasions his popularity among youth.

I must say that, even now, when I hear governments being pressured to make commitments before they have completed the work necessary to determine the directions that have the greatest likelihood of effectively serving the public good, I experience frustration.

On many occasions, I also found myself considering the political science concept of comparative development in the context of public policy that could impact different segments of society in very different ways. I understood that sometimes we must take steps to bring equity to situations that, if left on their own, might further divisions that already marginalize certain members of our society. An example of this had to do with child care. Inadequate and insufficient access to affordable, reliable, quality child care has long been identified as a significant barrier in allowing parents to leave social assistance behind and to secure employment.

When it was revealed by the media that there were child-care centres in subsidized housing complexes that had been permitted to retain their licences to operate while they corrected shortcomings related to their sanitary conditions, I had no difficulty accepting responsibility for the decisions made by my ministry officials. I knew that, had we closed those centres, we would have put those children at even greater risk because they might have been left un-supervised with nowhere else to go while their parents were out trying to earn a living. As minister of children and youth services, I stood by my ministry officials when they were criticized for not shutting down child-care centres where income levels of parents qualified them for the highest levels of subsidies, when they had found mouse droppings in the centres. I knew we were doing what was best for the children, who would have been at risk of being apprehended by the child-protection system owing to perceived neglect when their parents would have to continue going to work, leaving their children unsupervised or, alternatively, risk losing their survival jobs. Rather than closing those centres, the best solution for the children was for the inspectors to issue warnings and ensure that the centres got rid of the mouse droppings and, of course, the mice. Accepting ministerial responsibility included making a com-mitment to publish inspection findings at each centre and online, so parents could be better informed. By receiving more information about their children's child-care centres, the parents could also help government to hold the operators of their centres to a higher stan-dard, rather than either putting the children's health and safety at greater risk or threatening the parents' ability to hold on to their jobs.

It is also possible that the minister's power might be limited in several ways. Limitations can result from priorities blessed or decreed elsewhere, such as the premier's office or mandates that have joint carriage and require actions to be taken by more than one ministry.

Challenges to the effective implementation of government dir-ectives can also come from the fact that delivery of services takes place not only through a huge public service–run system, but also through hundreds of transfer-payment agencies that are funded to deliver services on behalf of government but are governed by their own boards of directors and operated by people they employ. It sometimes appeared that some of these agencies preferred to believe the provision of funding was the full extent of the government's responsibility.

Achieving an environment that helped people to strive toward higher levels of performance, an environment that caused people to feel motivated to be their best, was my objective. A collaborative environment, without hidden or political agendas and where communication was clear and information flowed freely, would help teams to work both effectively and efficiently.

Funding accompanied by agreed targets and unambiguous objectives that enabled everyone involved to understand and work toward the achievement of those goals would also lead to improved accountability. I saw the Freedom of Information and Protection of Privacy Act as well as cooperation with the media as part of that accountability. I believed ministerial responsibility involved being accountable for outcomes that reflected successes as well as outcomes that reflected shortcomings or failures we may or may not have been able to mitigate.

Chapter 13

Wards of the Crown

MY MOM PASSED AWAY ON January 4, 2006, in a Scarborough hospital, after undergoing emergency surgery to repair a complex fracture. She was ninety-four years of age. Our family was scheduled to return to Canada from a vacation in Mexico the following day. I was somewhat consoled that my sister, Pat, was with Mommy when she died. The finality of her passing registered fully when Chris drove me to the funeral home to make preparations for the funeral and I spotted two hearses parked across from the main entrance to the building. I remained seated in the car for a while until the tears stopped flowing, leaving a burning sensation in my eyes.

While I was downstairs in the funeral home, making my way through the coffins on display, wondering which one to choose — neither extravagant nor too simple, remembering that it was meant to be only temporary — my cell phone rang. It was Premier McGuinty calling to convey his condolences. He wanted to assure me that Mommy must certainly have been proud of me. The tears returned. I could only listen and say "thank you" at the end.

I chose a stunning, geometrically cut, heavy, clear-crystal urn for Mommy's remains. Mommy had always liked crystal. Unlike the coffin, the urn would be permanent. The people at the mausoleum told me they had never seen one like it before. The niche that houses the urn at the mausoleum has two marble walls and two glass walls and is positioned in such a way that during the day, when the sun shines directly through the large picture window across from it, the urn becomes a prism displaying an array of beautiful colours.

Paying tribute to my mom is something I have continued to do in a variety of ways, most often in private, and especially when I need to draw on her for inspiration and strength.

———

One evening, two or three weeks after my mom had died, I was having dinner at the Pape Adolescent Resource Centre (PARC), with a group of teenagers who were transitioning out of the care of Ontario's child-protection system. I told them I would be attending an event hosted by an association of foster-care providers. The timing was perfect because it gave me an opportunity to hear the thoughts of youth with lived experience, which I could share with my hosts the following evening. It was always helpful to be able to flavour my formal briefing notes and speaking points with real-life examples.

"What would you like me to say to the people I will be meeting tomorrow?" I asked the youth.

"Tell them we wish we could help ourselves to food from the refrigerator without first having to seek permission."

"We wish we could be treated like the biological children of our foster parents who are not subject to curfews and have their own keys to the house."

"Tell them we wish we could be allowed to bring our friends home."

As I felt my heart sinking, a girl who had not spoken before made a different kind of request. "Remember to thank them for taking us in and providing us with a home."

This entire experience was particularly overwhelming for me, so much for me to process. The loss of my mother was still fresh. I was still coming to terms with that. Listening to the young people as they shared their thoughts about foster care with me reminded me how fortunate I had been not only in my childhood but even as an adult. The tears were impossible for me to contain, causing the young people to question and comfort me with a warmth that was incredibly generous, particularly given their own experiences. One girl told me she hoped to be reunited with her biological mother soon.

Imagine a world where every child knows they are loved. I knew I was loved. I knew my parents and my teachers thought I was special. I was so sure about that, it must have been implanted in my brain for life. That's powerful.

I was free. I was safe. Nothing would ever harm me. I was confident. My teachers had given me tasks that children my age, then and now, wouldn't normally be given. So I tried to live up to their expectations. When my parents told me I was wonderful, even on days when they knew and I knew there was room for improvement, I felt I couldn't risk disappointing them. Very powerful.

As Ontario's minister of children and youth services, I came to understand clearly that children who found themselves as wards of the crown were experiencing life in a very different way. While there are youth who speak of the positive experiences they have had in foster care, no child deserves to be a ward of the crown. I disliked the term "apprehend," the term used to describe when a child is being taken into the care of the child-protection system. Perhaps it's the adults who have let those children down who should be apprehended and taken into a different kind of custody.

The weekend after I was assigned the children and youth services portfolio, I attended a community event where a man introduced himself to me as being one of my stakeholders. I asked him to tell me more. He told me he owned four foster homes. I asked him who attended the parent–teacher interviews at the children's schools. He looked at me like I was of unsound mind and walked away. I would learn that there were people who owned a lot more than four foster homes.

I also learned that some of these homes provided residential services for children and youth with severe special needs in a group setting. I would find myself having to ask and respond to questions about the administering of prescribed psychotropic medications and their effect on some of the children in these settings. While the medication had been prescribed by physicians, were children and youth in care being monitored sufficiently for how they were reacting to these powerful mood-altering substances? It seemed to me that the focus in some of these residential settings was on managing behaviour to achieve compliance, and I wondered if these residences were more about the provision of housing than providing a caring and supportive home environment. I was even asked, by members of the media, to comment on why police would be called to a residence because two children were slapping each other with tea towels. I heard that such calls for police intervention were a regular occurrence. How could I comment on that except to say I would never call the police to intervene if my sons were slapping each other with tea towels?

A woman called me at my constituency office to complain, angrily, that officials in my ministry were taking too long to inspect the rooms she had added to her home. Her plan was to provide foster care for children and it was taking too long to put the rooms into service. In the meantime, she was struggling with the debt she had assumed in order to get the construction work done. I suggested she put the rooms up for rent since it seemed her project had been about providing herself with a source of income rather than providing children with a safe and caring home environment.

Thora Espinet, a family lawyer, was one of the first people to reach out to me. Thora told me that some communities had a better understanding of how the child-protection system worked and how to prevent their children from being taken into care. They would appear at court hearings, sometimes in groups, to demonstrate that they could provide support to families experiencing difficulties. Their efforts would often be successful. Supports such as counselling for families could be very helpful during times of crisis that might otherwise deteriorate into allegations of suspicion of neglect.

Expanding the definition of "places of safety" to include people beyond biological relatives who were known to the child would also become one of the amendments that we made to the Child and Family Services Act. Consistent with that approach was our response to Indigenous leaders who told us about their practice of customary care. They explained that in their communities, children would be cared for by the community, not just by their biological parents. They also told us that when a child-protection worker visited a home and found what would really be evidence of poverty rather than evidence of neglect, the child would be taken away and placed in foster care sometimes far away from their reserve. That foster-care provider would receive funding to assist with the expenses related to caring for the child. Indigenous leaders wondered why their own families could not be provided with those financial supports so that they would not have to lose another child. I knew that the painful memories of residential schools were ever fresh in their minds and had no difficulty understanding the distress that Indigenous leaders described to me. Customary care was introduced in an amendment to the Act, and perceived neglect lost its previous power.

Some of what I learned made me realize, without any doubt, that my privileged life had sheltered me from many of life's harsh realities.

Some of the children's aid societies were not supportive of a change our government made to the Child and Family Services Act, which eliminated several of the barriers to adoption. Some wanted me to extend the age at which young people could be in their care. My objective was to provide children and youth in the child-protection system with the opportunity to have permanent homes rather than changing foster homes as often as eight times per year, as was the experience of some Crown wards. That could also mean having to change schools, or not feeling a part of a family, or not being able to assume that they would celebrate with "their" family on special occasions.

I have been touched by the resilience of so many children and youth I have felt privileged to meet. I cannot imagine that I would be the person I am without the love I received and the assumptions of permanence I was able to enjoy as a child. For sure, the challenges are too much for some to bear, but there are also amazing success stories.

One of my last initiatives as minister was, in 2007, to introduce and shepherd the passage of legislation to establish Ontario's first independent provincial advocate for children and youth. This was not without resistance from those who felt that independent officers of the legislature served to embarrass governments. I didn't deny that an independent advocate would lead to increased accountability. That was precisely my objective. I felt, very strongly, that children and youth who were receiving government-funded or government-administered services should be better off because of government's involvement in their lives. We couldn't change their pasts but we had an important role to play in improving their prospects for the future.

Prior to the proclamation of the Provincial Advocate for Children and Youth Act 2007, while Ontario had had a child advocate, the position was not independent of the government and as such did not report to the legislative assembly but rather to the government of the day. With that came the risk that observations and recommendations could be left unnoticed or even unavailable to the public.

It was in January 2006, less than two years before the Act was proclaimed, that I had the privilege of meeting Irwin Elman, who at that time was the manager of PARC, the transitional program for youth in and leaving care. That was when I had met the youth who consoled me as I cried uncontrollably after listening to what they shared with me about their experiences in foster care. I was struck by the respect and space that Irwin had provided the youth to express themselves, to share their thoughts and concerns with me. They were obviously in charge of the meeting with the minister. At PARC, Irwin empowered the youth and helped them feel confident about themselves while providing the kinds of support they needed to pursue their dreams. Between 2003 and 2007, he received the Ontario Association of Children's Aid Societies Outstanding Youth Service Award, was named a Canadian hero by *Maclean's* magazine and received the Ministry of Children and Youth Services' Outstanding Achievement Award.

In 2008, Irwin Elman was appointed provincial advocate for children and youth, pioneering the establishment of the Advocate's Office with the Act, the principles of the United Nations Convention on the Rights of the Child, and his prior experience working with and on behalf of children and youth, as his guides.

The purpose of the Advocate's Office, as defined in the Provincial Advocate for Children and Youth Act 2007, was to

- provide an independent voice for children and youth, including First Nations children, and youth with special needs, by partnering with them to bring issues forward;
- encourage communication and understanding between children and families and those who provide them with services;
- educate children, youth, and their caregivers regarding the rights of children and youth; and
- conduct investigations and make recommendations to improve children's aid society services and services provided by residential licensees where a children's aid society is the placing agency.

Irwin Elman undoubtedly held the government's feet to the fire but always did so in a thoughtful, sensitive, constructive, and solution-oriented manner. Several reports produced by his office clearly and in great detail described the experiences of children and youth whether in the care of the child-protection system, in youth-justice and other residential facilities, or in need of mental-health interventions. The Advocate's Office recruited youth amplifiers to ensure that the loudest voices were those of the children and youth, conducted listening tours across the province, and held conferences at which children and youth had the opportunity to have their voices heard by legislators, policy-makers, and service providers. Heart-wrenching situations in residential services, some most unfortunately requiring the involvement of the Office of the Chief Coroner, were brought to the attention of government and the public in objective, reliable, informed and informative, professional, genuine and passionate, but non-sensationalized ways, even as the Advocate's Office worked with the respective ministries and agencies of government toward achieving improvements to various aspects of the system.

Children and youth were provided the tools and resources to enable them to participate in legislative committee hearings on proposed substantive changes to legislation such as the Child, Youth and Family Services Act (2017). Irwin Elman created an atmosphere grounded in respect, self-esteem, and empowerment that provided development opportunities and built resilience among children and youth. With the primary office of the provincial advocate located in Toronto, he also established an office in Thunder Bay, bringing the presence of the provincial advocate closer to Indigenous children and youth in northern Ontario. Staffed with people with an understanding of the workings of the provincial systems from their own lived experiences — having themselves been recipients of such services, and who beyond that experience had also professionally qualified themselves at undergraduate and graduate levels of post-secondary education — the Advocate's Office under the leadership of Irwin Elman provided mentorship and modelling in Canadian settings beyond the province of Ontario, as well as internationally.

A humble and unassuming individual, yet one who has been unequivocal in speaking "truth to power" in the most effective and enabling ways, as the provincial advocate for children and youth in Ontario, Irwin Elman epitomized the concept of servant leadership.

Just months after taking office in October 2018, the new Ontario government closed the Advocate's Office and, in May 2019, repealed the Act that had created it. My heart still hurts whenever I think about that.

Chapter 14

The Autism Challenge

IN 1988, DUSTIN HOFFMAN AND Tom Cruise starred in a multi–
Oscar winning movie called *Rain Man*. I recall from the movie that
when Tom Cruise took his older brother to see a doctor and filled
out the required form for new patients, the office assistant asked
what he meant when he had written that his brother was "artistic."
On the form, Tom Cruise had actually written that his brother was
"autistic." That might have been an indication of how little awareness there was, thirty years ago, about autism spectrum disorder.
The character played by Dustin Hoffman would become a resident
at a mental-health institution, but his exceptional memory skills
and ability to perform numerical calculations involving large numbers, in his head, were truly remarkable and added to the mystery
and complexity of his condition.

There is still so much to be learned and so much more to be
done to support children with autism and their families. Autism
spectrum disorder is an excellent example of the complexities of
implementing public policy where doing the right thing for some

members of society might require drawing resources from support for other members of society.

My party's campaign platform promised to eliminate the age six cut-off for intensive behaviour intervention (IBI) therapy for children with autism. The age of six was criticized as being arbitrary, not supported by scientific research. Parents feared the withdrawal of IBI therapy would lead to deterioration in their child's condition. Less intensive therapies, while perhaps less expensive, were believed to be less effective. Parents saw little in the way of continuation of supports of other kinds for their children.

Our government inherited a court challenge by a group of parents who sought supports for their children. Those parents were professionals, well educated, well informed, some financially independent, some with more than one child with autism. They also had highly respected and capable legal counsel. That case had already been under way against the previous government for a few years, and the counsel in the attorney general's ministry who was in charge of the file on behalf of the government had maintained the position that only the government had the constitutional privilege of knowing what the full extent of priorities were and how resources should be allocated in support of various priorities.

The capacity of the system was inadequate. Parents of hundreds of children on wait-lists for IBI feared their children would age out while waiting to access services, while other parents feared that their children would be able to access only a fraction of the services they required because they would get to the head of the line only a short while before they would be cut off at age six. In order for a child on the wait-list to receive IBI, another child would have to end his or her access to IBI. There was also a shortage of qualified behaviour therapists, so even parents with the financial capacity to employ therapists had difficulty finding them.

In 2005, when I was appointed minister of children and youth services, the prevalence of autism spectrum disorder was about one in one hundred and fifty and growing. Children were typically given a diagnosis at around two years of age. Parents told me that some doctors preferred not to convey the diagnosis because of its lifelong challenging effects on families. Some family physicians felt they were not familiar enough with autism spectrum disorder to be confident in its diagnosis. The U.S.A.'s Autism and Developmental Disabilities Monitoring Network reported that in 2016, the prevalence of children with autism spectrum disorder was one in fifty.

Parents of children with autism proved to be well-organized and determined advocates. They often staged protests at Queen's Park, at constituency offices around the province, and elsewhere. Within a week of my appointment to the children and youth services portfolio, they staged a protest at my constituency office. It was a day when I would normally be in my minister's office, but I knew I needed to be at my constituency office to meet with those who would be holding their protest there that day. This would be my first real opportunity to understand what I needed to know about autism, and who better to learn from but the families of children with autism?

When I went outside to listen to what they had to say and to promise my support, I noticed a woman standing off in the distance on her own. I went over to introduce myself to her and to hear her story. "Are you here for the protest?" I asked.

"Yes," she said. "I have never joined these protests before but I thought it was time that I show my support for the other families who have been so committed to the cause."

"Will you tell me your story?" I asked.

The woman looked down toward the sidewalk sadly as she told me that she had a son with autism. She had had difficulty keeping a job and, in fact, had just been told by her employer of about a week that, although he had appreciated the high quality of her work, he needed someone he could rely on to show up for work every day. The problem was that her son had had another crisis that week and she had had to miss a day of work. To make matters worse, her husband had suffered a nervous breakdown some months before due, she believed, to the stress of having to cope with a child with autism. He seemed to have recovered from the nervous breakdown, but on the day before the protest at my office, she came home from work to find a note he had left for her, saying that he could no longer be there for the family. In addition to now having to cope with their son's challenges on her own, she also now had to cope with losing her husband. This woman's story served as a compelling introduction, for me, to the tremendous burden that autism can represent for families.

Some months after the protest at my constituency office, at the end of a meeting in the boardroom adjacent to my minister's office, I noticed that one of the women who had attended the meeting was obviously waiting for others to leave the room ahead of her. As was my normal practice, I was standing by the door, saying goodbye as people left the room. I had not recognized the woman who was waiting as someone I had met before. It was not unusual for stakeholders to join different groups for meetings with me. I assumed there was something she wanted to say to me privately.

"When I told my daughter I would be meeting with you today, she asked me to say hello for her," the woman said when it was just the two of us together in the room.

"Your daughter?" I said, revealing my surprise and the fact that I needed help to recall who her daughter was.

"Yes," the woman said. "My daughter remembered that we were at the autism rally at your constituency office. She remembered you had invited us to use your washroom even after we were so 'nasty' to you."

As the protest had been ending and families were starting to leave, I thought of the fact that there was no convenient location nearby where they could use washrooms if needed. No McDonald's, no Tim Hortons. Imagining that if I had been out with my children for that length of time, they might need those facilities, I invited the families to use the washroom in my office. A few of them did. I had forgotten about that. It had not seemed like a big deal.

I was touched that the woman's daughter, a child with autism, had recalled the experience and also expressed her memory of how I had been treated, with such empathy.

I would later meet parents of two sons who showed me bruises from attacks they had experienced after they had gone to sleep at night. Some children had difficulty expressing themselves verbally and managing their emotions, sometimes resorting instead to physical expression. I visited a treatment centre in southwestern Ontario where children and youth would be held in isolation, sometimes for days, while they recovered from their crises. Staff stayed close to the youth as I spoke with them, keeping us some distance apart.

I also visited a program in Ottawa where children and youth with autism were provided with camp-like activities. The program was run by individuals, including parents and students from universities in the Ottawa area. I was told that after working at the autism summer program, some students would change their majors in order to focus on studies about children with special needs. The program was a favourite with parents because of its emphasis on physical activities. The children would be exhausted by the end of the day and ready for a full night's sleep, a relief for the parents. Bus drivers who transported the children to and from the program each day were given an introduction to some of the characteristics displayed by children with autism. Factors such as familiarity with routes and routine were important. Increased awareness of the behaviour characteristics of children with autism could make a huge difference to everyone involved.

I learned that opportunities in the form of time away from their children with autism, respite, were important to the well-being of families. This typically involved expenditures often difficult for the families to afford.

Autism spectrum disorder and its low- to high-functioning characteristics also made for interesting learning. Among those who are high functioning, skills that involve repetition, attention to detail, and focus, as well as artistic skills are common. According to Autism Speaks, a North American research, advocacy, and awareness organization, approximately 44 percent of children with autism spectrum disorder have IQ scores in the average to above-average range, an IQ greater than 85.

Government funding for behaviour therapy was provided through service providers and transfer-payment agencies. Two options existed: direct service and direct funding. The direct service option funded the agencies to deliver the services to children. With the direct-funding option, the agencies transferred the funds to parents, who then sought their own services and service providers. Government had no direct contact with families. In fact, government had no identity or contact information for the families. This reality created some challenges for the government and for families. For example, when I announced the elimination of the age six cut-off, the announcement was made through newsletters distributed to the service providers and posted on the ministry's website. While the media also reported on the announcement, there were parents who said they were not aware of the announcement, and my ministry learned that some service providers were either simply placing the newsletters in their reception areas, or not even doing that. Some parents accused the government of not really wanting to inform them that the age six cut-off had been eliminated. There were also parents who informed the ministry that their service providers were unwilling to offer the direct-funding option because in doing so, funds would be diverted away from their agencies. Those parents told me that they could use the funding more cost effectively by engaging their own therapists rather than being limited to the services being provided by the agencies.

While the elimination of the age six cut-off resulted in children receiving services for a longer period of time, it also resulted in more children qualifying for access to services. This contributed to a substantial increase in the number of children on wait-lists for services.

Parents of a boy who was just about to turn six told me they had heard that the government of Alberta was providing funding beyond the age of six. They put their home up for sale and prepared to resign their jobs and move to Alberta. Our government's announcement of the elimination of the age six cut-off had happened just in time for them. My ministry also learned that while Alberta, at that time enjoying a very strong economy, had the funds to assist parents, a shortage of therapists meant that parents had money but also had difficulty finding therapists to employ.

In Ontario, qualified behaviour therapists also existed in limited numbers. Parents also needed help in accessing information on the qualifications, experience, and whereabouts of therapists they could hire on their own with the help of the direct-funding option. We worked with an autism-support organization to develop an online registry of behaviour therapists that parents could access on their own.

With the increased demand for services that followed the elimination of the age six cut-off, it was obvious we would need to help build a system with greater capacity to serve a larger number of children. We engaged a professor at George Brown College in Toronto to design a certificate program in autism and behavioural science and worked with several community colleges in the province to add it to their course offerings.

The day before I made the announcement about the new program to be offered at community colleges, my staff told me that a mother of two sons with autism had asked to be allowed to introduce me. Being unsure of what the mother might have in mind, staff asked her to share her intended remarks with them before they could agree to include her on the program for the announcement. My staff were so touched by the mother's remarks that they shared them with me. I cried when I read what the mother wanted to say, I think because it had been so difficult to secure the support needed to make meaningful advances for families living with the huge challenges autism presented. The following day, as I walked out of the ladies' room at George Brown College on my way to the room where the announcement was to take place, I met the mother in the hallway.

"I am glad I had the opportunity to read your remarks before you presented them today," I told her. "I preferred being able to cry in my office in private rather than crying in public today."

"Minister, you obviously don't get thanked enough," was her response.

Individuals interested in qualifying as behaviour therapists weren't the only ones doing the program. The program was also of interest to parents who needed to be better equipped to care for their children. The college program proved to be so popular that soon there were more colleges including it in their offerings.

Caring for children with autism can be physically, emotionally, and financially overwhelming for parents. The annual cost of therapy was around $50,000 when I was the responsible minister. Owing to the intense nature of behaviour therapy, more than one therapist would likely be necessary for a child. Giving their children the ability to achieve their best potential, whatever that might be, also involved struggles with the education system. The preference was to have their children in integrated environments; however, that could also strain the public school system, given the challenge of teachers and education assistants having to share their attention with special needs children in otherwise regular classes. While I met an amazing teacher who told me that children with special needs helped to teach other children empathy, so integration was a good thing, the typical reaction was that having children with autism in their classrooms was very challenging for teachers. Parents also shared experiences of children reacting negatively when being dropped off at school without having their therapists accompany them. So it seemed obvious to me that the solution was to allow children's therapists to be with them at school, thereby satisfying the children's need for familiarity and special attention as well as easing the burden for teachers and their regular education assistants. Yet, it turned out to be not that simple or obvious a solution to implement. I was told that having the children's therapists with them at school could present a threat to the job security of regular education assistants.

Sometimes serving the public good can be very challenging. The complexities of public policy-making require compromises, emotional and values-based judgments, and expenditures to be borne by all taxpayers for the benefit of some.

A senior policy adviser in the premier's office would later share with staff in my minister's office his opinion that from a political perspective, had the minister's (my) position in support of families been embraced earlier, rather than pursuing the legal stance we had inherited, our government would have been better served.

More recently, questions have been raised as to who should bear the high costs of supports for children and families living with autism, and with what conditions. There have been suggestions that government funding should consider families' ability to pay for those supports; that is, the level of support should be based on income. The challenge continues, with public policy still evolving on the autism file. There have been calls for a national autism strategy.

Even as the prevalence of diagnosis has increased, the nature of supports and the commitment to adequate funding continue to be complex issues. While the numbers of children receiving IBI and applied behaviour analysis have increased, so have the numbers of children on wait-lists for those interventions.

Chapter 15

It Is Easier to Build Strong Children Than to Repair Broken Men[2]

THE YOUTH CRIMINAL JUSTICE ACT (YCJA) governs Canada's justice system for those who are between the ages of twelve and seventeen when they come into conflict with the law. The Youth Criminal Justice Act (2003) replaced the Young Offenders Act. Skeptics suggested that YCJA stood for You Can't Jail Anyone. It is the case that rates of youth incarceration in Canada have been steadily decreasing over the past several years, and I believe that should be viewed positively. A youth-justice system that focuses on rehabilitation, effective reintegration into society, a reduction in recidivism, restorative justice, and restitution recognizes that statistically, teenagers have many more years ahead of them than behind them and society will be better served if those who find themselves in conflict with the law are provided with opportunities for personal development that might serve to set them on a better path going forward.

---

2 Frederick Douglass (nineteenth-century American abolitionist born in slavery).

The YCJA also required that youth be moved out of custody facilities they had previously shared with adults in the justice system. When I visited one of the last secure-custody facilities in Ontario that was shared by adults and youth, I heard a young man who was entering the cell area call out from behind me, "That's Mary Anne Chambers."

A secure-custody facility is not exactly the kind of place where you want to be recognized by someone in residence. The protocols for what the minister can say to youth in the justice system are quite strict, especially in relation to the identity of the youth. I turned to the young man and said, "That's correct."

"You came to my school."

"Which school was that?" I asked, as staff at the facility tried to hurry him along and away from me.

He named a vocational school, an alternative high school I had visited on a number of occasions. I had even taken my young granddaughters with me on one of my visits. The teachers were obviously very committed to their students and the students were always warm and welcoming. The school had a great cooking program and on more than one occasion, I had purchased delicious butter tarts the students had made.

I would usually be asked to say a few words to the students assembled in the auditorium. The principal and the teachers always seemed happy to have me visit. They also seemed keen on hearing what I had to say. Contrary to the energy I would observe when I saw the students outside while I was parking my car, at the assemblies they often looked tired and uninterested in what I had to say. It would sometimes feel like I was talking to myself and it would take all the energy I had in me to get me through my remarks.

So when this young man revealed that he knew my name because I had visited his school, I was surprised and it made me want to know more. Throwing protocol out the window, I asked, "Why are you here?"

"It was a misunderstanding," he said with a slight smile, adding that one night he was driving a car he had borrowed from a friend when he was stopped by the police. The police searched the vehicle and found a firearm under the driver's seat.

"You will have to learn to choose your friends more wisely," I responded.

Another young man at the shared custody facility spoke to me from behind the bars of his cell. He told me that the time he was spending there was just a temporary setback. He had plans to return to school, complete his education, and be successful in life.

This facility gave me a sense of what jails for adults must have been like. The cells were shared by two people. Beds were hard surfaces, stacked bunk-style. The metal bars of the cells afforded no privacy even as the occupants of the cells were required to share a small washbasin and a toilet. I shuddered at the thought that two strangers would be living like that. It was impossible to imagine rehabilitation or the objective we had for reducing recidivism having any success in an environment such as this. It's no wonder the YCJA called for youth to be removed from facilities shared with adults.

At a secure-custody facility for younger youth, I met a soft-spoken, shy twelve-year-old boy who looked even younger than his age. It was mid-afternoon and he was sitting alone at a table in the cafeteria, eating a freshly baked cookie. The cook had told me he had worked at that facility for many years and loved being there "for the kids." I asked a youth worker about the boy and was told he had just returned to the facility. The worker told me the boy had previously been released, having served his sentence, and had immediately stolen a car, his intent being to be returned to the facility. The youth worker also told me that the boy was from a large family and had been repeatedly bullied at home. For that boy, secure custody meant protection for himself, a safe place. I left that facility wondering what the future might hold for that boy.

Sentencing options in the youth-justice system were secure custody, open custody, or community supervision, based on the severity of the offence. Under community supervision, youth would live with their families or in their communities but be required to check in with probation officers according to a specified schedule and frequency.

Open custody happened in group homes that looked like other homes in the neighbourhood, often without the knowledge of other residents in the community that they were youth-justice facilities. Time in open custody could be the actual sentence or part of the transition from secure custody to community supervision. Youth workers accompanied residents on outings such as trips to the library or community centre. Youth workers were not armed and outings were subject to an assessment of risk based on the progress the particular resident was determined to be making in their rehabilitation. I visited an open-custody group home after a young man who was in transition from secure custody to community supervision had obviously placed more emphasis on the *open* than on the *custody* element of his status.

The media became aware of the escape and the severity of the crime he had committed. I waited until later in the day when the media frenzy and surveillance of the home, from the air and on the ground, had subsided, then I paid the home a visit. There I met another resident, who had made a habit of teasing and bullying the one on the loose. He had reacted with shock to the news that the fellow who was out had committed such a serious crime. Only then did he realize that he might have been playing with fire. I did a tour of the home and saw the room, on the uppermost level of the house, where the missing young man was staying. It was the room reserved for the resident who was making the greatest progress. Adjacent to the room, on the outside of the house, were stairs — a fire escape that led to the ground. It was those stairs the young man had used to leave the home.

While at that home, I had a very interesting conversation with a psychologist, an elderly gentleman profoundly committed to the work he did with youth in the justice system. He told me with great pride that in the several decades he had been working with troubled youth, not one had ever re-offended. He expressed concern about the shortage of child psychologists and child psychiatrists in Ontario.

Within a day or two, the young man who had created the excitement made contact with his relatives, who saw to his return to the open-custody facility.

Not all workers in youth-justice facilities subscribed to the intent of the YCJA. I travelled to a secure-custody facility that had been the subject of reports in the local newspaper that youth were being treated too well. There I met a staff member who told me he was new to the youth-justice system, having recently moved from an adult corrections facility to be closer to where he lived. He told me youth at the facility were being "coddled," unlike the adult inmates in his previous facility, where he would simply check from time to time to ensure that they were still alive. Other youth workers and the management at the youth facility were unhappy about the reports in the local newspaper, which they considered misleading and unfair. The unprompted feedback I received from the new staff member from the adult system while I toured the facility was shared with the management of the facility and I was relieved to learn, very shortly after my visit, that the man from the adult system was no longer working at that youth-justice facility.

Working with the youth-justice file also gave me an understanding of the meaning of "in lieu of time served." There was different language used to describe the status of youth in secure-custody facilities. Youth who were serving out their sentences were in detention. Youth who were in custody awaiting trial were on remand. It seemed to me that there were far too many youth in custody awaiting trial. I acquired an appreciation of the saying "justice delayed is justice denied."

Margaret Parsons from the African Canadian Legal Clinic intercepted me as I was leaving an event late one Saturday night. She introduced herself and said she needed to meet with me. She told me there were a lot of problems with the system. Determined to get some kind of response from me, she repeatedly stressed that there were problems I needed to know about. It seemed I was not going to be able to leave the event without making a commitment of some sort. I told Margaret I didn't just want to hear that there were problems, I wanted to hear what solutions she could propose, and I promised her I would read whatever she submitted for my consideration.

A few weeks later, I received a very thoughtful and well-developed proposal for the African Canadian Youth Justice Program. Ministry officials and staff from my office met with Margaret and another lawyer from the African Canadian Legal Clinic to discuss the proposal. The rationale for the proposal was that Black youth had little or no understanding of how the justice system worked. As an example, they were often uninformed and unaware that the severity of their situations would increase if they failed to check in with their probation officers in accordance with the conditions associated with their sentences. The proposed program would provide for youth-justice workers to be located in the courts for the purpose of providing youth with information on how to navigate the system and an understanding of what the courts expected of them. The Ministry of Children and Youth Services approved funding for the program.

The African Canadian Youth Justice Program proposal also included a position description for a senior role to oversee the program. The qualifications and experience described were demanding enough that staff in the ministry's youth-justice division expressed doubt that anyone who met the stipulated requirements would be interested in applying for the role. I was pleasantly surprised when a young, suitably qualified Black woman who was actually on staff in the ministry's youth-justice division applied. The position she held in the ministry was a relatively junior one and it did not escape me that more senior officials had apparently not been aware of the talent in their midst. Judges in Ontario applauded the program, and the province of Nova Scotia reached out to the African Canadian Legal Clinic for help in establishing the program in Nova Scotia.

An initiative to create a new secure-custody youth centre was under way before I was appointed minister of children and youth services. With the YCJA requiring the separation of youth and adult custody facilities, the new centre was also set up to provide designated space for worship, a school, indoor and outdoor exercise areas, individual rooms that provided greater privacy for the youth, and a layout that allowed for proper line of sight and monitoring by staff. Along with the physical design, there would be programs provided by community organizations.

Centres were typically named to reflect where they were located. I wouldn't expect that having a custody facility named after an individual would be highly sought-after recognition. However, I saw the naming of the centre as a way to reinforce the progressive, rehabilitative aspects of the YCJA, and our government asked the Honourable Roy McMurtry to lend his name to that cause. I was thrilled when he responded positively to the request. I was also extremely grateful for the wisdom and patience he showed when protests against the creation of the centre unfairly targeted him as he accompanied me at my announcements. I saw the protests as misguided at best. The new centre would be a vast improvement over previously existing facilities. The protests also seemed to ignore that the youth centre was not where decisions regarding guilt or sentencing took place.

In marking the official opening of the Roy McMurtry Youth Centre, the Ontario government presented Roy McMurtry with a plaque with the inscription "In tribute to the Honourable Roy McMurtry, in appreciation of your many years of dedicated support for the rehabilitation and just treatment of the youth of Ontario. The Ministry of Children and Youth Services, by order of the Premier of Ontario, hereby proclaims that the new youth centre to be opened in Brampton in 2009 be named in your honour." It's quite possible that most people would prefer a youth-justice facility not be named in their honour, but the symbolism was important. Roy McMurtry is indeed a man who epitomizes the *just* in *justice*. As a separate initiative, Roy McMurtry was asked by our government to co-author, along with Alvin Curling, a report titled the *Roots of Violence*.

Roy McMurtry was attorney general of Ontario from 1975 to 1985, serving while William G. Davis was premier. They were, and still are, both highly respected and admired in the legal and education arenas and well beyond the membership and supporters of their Progressive Conservative Party. Roy McMurtry also served as chief justice of Ontario from 2003 to 2007. It was during those years that I came to know him. When he extended an invitation to me, a Liberal cabinet minister, to join him for lunch at his office, I accepted without hesitation. I looked forward to those informal lunches. They continued beyond my time in government and beyond his time as chief justice. They were opportunities for me to learn from his invaluable experience and insights on serving the public good.

From 2008 to 2014, the chief, as I have always called him, served as chancellor at York University. In 2013, in his capacity as chancellor, he presided over the convocation ceremony at which that university awarded me an honorary degree of doctor of law "to recognize your leadership in the fields of education, social services, and health care in both the public and private sectors, as well as your service to humankind through your work increasing access to opportunity for marginalized people, which has had profound impact on communities throughout Ontario and abroad."

I know very little about the adult-justice system but what I learned about the youth-justice system convinced me that it was important to understand the reasons why some children and youth find themselves in conflict with the law.

Staff in the youth-justice division of the Ministry of Children and Youth Services told me that it was their observation that learning disabilities were the most common reason why youth found themselves in conflict with the justice system. Some staff brought books from home, which their young children enjoyed reading, for the youth in the facilities because that was the developmental level at which many of the teenagers were functioning.

Teachers at the school at Brookside Youth Centre, a secure-custody facility for youth in the justice system located in Coburg, Ontario, told me they were compressing the curriculum so that the youth who spent time there could return to their communities with at least one new high-school credit. These teachers had also established a partnership with an association of skilled tradespeople in Coburg, so that youth from the centre could acquire marketable technical skills as apprentices. The ultimate objective was that the youth would leave the centre better qualified than they were before, better equipped to succeed in the real world than when they arrived at the centre. Those teachers were very creative and fully committed to the success of their students, young men who otherwise would likely find it difficult to detach themselves from a life of conflict with the justice system.

I heard a lot about the importance of education. I learned that the odds were poor for youth who did not complete their high-school education. There was more I would learn even after I was no longer in government.

In 2009, in his capacity as director of the York Centre for Education and Community (YCEC), York University's first organized research unit in its faculty of education, Dr. Carl James invited me to serve as the founding chair of the advisory council for the centre. I served in that role for three years. A judge in the Ontario Court of Justice who was also a member of the advisory council wanted to know why so many of the youth, teenagers, who were appearing before him in court were illiterate. They could not read or write adequately. They demonstrated learning deficiencies and disorders. He wanted to know how their teachers could not have noticed and intervened.

Through my involvement with the YCEC, I had the opportunity to observe Dr. Carl James's outstanding commitment to equity in education, his high expectations of the graduate students whose work he supervised, his engagement of fellow university faculty, his outreach to school boards and teachers and his embrace of schools in diverse communities as models for the achievement of excellence for their students. In addition to his own body of research and numerous publications, Dr. James led the mobilization of knowledge gained from the research done in the YCEC, and through conferences and advocacy initiatives targeted at policy-makers in municipal, provincial, and federal governments. He worked to increase the awareness of equity-related factors by practitioners in the education system, recognition of the importance of understanding the impact of mental health on student success, and factors contributing to the over-representation of Black and Indigenous youth in the justice system. For Dr. Carl James, support for student success also had to include support for parents.

The significance of all of these factors and stakeholders was reflected in his work with the YCEC. In an era when the importance of disaggregation of race-based data was viewed as too controversial for politicians to pursue, Dr. James was already working with school board researchers on the importance of this data, with the belief that progress could not be made in the achievement of improved results for underperforming students without an understanding of who they were and the socioeconomic and cultural factors that defined their lives. He has also had a long-standing belief that the participation of community is vital to the achievement of success in education. Since 2016, Dr. Carl James has held the Jean Augustine Chair in Education, Community, and Diaspora at York University.

In *Towards Race Equity in Education,* a 2017 report on a Greater Toronto Area study led by Dr. James, it is revealed that by the time Black students finished high school, 42 percent had been suspended at least once, compared with 18 percent of white students and 18 percent of other racialized students.

In the Toronto District School Board, 48 percent of students expelled between 2011 and 2016 were Black, 18 percent were white. These statistics suggest that almost half of Black youth in the largest school board in Canada are on track for failure, not only in school but, by extension, in various other aspects of life.

Statistics like these should be of great concern not only to the young people who are directly involved, and their families, but also to the wider society. As a society we cannot be successful if nearly half of any large group of young people are at risk of not achieving their potential.

I am definitely not suggesting leniency or turning a blind eye to dysfunctional behaviour. I do believe that it is important to consider whether conscious or implicit bias might be involved. Stereotypes, especially negative ones, are not usually helpful in determining a young person's potential.

With the ability to record and track race-based statistics, school boards can look at trends like where and by whom decisions such as suspension and expulsion are taking place. By analyzing why, to whom, and by whom these actions are happening, it should be possible to determine whether there are trends that point to the kind of remedial action that needs to be taken.

Disaggregated race-based data also illustrates that broad classifications like "visible minorities" or "racialized people" are not very helpful because there are significant differences in the experiences of people who are Black versus the experiences of other visible minorities or other racialized people. This is especially important for policy-makers and providers of any kind of public service to understand.

Years after I served in government, my husband and I joined the founder, Rick Gosling, and a few other supporters of an organization known as Second Chance, to have Christmas dinner at a secure-custody youth centre east of Toronto. Roy McMurtry was one of the patrons of Second Chance. Through their support for Second Chance, lawyers and judges had equipped secure-custody facilities with library books and helped to raise funds for scholarships to enable youth to pursue post-secondary education.

While seated with some of the youth at the centre, I asked them if they kept in touch with their parents. Two responded, "Yes, Miss." One of the others held his head down as he said, just loudly enough for me to hear, "No, Miss, but my father will never be able to hurt my mother again." I thought it best not to probe. Instead, I took the conversation in a different direction.

My reason for asking the youth if they had kept in touch with their parents while they were in custody stemmed from experiences I had had as minister of children and youth services. On a few of my visits to secure-custody facilities, sometimes while playing basketball with the youth, I would ask them if their parents visited often. My heart would hurt when the response was, "No, Miss, never," or "Not really, Miss," or "Only once, Miss."

I don't know how I would have dealt with feeling like I had been abandoned by my parents even if it could have been argued that I had earned that kind of treatment. This caused me to worry about how youth might decide where to turn for acceptance when their terms had been served. I also tried to imagine what it must be like for the parents of youth in the justice system.

Chapter 16

I Am What I Aspire to Be, Not What I Now Am. I Am What I Do with My Mind. I Am What I Do with My Youth.[3]

THE CHILDREN AT THE SUMMER school where I taught as a child myself, and the men who worked in the factories that I came to know through the Jamaican government's adult literacy program, saw education as a source of hope and an opportunity to better their lives. But even then, I didn't ever see myself as a teacher because I learned more from them than they did from me. One of the things I learned was how fortunate I was. I also learned that everyone has abilities, that everyone has potential. At the same time, it was obvious to me that some people might need others to help them to achieve their potential.

My work as MPP for Scarborough East was quite different from my work as a cabinet minister. As a cabinet minister, my focus was the particular portfolio for which I was responsible. It

---

3   Benjamin E. Mays (American civil rights leader, president of Morehouse College).

often seemed that as an MPP, I was expected to assist residents in my riding with any concern they had, even if the responsibility for the particular issue resided within some other jurisdiction or authority.

One day, a constituent called me to complain that the government no longer provided funding for reading recovery. She told me that her child needed the help and her school no longer provided that help. But I knew the funding had not been cancelled, because I had had the opportunity to observe a reading recovery session at a school in my riding. That school had been able to obtain a part-time resource specifically for that purpose. I discovered that the funding was managed by the Toronto District School Board's superintendent for that area and had to be requested by the schools. The principal of the school where I had observed the reading recovery program being offered had identified students who needed that extra help and had gone after the funding for the resources he needed to help his students succeed. So, it came as no surprise that within a couple years after that principal's arrival, that school was recognized as the most improved school in the province, based on their Education Quality Assessment Ontario test results. That school's principal was a champion and an advocate for the needs of his students. The school was Galloway Road Public School, and that principal was Winsley Belille.

I met Winsley Belille when I was the MPP for the riding of Scarborough East, from October 2003 to October 2007. Many of the students at Galloway Road Public School came from a cooperative housing community across the road on the east side of Galloway Road or from subsidized Toronto community housing buildings across the intersection of Kingston Road and Galloway Road to the south of the school. The Gabriel Dumont housing complex, home to one of Toronto's largest Indigenous communities, is located on the other side of that intersection.

Winsley Belille hailed from the Caribbean nation of Trinidad and Tobago. After his father passed away, his mother, having become the matriarch of a single-parent family, worked hard to provide for her three children. Winsley was the youngest of his siblings. Seeing his mother's struggle, he decided to leave school and find employment so that he could give her some support. But he continued his education on his own, outside of the formal school system, and was so successful that he was accepted by Mausica Teachers' College, a post-secondary institution funded entirely by the government of Trinidad and Tobago. Canada would later become the beneficiary of yet another outstanding member of the Caribbean diaspora.

Mr. Belille knew every student in his school by name and they knew him. His teachers loved working with him. Parents participated in the school's activities. On one of my visits to the school, a male student bumped into me a few times as we walked through the hallways. He was physically taller and heavier built than the other students and he seemed to be bumping into me intentionally. I asked Winsley if that student would be okay. He told me he was confident he would be okay. He went on to say that the young man had been suspended only three times that year, a significant improvement over the previous year, and that he had learned to negotiate effectively on his own behalf. Winsley Belille had faith in his students. It showed, and it was obvious to me that his students knew it.

Shortly after the summer break one year, I was scheduled to meet with Winsley. When I arrived for our meeting, he came out of his office, closed the door behind him, and led me to another room for our brief meeting. He explained to me that we could not meet in his office because there was a student there who, during the summer vacation break, had been sexually assaulted by her brother. For weeks after the assault, she had refused to speak about what had happened to her. Eventually, when a child-protection worker from the Toronto Children's Aid Society pleaded with her to identify someone, anyone, with whom she would feel comfortable speaking about her traumatic experience, the young girl said she would be willing to speak only with Mr. Belille. In her time of emotional need, it was Mr. Belille, her school principal, who was her confidant, her consoler, and her counsellor. Winsley Belille's dedication to helping his students achieve their personal best was obvious. He knew how best to serve his students and, by extension, their families and their community.

The University of Toronto Scarborough was also in my riding. While there attending a conference for students in a concurrent teacher education program, I wandered among the students during a break asking them, individually, why they wanted to be teachers. The responses I received varied. One individual loved mathematics and wanted to share his love of the subject with others. Another student told me she had had some terrible teachers when she was in school. What she had experienced had inspired her to become a teacher, and she was determined to be an excellent teacher. In most cases, the motivations the students shared with me reflected their academic interests. I knew they would come to know that the reality for teachers goes well beyond academics. We know teachers to be educators. They certainly are, but they are more than that.

Teachers matter. They matter a lot. The following note from a parent to his son's high-school teacher illustrates that well. My daughter-in-law, Minka, is the Mrs. Chambers, but Jason is not the student's name.

> Hello, Mrs. Chambers. I just wanted to let you know how much the above course has meant to Jason so far. He started seeing a psychologist yesterday to help with his anxiety and confidence and he told her that for the first time in his life, he actually looks

*forward to a class and it's easier for him to think about going
to school. It has impacted him so much I had to let you know.
He normally suffers from his IBS [irritable bowel syndrome]
about three days a month but since he started this semester,
he hasn't had to miss school due to illness because his anxiety
is much better. Clear instructions are always so important for
him; he gets confused easily and stresses a lot about not doing
the right thing or misunderstanding and not being in the right
place. I wanted to mention that so that any instructions given
to him should be given one instruction at a time. Thank you so
much for teaching this course and making it fun. It is doing so
much more than just educating Jason — it is the greatest help
in improving his mental wellness.*

That parent was very clearly telling my daughter-in-law, the
teacher, that she mattered.

––––––

The year was 2007 and my last personal pledge of support to the
university had been fulfilled. That pledge had funded a fully accessible workstation in the academic resource centre at UTSC. I had
told the acting principal that my next commitment would need to
be for an initiative that would make the university more meaningful to young people in Scarborough East. I was approaching the
end of my term as the MPP for Scarborough East and, while I had
not yet revealed my decision publicly, I knew I would not be seeking re-election. The acting principal at UTSC assigned Rashelle
Litchmore the task of preparing proposals for my consideration.

When Rashelle came to Toronto from Jamaica to complete high
school, she observed that many of the Black students at her school
were not doing well. Statistics released by the Toronto District

School Board confirmed that a high percentage of Black students were not completing high school. Rashelle went on to study at UTSC and, as president of the Black Students' Association, worked with other members of the association to create an academic mentorship program for Black middle- and high-school students, where the mentors are high-achieving Black students at the university and great role models for the younger mentees.[4]

Just months after my meeting with Rashelle and UTSC's acting principal in 2007, and while I was still serving as MPP and Ontario's minister of children and youth services, it was my pleasure to participate in the installation of Professor Franco Vaccarino as UTSC's ninth principal. It was not in my political capacity that I had been asked to speak, but rather as an alumna of UTSC.

On that occasion, I noted that being a UTSC alumna was a source of great pride for me, but it was also clear to me that, for that pride to remain justifiable, UTSC would need to be relevant then and into the future. I defined the boundaries of relevance as the community in which UTSC is located, the province of Ontario, Canada, and indeed the world. I pointed to the rich diversity of UTSC's student and alumni population as assets in the achievement of UTSC's relevance. I also recognized the impact that mentorship can have in the life of a young student who, if fortunate enough to receive such support, could be the first in their family to acquire a university education.

Throughout his six years as UTSC's principal, Franco Vaccarino committed himself to the leadership of UTSC not only in terms of achieving the highest academic standards and the introduction of a broader offering of programs at both undergraduate and graduate

---

4 In 2019, shortly after earning her doctorate at the University of Guelph, Dr. Rashelle Litchmore was appointed assistant professor in the Department of Human Development at Connecticut College.

levels, but also to elevating UTSC's presence and contributions to the Scarborough community and beyond. Principal Vaccarino led the engagement of UTSC in socioeconomic partnerships with community organizations. His support for the Imani Academic Mentorship Program and the creation of other experiential learning opportunities for UTSC students through these partnerships has benefited students in several elementary and secondary schools while enriching the development of UTSC students.

On a visit to see how things were going with the Imani Academic Mentorship Program, I met a teacher from one of the middle schools, who had heard I would be dropping by. She told me one of her students had invited her to see what he did at the university. He was actually the second student she had referred to the program because she had been so impressed by the positive impact the program had had on the first student. I thanked her for recognizing that sometimes students need support beyond what teachers can provide in the classroom. I also thanked her for believing in the potential of her students. Her eyes reflected how emotional the experience had been for her.

I also met a young teacher at Cedarbrae Collegiate Institute, who wore his hair in dreadlocks, whose commitment to his students was unmistakable. It was he who ensured that students from his high school participated in the Imani program. And when I learned that students from St. John Paul II Catholic Secondary School, the school that my sons had attended, had joined the program, I was thrilled.

A janitor at the university had observed that Black kids would arrive at the university in groups and inquired as to what they were doing there. He shared with staff in student affairs that his daughter, Annie, had been told by her teacher that she would not be successful. He believed otherwise and he asked if his Annie could be allowed to participate in the program although she did not attend one of the schools that were part of the program. Staff told Annie's father that she would be welcome. Annie graduated from high school and was accepted to study at UTSC. She became a mentor and ambassador for the Imani program while successfully pursuing her studies at the university.

Speaking directly to the mentees at annual graduation events, I have encouraged them to embrace the possibilities that exist for their future success. I have asked them to recognize their mentors as role models, not much older than they are, who are not only excelling in their personal pursuits but have also demonstrated their commitment to helping their younger mentees to succeed. I emphasize my belief that young people are capable of leadership. They are capable of making good things happen not only for themselves but also for others. I ask the mentees to not ever take anything for granted in life. I want them to be hungry for success and I want them to remember that they get to define what's important in life, who they want to be, and what it means to be a better person. I tell them to have confidence in their abilities, to appreciate the help they receive along the way, and to do their part to help others succeed. Real success requires hard work and commitment, wisdom and good judgment, setting high standards for themselves, and making the right choices.

I am grateful to staff and faculty of UTSC for embracing the Imani Academic Mentorship Program. Their commitment to the program and other similar experiential learning initiatives for their students has also served to increase the university's impact and relevance in and well beyond the Scarborough community. My gratitude is also shared with former UTSC staff member Liza Arnason, then with student affairs, who did most of the program's heavy lifting for many years.

In Swahili, a language spoken in several countries in East Africa, Imani means *faith*. In 2015, in its annual *Vital Signs* report, the Toronto Foundation described the Imani Academic Mentorship Program as one of the "ideas and innovations that point the way forward for Toronto." The Imani Academic Mentorship Program has served some thousand mentees since it was established. In recent years, Scotiabank has supported the Imani program. That support, along with an increase in the University of Toronto's financial commitment, has enabled an increase in the number of participants who are benefiting from the program.

———

For many years, my family sponsored Basic Schools in Jamaica, early childhood institutions for children between three and six years of age. My son Stefan accompanied me on a short trip to the island, the primary purpose of which was to visit a few of the schools we sponsored. I have never had to convince either Nick or Stef to travel with me to Jamaica. While the purpose of those trips would always be related to work of one sort or another, I have always enjoyed the opportunity to spend precious one-on-one time with my adult sons.

On a visit to Wait-A-Bit Basic School, which is located in the mountains of the parish of Trelawny, the children fell in love with Stef. I had probably been spending more of my time with the two women who ran the school in this lush countryside area, understanding their challenges and their needs. These schools are run by individuals, many of whom have not had formal training as teachers but who care deeply about the children in their towns and villages. Small-scale agriculture is the primary source of income for the residents of Wait-A-Bit, a small, quiet town with little sign of wealth beyond the fertile, stunningly beautiful surrounding landscape, cooled by its high elevation. Even the treacherous sections of the road to get to Wait-A-Bit could be viewed as a deterrent to all but its small population.

While I was talking business, Stefan was having fun with the children on the grounds outside the school building. They wanted to know when he would be back to visit them again. His assessment of them was that even if they did not become the proverbial rocket scientists, they would be good people. Their school uniforms were beautifully kept, and their attendance was high. It seemed they had not yet developed an understanding of poverty. They seemed not to find it at all strange that before they had lunch each day, they would all wash their hands together, sharing a basin of water that their teacher would put out for them, along with a small piece of soap.

The principal had asked me for a computer for the school. She was not at all concerned that there wasn't proper plumbing for the toilets at the school. What she really wanted was a computer so that her students could be exposed to greater learning opportunities. Stefan and I delivered a brand-new IBM personal computer to the school that day.

Perhaps inspired by that experience, on a subsequent visit to Jamaica, Stefan also donated a personal computer to a Basic School that he sponsored. That school, located close to the cruise ship pier in Falmouth, was also able to improve its washrooms thanks to his support.

———

From May 2010 to May 2014, I served as president of the Project for the Advancement of Childhood Education (PACE Canada), a volunteer-run charitable organization that brings together hundreds of sponsors, including people who are not members of the Jamaican diaspora, in support of Basic Schools and early childhood institutions for children three to six years old, as well as the training of early childhood educators. PACE (Canada) was originally known as Women for PAE (Canada). The organization was founded in 1987 by Jamaican-Canadian educator Dr. Mavis Burke in response to an appeal by the Most Honourable Edward Seaga, then prime minister of Jamaica. The prime minister asked members of the diaspora to support early childhood education through PACE. In an issue of the newsletter that we published twice each year, my president's message included the following story.

While in Jamaica last year, PACE (Canada) board member Dr. Fred Kennedy and I had lunch with the executive director of the Early Childhood Commission and three members of her senior team. As we were returning to their office, which is located in a busy mall close to the waterfront in downtown Kingston, I heard what sounded like a commotion among some of the street vendors in the mall. The noise seemed to be following us. I turned around and saw a woman running toward us, calling out something undecipherable as she approached. Richard Williams, a member of the team from the Early Childhood Commission, also turned around as the woman got closer to us, and it was obvious that he recognized her but seemed a bit embarrassed by what was happening. As the woman got closer to us, I noticed that she had a photograph, probably about 4" by 5" in size, of a little girl in a blue and white school uniform, on a strap around her waist. Feeling mischievous, Fred and I made comments alluding to what the possible nature of the relationship between the woman and Richard might have been. Our comments obviously did not amuse Richard. By then the woman had caught up with our group. She raised the photograph of her little girl and proceeded to tell us that Richard had been her daughter's first teacher, and that he had been her daughter's best teacher. She went on to tell us that her daughter was now in medical school studying to be a doctor. The woman was bursting with pride. The shy, unassuming Richard, while obviously uncomfortable with his rock star profile, instantly became my poster boy for what we all know to be true, which is the undeniable influence and impact of a competent and conscientious teacher.

Dr. Fred Kennedy, an educator for decades and more recently an author, is a dear friend. Fred served as principal at St. George's College in Kingston, Jamaica, from 2004 to 2006. There was a long tradition of Jesuit priests being principals at that Roman Catholic high school, the one where my brother, Keith, had been a student in the late 1950s. St. George's College has a proud reputation for producing graduates who have become Rhodes scholars. As principal, Fred broke another tradition at that all-boys' school when he welcomed girls to study there in the most senior, pre-university years of their program.

Studies have revealed that as much as 50 percent of children's academic achievement can be attributed to their family environment. It has also been observed that the parents that teachers really need to meet are often the ones who, for a variety of reasons, don't typically show up for parent–teacher meetings. I believe the ideal support system for children exists when parents and teachers are able to work in partnership with each other.

On occasion, I have been saddened to learn that the recipient of one of my scholarships has not been accompanied by a parent to the scholarship awards event. In one case, I asked the young lady who was receiving my award if her parents were at the event with her. Her response was that she didn't "have that kind of support system." She had been accepted to pursue studies at a Toronto university.

I met Wendell at a scholarship awards event. Then a youth worker in Toronto's Jane and Finch area, he thanked me on behalf of the young man who had just received my scholarship. Wendell told me that the scholarship meant a lot to the young man who had been accepted by Toronto's George Brown College for their chef's program. There was no family at the awards event to celebrate with the young man, only Wendell, his youth worker. To my pleasant surprise, Wendell also told me that we were connected in another way. He told me that my son Nick was one of his mentors. Wendell, a brilliant young man who hails from Ghana, received offers of acceptance and scholarships to further pursue his graduate studies from American Ivy-League universities; not very long after we met, he left Toronto to study at Yale in New Haven, Connecticut. His work in academia has earned him recognition and awards from Yale University, Princeton University, the University of Pennsylvania, Harvard University, the Massachusetts Institute of Technology, the University of Toronto, the Pierre Elliott Trudeau Foundation, and Canada's Social Sciences and Humanities Research Council. Dr. Wendell Nii Laryea Adjetey is now an assistant professor in the Department of History and Classical Studies at McGill University in Montreal.

Parents. Teachers. Mentors. Financial sponsors. Community organizations. Academic institutions. Businesses. Government. It really does seem to take a village to raise a child.

There are countless examples of the impact young leaders can have in moving the rest of us forward. The students behind the proposal for the Imani Academic Mentorship Program, and those who have kept the program going through their commitment to helping to improve the trajectory for the mentees, serve to illustrate that the power to be changemakers resides beyond the traditional sources of influence and authority. It is for this reason that I continue to seek and embrace opportunities to spend time with young people. They might see me as their mentor, but what I learn from them refreshes and uplifts my life. I admire their appetite for exploration, their thirst for new and better ways of solving problems, and their willingness to ask "why not?" rather than to resign themselves to the acceptance of how things have traditionally worked. I have also appreciated the clarity with which they view matters that older, more established people sometimes struggle with, perhaps because their judgment might be influenced by a desire to preserve what they have already achieved and acquired or a desire not to be seen as rocking the proverbial boat or threatening the dominant status quo.

Our young people are remarkably wise. When we support and guide them so they can rise above the challenges many face every day, we help them to believe in themselves, and we give them hope. When we emphasize the importance of education, we help our youth to appreciate the opportunities that education can provide. When we help them to recognize and respect the value of honest work and the joy of seeing what their skills and efforts can produce, we help them to experience genuine pride. And when we show them how to love themselves and how to love others, we give them the very best gift of all.

Chapter 17

Stigma, Shame, and Blame

MY STORY INCLUDES A MIX of personal experiences that have influenced how I think of mental health. My story spans a lifetime of growth and I continue to grow. There is no science involved, only observations, impressions, and a genuine interest in humanity.

In 1970, when I signed up as a volunteer teacher for JAMAL, the Jamaican government's adult literacy program, the teacher training program I completed encouraged us, the teachers, to hold classes in places where adults would feel comfortable. Adult learners would be more comfortable in places like churches than school premises, where people might conclude that they could not read or write and thus be judgmental rather than supportive of their interest in bettering themselves. We were also told to use ice breakers, lighthearted small talk, at the start of each class, to help our students to relax and feel comfortable about being there. At the end of my workday, I would go to the manufacturing company where the men, my students, worked, and they would meet me in an area normally used as a lunch room, at the end of their workday. I was finding it difficult to break the ice at the start of each class. The men were tired but more than that, they seemed uncomfortable communicating with me. It seemed they felt they had nothing in common with me.

I was also tired. I was in the first or second trimester of pregnancy but I really wanted to teach these men to read and to do simple arithmetic and I knew they really wanted to learn those skills. But, after a few weeks in which I struggled to find lighthearted ways to start each class, my pregnancy had become obvious and to my pleasant surprise the men started to ask me questions about the baby. I realized this was a topic they were comfortable with. I was thrilled. The communication with my students improved so significantly that one evening, I seized the opportunity to seek answers to a question I had always wondered about. I asked the men how they could justify having more children than they could afford to care for. The answer I received caused me to realize that they might have been working hard to learn their multiplication tables, but they already had a clear interpretation of the concept of probability. They told me that the chance of having a child turn out well enough to look after them in their old age was greater if they had several children than if they had only one or two. I was concerned about giving the children a fighting chance at being successful. They were concerned about providing secure futures for themselves.

In hindsight, I have wondered if that response might have had a connection to that old belief that every family will have black sheep. Was there a culture that simply accepted this as inevitable? Was there also an assumption that there was nothing that could be done to provide hope and a better life for those individuals?

While I was Ontario's minister of training, colleges, and universities, I toured the Centre for Addiction and Mental Health (CAMH) to learn about internships for physicians and nurses taking place there in partnership with the University of Toronto. That orientation to the mental-health sector caused me to remember a few promising young friends of my sons who seemed to have everything to live for but whose lives had sadly been cut short. In each case we wondered if there might have been warning signs, if each tragedy might have been preventable. During the tour, I asked Dr. Paul Garfinkel, CAMH's president and chief executive officer (CEO), if there was material I could read that would help me to learn about depression. Just days after my visit to CAMH, Meg, my chief of staff in my minister's office, brought me a large brown envelope that had been delivered to the office. It was addressed to me and marked in large letters "Strictly Private and Confidential" on both sides of the envelope and it had no return address. Meg did not open the envelope but she offered to sit with me while I opened it myself. To our relief, it was material on depression, sent by Dr. Garfinkel in response to my inquiry.

It occurred to me that had I asked the president of my local hospital for information about a physical health matter like diabetes, for example, it would likely not have been sent in a brown envelope with no return address. The envelope might have been marked "personal" to ensure that I received it, but I doubt it would have been so prominently marked "strictly private and confidential" in an obvious attempt to protect me from those who might have chosen to question my ability to perform my duties as minister. That experience helped me to understand the significance of the stigma often associated with mental illness.

According to a 2006 report entitled *The Human Face of Mental Health and Mental Illness in Canada*, 70 percent of mental-health problems have their onset during childhood or adolescence.

It seems that the danger of the characteristics of stigma, shame, and blame were all too common, starting with assumptions about attention deficit hyperactivity disorder (ADHD) in children and the tendency to be quick to make such diagnoses even by people not qualified to do so. ADHD is typically included in statistics on mental illness, although it can often be misunderstood and confusing because of its manifestation among what we might simply describe as the behaviour of very active or perhaps even bored children. I found it distressing to learn that there were schools that had refrigerators in which Ritalin was kept. I heard stories about parents being called by their children's school to come pick up their children because they were hyperactive or their behaviour was disruptive. Parents, desperate to keep their children in school, would be advised to take their children to a doctor in order to receive a prescription for medication to settle them down. But sometimes that could result in the development of a dependency that could be harmful to the child.

There also seemed to be no consideration that perhaps children's diets might be a factor in how they behaved. A retired school principal told me that on Halloween, she would remind her teachers that the following day, their students would be "on the ceiling." She would tell them to remember how much sugar the students would have received and consumed from the treats they received for Halloween. Zanana Akande was that wise principal. In 1990, Mrs. Akande was elected to represent the Toronto riding of St. Andrew–St. Patrick, making her the first Black woman to be an MPP in Ontario. She would also become the first Black woman to be appointed a cabinet minister in Ontario.

After I left government, I accepted an invitation to join CAMH's board. As part of my orientation, I participated in a meeting where attendees were invited to introduce themselves. We were also told we didn't have to share anything about ourselves that would make us uncomfortable. In other settings, I don't think that comment would have been made. I think, instinctively, we know it might be best not to share some things about ourselves with strangers.

At least, that's what I thought before the onset of the questionable revelations that social media seems to encourage. The hosts of the meeting obviously knew why they had made that well-intentioned statement, but I pushed back with the claim that CAMH, of all places, should be understood to be a safe, non-judgmental, comfortable place. I spoke about my brother and how I wished I had known about mental illness much sooner.

My brother, Keith, the eldest of my siblings, frequently exhibited problematic behaviour. Had I known, fifty or so years ago, what I know now, I would have realized that he needed help. But in that era, families consoled themselves with the argument that every family had a troublesome child. The one whose antics disrupted class at school and caused our parents to be summoned to the headmaster's office on a regular basis until his chances were exhausted. The one who had to be moved to another high school many miles from home but would walk for hours to come home on weekends then be driven back to school on Sunday evenings. The one who drove faster when police tried to stop him for speeding. The one who took his friends out to dinner then told the restaurant to send the bill to our father. He never seemed to have any money and his first wife was a woman old enough to be his mother.

Keith certainly had his challenges, but he was also talented, artistic, entrepreneurial, kind, gentle, and very handsome. Sadly, he succumbed to non-Hodgkin's lymphoma in his forties.

I had little or no reason to believe that the society in which we grew up was equipped to provide appropriate care and support or even enlightened enough to understand the possible potential of people with mental illness. Given the history of past practices, even here in Canada, where isolation and confinement were the common responses, with no apparent sense of the potential individuals might have if there was access to appropriate treatment, we have come a very long way. There is still more to be done, however — not only in the provision of sufficient and supportive access to care, but also in the fight against stigma.

Late one night some years ago, as my family approached the entrance to the Metro Hall parking garage after enjoying a production of *Les Misérables* at one of the Mirvish theatres across the street, I could tell, even before I got really close — even with the hood of the track suit partially covering the person's head, along with a baseball cap, perhaps as a disguise or perhaps as protection from the harsh cold — that the person holding the door open was a very young woman, likely a teenager, obviously new to life on the streets of downtown Toronto. Her cheeks were unblemished and she was obviously uncomfortable, standing there. In the hand that was not holding the door open she held another cap, timidly extended in a silent ask toward the people who were going through the door to the garage. I slowed down, letting the others go ahead of me.

"It breaks my heart to see you here," I said as I dropped something into her cap.

"I am so sorry, Ma'am," she responded softly, her voice sounding frail as her head hung a bit lower.

I have often thought about that young woman. I have wondered what her story could have been. For years, whenever I was in that area, I would wonder if that was her sleeping under the blanket on the sidewalk, or if she had moved to another area. I wondered if I would recognize her, if the street had taken its toll on her pretty face or her state of mind. I would wonder if she had gotten more aggressive. Most of all, I hoped that she was doing better and no longer living on or having to make a living from the street.

I thought about that soft-spoken, pretty young woman again when, not long after that encounter, I visited a women's hostel in Toronto. I imagined I was again hearing her voice say, "I am so sorry, Ma'am," when a staff member at the centre spoke with empathy and sensitivity about the hardening impact that living on the street can have on the women she cares for at the hostel. I asked the staff member about the women's stories. She told me that while they were unique in some ways, they had all experienced a significant decline in their mental health. A few days living on the street was all it took for that to happen, she told me.

Some years ago, I heard from a distraught mother who sought my advice on how to deal with the elementary school her young son and daughter attended. She had started a new job a few months before as a receptionist and administrator in a doctor's office. She was the only person on staff there and was afraid that she would lose her job if she had to keep leaving the office to collect her children from school every time the school called to complain about them. The children were under seven years of age and she was a single mother without a strong support system. She felt she was entirely at the mercy of the school. I offered to accompany her to meet the school's principal.

It actually seemed to me, from the behaviours that were described, that these children were just being children, children with a lot of energy, who wanted to have fun even after playtime was officially over. But their behaviour was deemed to be disruptive. During the meeting, the principal asked me why it was that she thought she knew me. While I could think of at least a few reasons why she would have known who I was, I told her I had no idea. It was obvious to me that being present as an advocate for the mother and her children was important. I think just the fact of the principal being aware that the mother had someone who was willing to be there with her helped to move the conversation to a constructive place where it was determined there were actions that both the school and the mother could take to improve the situation.

I attended a session at my granddaughters' high school, which the students had organized in support of mental-health awareness. The speaker was a nice-looking young man from a community support agency in the area. I thought he was a great choice for this all-girls' school. He certainly had their attention. But his message was serious, thoughtful, and wise.

Knowing that these young ladies were very likely customers of Second Cup, he asked them if they knew anything about a co-founder of Second Cup, a man by the name of Frank O'Dea. Frank O'Dea had struggled with mental-health challenges and lived on the streets of Toronto as a young man, a homeless panhandler, before finally using his last coin to make a phone call for help that, according to him, would change his life. Frank O'Dea went on to become a very successful businessman. I came to know and admire Frank when we served together on the board of Cuso International. The young man also asked the young ladies at my granddaughters' school if they knew Michael Phelps, the now-retired competitive American swimmer who, not long before, had captured the world's attention as an Olympian swimmer. With his mother's help and encouragement to focus his attention on swimming, as a child Michael Phelps, who is now in his thirties, learned how to manage his mental-health challenges and excelled at swimming. He holds the record for the most Olympic gold medals ever. The young man also spoke about Abraham Lincoln, who, as president of the United States of America in the nineteenth century, is known to have said, "If slavery is not wrong, nothing is wrong." In recognizing his contribution to the elimination of slavery, the young man also shared with the students that Abraham Lincoln had lived with depression.

These individuals and others, he said, had succeeded because they had been given reason to be hopeful. Without hope, he said, people like Abraham Lincoln and Frank O'Dea and Michael Phelps would not have gone on to achieve such significant success and to positively impact the lives of millions of people.

He also encouraged the young ladies at my granddaughters' school to pay attention to changes that they might recognize in the behaviour of their friends. He stressed the value and importance of providing hope in order to overcome despair.

The list would actually be quite long if we were to record the names of brilliant, gifted, well-known individuals — scientists, artists, composers of music, award-winning entertainers, and others — who, despite their own mental-health challenges, have enriched our lives in a variety of ways.

It seems my story began in much simpler times. Friends were people I actually knew. We didn't count "likes" and we didn't publicly "unfriend" each other. Bullying involved fist fights in the schoolyard, not far-reaching humiliation by mysterious actors on social media. Recreational drugs were almost unheard of, certainly socially unacceptable, and my understanding of ganja was that it had a religious purpose, maybe something like communion for Catholics. In fact, my first encounter with marijuana was when I smelled it in a stairwell in my office building in Toronto. I left Jamaica in my twenties not even knowing what the plant looked like.

A recent report by University of Guelph researchers published in the *Canadian Journal of Addiction* claims that even a single exposure to vaping cannabis can cause prolonged changes to brain patterns and function, changes similar to those associated with schizophrenia. The report's findings are particularly relevant to youth, according to the researchers, because adolescence is a critical period for brain development. According to the 2019 report *Cannabis Use, Harms and Perceived Risks Among Canadian Students* by the Canadian Centre on Substance Use and Addiction, nearly 30 percent of youth in grades 7 to 12 used cannabis in the previous twelve months. It is estimated that there was a 50 to 60 percent increase in use by high-school students between 2017 and 2018. According to that report, the "cognitive effects of cannabis vary with how it's ingested, frequency of use, and concentration of

THC (tetrahydrocannabinol) and the non-psychotic cannabidiol (CBD)." THC is the principal psychoactive constituent of cannabis, the chemical known for producing the high.

Stigma has also played a part in the public's perception of mental illness, and users of non-prescription drugs have been seen as addicts who have brought the problem on themselves. A lack of understanding of some of the circumstances and issues involved has led to a lack of empathy in the public arena. Advocates such as those involved in harm control have struggled to be heard while governments have felt more pressure to see the situation in the context of public discomfort rather than a problem to be addressed from a public health perspective.

Life certainly seemed simpler in my formative years. I pray constantly that my own children and grandchildren, even as the adults they are now, will be resilient in their ability to cope with and overcome the challenges that life will present them with from time to time.

Chapter 18

Serving the Public Good

THE ANCIENT PHILOSOPHERS DEFINED POLITICS as serving the public good. I don't think they were referring only to people who hold political office. While the reach and impact of government can be greater than that of any other institution, my own experience has reinforced my belief that people need not hold political office to be able to make a difference. I believe that governments would accomplish less without the commitment and nudging of people who care, not simply about their organization's success or the services that are important for their own families, but rather for the public good. My passion for what I was able to achieve during my four years in government was fuelled by the committed advocates who were relentless in their calls for action on the issues they cared about and government needed to care about.

While I would always remember that there were minority voices I needed to bring to the table, such as the voices of people from underrepresented or marginalized communities, people whose voices and issues were often unheard or discounted, I also knew I had been elected by a broader society. I believed it was my responsibility to unite the needs of the minority voices with those of the rest of society, so that all could understand the importance of improving the quality of life not just for some people but for as many people as possible. In doing so, I served not only minorities, but also the broader society. I served the public good.

It is not easy being a minority in politics. We need to be very strong. We need to stay true to our desire to serve, and we need to avoid being overcome by a desire to feel accepted or popular lest we be inadvertently co-opted or submerged by the dominant culture in which we might find ourselves.

I believe all who hold positions intended to serve the public good must take care not to view themselves or the office they hold as important, but rather to always be aware of the burden of responsibility they bear, to serve the public good.

The burden of responsibility is even greater for minorities. Members of minority communities expect minorities in positions of influence and authority to make their particular needs their priority. I constantly found myself wishing that there were others like me to share the burden.

———

Doris McKeogh, who had volunteered on my campaign team, agreed to be my executive assistant in my constituency office. The title is somewhat misleading as it could imply that I led the team in the office. On the contrary, the executive assistant ran the office. Doris was very competent. As a retired public servant, she was familiar with how government worked. She had also been involved as a volunteer for organizations in the community and knew her way around the riding.

We hired UTSC students for co-op placements along with recent university graduates. I felt really good about being able to help students in this way. It has always concerned me that some employers "hire" students and new graduates as unpaid interns, justifying that practice as providing opportunities for these young people to acquire work experience. There also seems to be a practice of hiring interns with pay to fill temporary positions or to help cover periods of higher-than-usual workloads. The intern is hoping the placement will lead to full-time employment while the employer already knows that's not their plan. I wish employers would see their employees the way they would want to be seen and treated themselves. If only it were not so easy to forget what it felt like when they were seeking work opportunities and trying to build their careers.

The constituency office was staffed with professional, loyal, conscientious young people who displayed a desire to be of service and a willingness to do whatever research was necessary to get answers to constituents' questions and to provide them with the services they needed. They represented me well, sometimes even attending events on my behalf when my schedule did not permit me to be there in person. I typically spent Mondays to Thursdays in my minister's office and Fridays at the constituency office. Most weekends had me attending events in the riding, sometimes accompanied by a member of staff from the constituency office.

The constituency office was an interesting place. People met with me for a wide variety of reasons. Some wanted my support for their appointment to government-related roles. I often knew when this was about to happen because the conversation would start with a comment like "I had your sign on my lawn." But there were others who wanted my support for students from their schools to attend special camps or wanted me to be aware of mental-health services their organization provided to youth in Scarborough.

I met inspiring individuals like Agnes and Annie, who, having overcome their own significant challenges, were helping others to achieve success. Agnes, a single parent who had come to Canada from Ghana with her four children, completed high school while living in a family shelter, continued her studies to become a personal support worker, and has since been inspiring and supporting other women in the pursuit of better lives for themselves and their children. Agnes's four children have all earned graduate-level degrees and are all involved in community-building work. Annie, a soft-spoken but strong woman, wrote a book about her own experience as a victim of severe and prolonged domestic abuse. She also established an organization to help victims of domestic abuse through programs that helped women in Scarborough to develop self-esteem.

There were also those who sought my support for the establishment of programs that would be of benefit to the community, which had long been proposed to government without success.

Dr. Christopher Morgan, a young chiropractor, met with me to tell me about a community health centre that the Black Health Alliance had been trying to establish for a few years. Members of the Black Health Alliance were doctors, nurses, and other health-care practitioners. They had not yet been successful in securing the government's support. The new community health centre's intentional focus on serving the Black community would take the form of a holistic approach to health promotion and the delivery of primary health care, focusing on the social determinants of health, historically disproportionate impacts of chronic diseases, and cultural considerations such as dietary habits. George Smitherman, who was Ontario's minister of health at the time, seemed receptive when I shared with him what I had learned. The Malvern community of Scarborough, which was not within the boundaries of my riding, was the location favoured by the Black Health Alliance. There was already a community health centre in my riding, the West Hill Community Health Centre, with a heavy demand for its services. Malvern was a racially diverse community, challenged as well as underserved by a variety of definitions.

In 2004, George and I spent time with members of the Black Health Alliance, supportive representatives from other community health centres, and residents in the Malvern community to gain a stronger appreciation of their need and their capacity for success, and in November 2005 our government announced its approval for the new centre in Malvern. TAIBU Community Health Centre has since demonstrated the foresight and wisdom of its advocates, excelling by all measures and performance indicators under the leadership of Liben Gebremikael, its very capable executive director, and its committed board of directors. TAIBU, which is Swahili for "be in good health," is also a vivid example of an organization fully embraced as its own by the community it exists to serve. I am honoured that TAIBU refers to me as one of its founding members.

George Smitherman also responded positively to my advocacy on behalf of Rouge Valley Health System's Centenary Hospital's request for the government's support for their proposed family birthing and newborn centre. I was very pleased to be able to participate in the ground-breaking ceremony for the new centre. At that event, I was presented with a purple t-shirt with a message imprinted in white on the back that said, "Mary Anne *really delivers*."

The message on the front, accompanied by humorous caricatures, was the following:

The Longest Gestation Period Ever ...
Cat: 58 days   Pig: 112 days   Sheep: 144 days
Human: 266 days   Elephant: 645 days
The Regional Birthing and Newborn Centre: 3,650
days gestation and 18 months of labour!
Rouge Valley Health System

The message was certainly accurate. The fundraising campaign had started years before the hospital received the government's support. In fact, it was a few years before I became the MPP for the area that I had made a personal pledge to sponsor one of the family birthing rooms. The room still bears a plaque in appreciation for that support.

Careers fairs for youth organized by my constituency office team were a priority for me and I was determined that they take place in a post-secondary institution, to emphasize that they were meant to be aspirational. They were not meant to be job fairs like the ones often staged in shopping malls. With the willing support of Centennial College and UTSC, the location of the youth career fairs alternated between those two institutions. A broad range of exhibits on several skilled trades, community and private career colleges, and the university, as well as local community organizations that offer support services for youth, drew from the mandate of the Ministry of Training, Colleges, and Universities. Hundreds of young people, as well as parents, attended the fairs.

There were people who lived outside my electoral riding who would pretend to be my constituents so they could meet with me to discuss matters of importance to them. They would tell me they did not feel comfortable speaking with the elected members in their own electoral ridings. I would often also discover that they didn't vote. Their excuse was that they believed their votes didn't matter because their voices were never heard. I would tell them that they could expect to be taken seriously only if they voted. Votes are important. Votes are powerful. Votes matter to politicians.

But when I would passionately advance the issues of those whose voices had often been ignored, with strong and convincing evidence-based arguments for my proposed solutions, effective public policy, not only for the good of those minorities, but also for the good of the broader society, I would find little or no resistance from my colleagues in elected office. Instead, I think I earned their respect, because I always kept at the forefront of my mind why I had agreed to seek elected office, that being the desire to serve the public good. But it was also obvious to me that had I not brought those policy proposals forward, no one else might have done so. The minority voices might not have been heard.

This was important to remember as I considered who I could propose to the party as a candidate to replace me in the 2007 provincial elections. I was determined that my replacement would be a Black person.

Joan Lesmond was a member of the panel for the town hall meeting on health care that I had hosted during my election campaign. Joan was vice president of the Registered Nurses' Association of Ontario. Originally from the Caribbean island of St. Lucia, Joan was articulate, well versed in her field, professional, passionate, and grounded, an entirely impressive woman who travelled to a university in Rochester, New York, on weekends to study for her doctorate in nursing. I had not met her prior to the night of the town hall meeting. As we walked together to our cars after the meeting, Joan confided in me that she had political aspirations, but had a few things she wanted to accomplish before putting her name forward for consideration. I vowed to help her achieve that goal. We kept in touch and became good friends. When I decided not to seek re-election in 2007, I asked Joan if she was ready. This was an opportunity she very much wanted but the time was not right. A brother who was living in New York had been diagnosed with cancer and the prognosis was poor. One of several siblings, she believed it was her responsibility to be available to care for her brother. That had to be her priority and she could not see a way to combine that responsibility with the demands of political office. This just served to convince me that she would be an ideal candidate when the time was right. Joan's brother passed away not long after that. We continued to keep in touch and she kept her eyes on the political arena with the 2011 provincial elections in mind.

Joan began experiencing excruciating pain in her lower back, which she attributed to a fall while attending a conference in the U.S. I attended the 2011 YWCA Toronto Women of Distinction Awards, in honour of Joan being named a recipient, only to learn that she would not be at the event. Dr. Joan Lesmond had been diagnosed with cancer and admitted to the palliative care wing at Sunnybrook Hospital. We lost an outstanding human being who had so much yet to offer.

Paulette Senior had run for the New Democrats in the riding of Scarborough–Rouge River. In 1999, she ran provincially against Alvin Curling, who had held that riding for the Liberals since 1985. In the year 2000, she ran federally against Derek Lee, who had held that riding for the Liberals since 1988. It had seemed to me like the New Democrats had wasted Paulette by running her, a new candidate with great potential, against two very popular veteran incumbents. I was also unhappy that they had run a Black woman against Alvin, a Black man. I felt that there were too few Black people in political office to be running us against each other. It mattered not, to me, that Paulette had run for the New Democrats. I believed that if she was still interested in serving the people of Ontario as an MPP, the party she had previously run for might not be of primary importance to her. Paulette knew Scarborough well. She had served on the board of the Rouge Valley Health System where I had also served, and the boards of the Black Business and Professional Association, the Centre for Social Justice, and the Malvern Family Resource Centre. Paulette had also managed employment services in Scarborough for YWCA Toronto. In 2007, when I asked Paulette to run for the Liberals in the seat that I was about to vacate, she was CEO of YWCA Canada. I understood why it would have been difficult for her to say yes when she was doing so well, but I saw her success with the YWCA as further evidence of my assessment that she would have been viewed as a star candidate. Paulette continues to do well. She currently holds the position of president and CEO of the Canadian Women's Foundation.

Toronto city councillor Michael Thompson had represented the municipal Ward 37 of Scarborough Centre, now known as Ward 21, since 2003. I asked Michael if he would consider running in the upcoming 2007 provincial election as a candidate for the Liberals. I did not actually tell him I would not be seeking re-election in Scarborough Guildwood, as my riding was to become with the redistribution of ridings that was about to take effect provincially. He said no. Michael is now deputy mayor of the City of Toronto.

Ron Rock, the well-loved, long-time, just-about-to-retire executive director of the East Scarborough Boys and Girls Club, also said no. Ron told me the time was not right for him.

Margarett Best, a lawyer who had shown an interest in the world of politics and had been very supportive of me during my time as MPP, was willing to consider running. I introduced her to the party and they did what they needed to do to determine that she would be a good candidate. Margarett ran successfully in October 2007.

The provincial riding of Scarborough East had been represented by a New Democrat from 1990 to 1995. When I ran for political office in 2003, the incumbent was a two-term Conservative who had served from 1995 to 2003. Scarborough East and its successor, Scarborough Guildwood, have been held by the Liberals, provincially, since my election in 2003. Mitzie Hunter, the current MPP for the riding of Scarborough Guildwood, was elected in 2013.

When I announced, in 2007, that I would not seek re-election, I wrote a letter of appreciation to the thousands of people who had made my four years in elected office possible. Whatever I had accomplished was possible only because they had believed in me and supported me. The following is an excerpt from my letter:

I am writing to thank you for your support in enabling me to serve the people of Ontario as the Member of Provincial Parliament for Scarborough East and a member of the province's executive council, over the past four years.

With the Writ having been signed for an October 10th election, and my decision not to seek a second term in political office, I wanted to take this opportunity to share with you some of my accomplishments during my time in office. It is only through the support of people like you, who believed that I could make a positive contribution to the quality of life we all seek to enjoy in this wonderful province, that I am able to say with humility but also with confidence that I have in fact been able to make the kind of contribution that should justify the confidence you placed in me.

As minister of training, colleges, and universities from October 2003 to June 2005, my responsibilities included improving access to, and the quality of, post-secondary education and training. Our government's belief has been that it is the personal interest, initiative, and academic ability of our young people, rather than their families' financial position, that should enable them to achieve their potential. In 2005, we announced the establishment of income-based, non-repayable tuition grants for first- and second-year college and university students, reduced the parental contributions required for financial assistance through OSAP, increased the amount that students could borrow without increasing the maximum repayable for each year of full-time study, and eliminated the 12-month wait period for new immigrants and protected persons to be able to apply for OSAP. We also funded increased capacity in Ontario's medical schools and introduced grants to assist nurses to pursue graduate studies so that they could in turn train more nurses for Ontario's health care system.

*We strengthened the quality of education and account-
ability of the private career colleges sector, thereby enabling
better protection for students, through legislative changes to the
Private Career Colleges Act, which had not been subjected to
a significant review in 30 years. We created an Apprenticeship
Training Tax Credit to encourage employers to provide on-
the-job training opportunities for individuals interested in becoming licensed to work in the skilled trades, and substantially
increased the number of high-school students participating in
the Ontario Youth Apprenticeship Program. Industry estimates
indicate that approximately 50 percent of workers in the skilled
trades will retire by the year 2011.*

*During my term as minister of training, colleges, and uni-
versities, we also launched a review of the accreditation processes of Ontario's regulatory colleges that determine whether
or not internationally trained individuals can work in their
particular field in this province, because we know that Ontario
needs everyone contributing to their full potential in order
to ensure the economic and social viability of this province.
This review has since led to the appointment of Ontario's first
Fairness Commissioner. We also established several bridging programs to assist internationally trained individuals to
meet the accreditation standards of their particular regulatory
environment.*

*In June 2005, I was appointed minister of children and
youth services. Under that portfolio, we have led the transformation of Ontario's child-protection system to be more accountable to children and families, and to provide better alternatives
for the protection of children. We now have legislation that has
removed the barriers that prevented too many children from
being able to grow up in caring, stable homes, through adoption
or legal custody arrangements. The new legislation recognizes*

grandparents, extended families, and Indigenous customary care arrangements as potential places of safety, subject to appropriate safety assessments. We have also introduced differential response as a method of supporting and strengthening family situations where temporary difficulties have put children at risk, with the objective of avoiding having to take children into the care of the child-protection system. A new complaints process has been introduced, enabling families to take their concerns to an independent board for review. We have also created legislation for the establishment of an Independent Office of the Child Advocate, so that children receiving government services can have a stronger voice, without fear of political interference or suppression.

We have tripled the number of children with autism receiving Intensive Behaviour Intervention (IBI) therapy, and eliminated the age six cut-off for IBI, previously imposed by the Conservative government. The provision of more services and supports for children with autism spectrum disorders has required us to build capacity through investments in the training of education assistants and teachers in the school system, resource workers in the child-care sector and therapists to provide IBI for children at the more severe end of the spectrum. We have established a new college graduate–level program in autism and behavioural sciences, which has been offered by nine Ontario colleges, and has trained 203 new therapists over the past two years. This summer, I announced funding to enable three additional colleges to offer the program and, by 2008–2009, enrolment in this program is expected to rise to 220 full-time students per year. We have funded summer camps for 800 children with autism spectrum disorders and respite services for more than 3,000 families annually. We have also established a Research Chair in Autism at the University of

Western Ontario, because there is so much more that we need to learn about autism spectrum disorders.

Agencies serving children and youth with mental-health challenges have received two increases in their base funding over the past few years. This sector had not received an increase in their funding in 12 years, despite the extremely high prevalence of mental health challenges in children and youth. We have also increased funding for children's treatment centres, enabling these centres to provide more services to the benefit of 7,000 kids with complex special needs.

Ontario now has more than 22,000 new licensed child-care spaces, and as a result of legislation proclaimed this year, will have the first Regulatory College for Early Childhood Educators in Canada. This is part of our government's effort to improve the quality of early learning and child care in this province.

Finally, I must tell you about our Youth Opportunities Strategy through which the Ministry of Children and Youth Services has hired 65 full-time youth outreach workers, and funded a variety of summer jobs for 1,800 youth, 15 to 18 years of age, as well as 165 Youth in Policing summer jobs for 14- to 17-year-olds, in partnership with local police services, each year. All of the youth are from marginalized communities in Toronto, Durham region, Windsor, Ottawa, Hamilton, Thunder Bay, and London, and for the overwhelming majority, these have been their first jobs. The particular communities have been selected because of the lower-than-average income levels, employment levels, and academic levels achieved by their populations, which place their youth at a greater risk of dysfunctional behaviour. We have found, however, that these kids are eager to learn and willing to work hard. They just need to be given the chance to do so. Feedback from the youth, their families, and participating employers has been extremely positive.

If I seem proud of what I have helped to achieve over the past 4 years, and these are just some of the highlights, it's because I really am happy that you helped to give me the opportunity to make a positive difference in the lives of so many people. I hope you also feel proud of the fact that you helped to make these good things happen. Indigenous leaders have written to me saying, "the accomplishments of your ministry under your watch have been unprecedented." Parents who have previously felt it necessary to take government to court to fight for services for their kids have said, "thank you for your generosity of spirit and willingness to work with us." The bureaucrats who worked so hard for us refer to my "unwavering support and commitment to children, youth and families."

Polls conducted by the party before I announced I would not seek re-election revealed that I would have won in 2007 with an even greater margin than when I was elected in 2003. When I was a young girl, my wise mother would tell me that I should never overstay my welcome. She advised me that I should always leave while my hosts still want me to stay.

———

In December 2010, at the invitation of the independent expert on minority issues, I addressed the third session of the United Nations Forum on Minority Issues in the Palais des Nations in Geneva, Switzerland. It was a very special opportunity to meet delegates from all over the world who shared experiences that opened my mind to the variety of attitudes that exist toward what I assume to be basic human rights. The theme of that year's session was minorities and effective participation in economic life. The topic for my particular panel was minorities and effective political participation.

Some of what I shared when it was my turn to address the forum seemed pale in comparison to the struggles that others from other countries spoke about. A delegation from an Asian country spoke about a caste system that deemed women to be filthy. A delegation from the Middle East reported the murder of one of their associates that had taken place in their country while the forum was in progress. They expressed deep concern that they were all at risk. That night, as I boarded the local bus for the drive that would take me close to my hotel, I considered how fortunate I was not to have to be concerned I might not complete my commute safely. My remarks the following day included a reflection on the reality of my world at that time. They were thoughtful but hardly dramatic.

Currently, the only Black member in the Ontario legislature is a woman whom I invited to run in my riding when I decided not to seek re-election. There were a number of other Black candidates who ran in other electoral ridings, for all three political parties, but none of them were successful. Had my party not accepted the person I proposed, the current Ontario legislature might today be without a single Black member. While approximately 22.8 percent of the population of Ontario are visible minorities, there are only 11 persons of colour among the 107 members of the Ontario legislature. Most of the visible minority members are of South Asian heritage. One member is Chinese.

In Canada, visible minorities make up approximately 20 percent of the population. Approximately 4.1 percent are South Asian, approximately 4 percent are Chinese, approximately 3.8 percent are Indigenous, and approximately 2.5 percent are Black. As is the case in Ontario, visible minority representation in the parliament of Canada does not come close to being reflective of the country's demographics.

———

In a further attempt to foster greater diversity in the Ontario legislature, I invited Michael Coteau to lunch a few times. I had met him while I was an MPP and he was involved in community work in the Malvern area of Scarborough. Michael served for many years as a school trustee, and also as deputy chair, with the Toronto District School Board. I got the impression he didn't know what to make of my invitations to lunch. My motive was simple. I was interested in introducing him to the Ontario Liberal Party and I wanted to get to know him better before doing so. At first Michael didn't seem eager to pursue provincial politics, but there came a point when the time seemed right for him and I delivered his resumé to a senior member of the party. The rest, as they say, is history. Michael has represented the riding of Don Valley East since October 2011 and served as a cabinet minister from 2013 to 2018. In 2020, Michael Coteau and Mitzie Hunter both ran unsuccessfully for the leadership of the Ontario Liberal Party.

The Ontario legislature is certainly a more racially diverse place in 2020 than it was a decade before, when I addressed the United Nations Forum in Geneva. There are, as of the 2018 provincial elections, seven MPPs who are Black, five New Democrats and two Liberals. In April 2019, the New Democrats, currently Ontario's official opposition party, proudly announced the formal creation of a Black caucus group of five of its own members, the first Black caucus in the history of the Ontario legislature. The mandate of the group is "to ensure that Black perspectives are meaningfully incorporated into the work that New Democrats do on every file — from finance to health care, education, housing, the arts and beyond."

Chapter 19

The Time Is Always Right to Do What Is Right[5]

WE EACH GET TO HAVE a say in our destiny. I believed that what would define my success in government were the kinds of qualities and behaviours I had successfully developed and applied in other settings. That is not to say there would not be impediments along the way. Curve balls exist. Setbacks happen. How we handle those impediments defines who we are and how determined we are to succeed.

My only female boss in all my years at the bank, a brilliant and very successful woman whom I admired greatly, once told me I should exploit whatever made me different from others. She believed the factors that made me different also made me special. I could never bring myself to encourage people to see me as the woman or the Black woman they needed to help them achieve their equity or diversity objectives, but I understood what my colleague was trying to tell me.

---

5   Dr. Martin Luther King Jr.

I do remember telling the premier that I had not realized I was Black until I arrived at Queen's Park. It was my way of saying I was more than that and expected him to recognize that I didn't simply see my role as the MPP or minister for Black people. I didn't appreciate being singled out as the person who absolutely had to represent the government at the annual Caribbean Carnival parade. I expected my colleagues to also care about issues like the over-representation of, and better outcomes required for, Black and Indigenous children in the child-protection system; the difficulties faced by young people in underserved neighbourhoods seeking employment opportunities; and the challenges experienced by internationally trained professionals in becoming accredited to work in their fields of expertise.

People often ask me how different my work, or even the work environment, in government was to my experience in the world of business. I would have to say, perhaps not as different as many people think. I also found that my governance experience in the not-for-profit sector was tremendously helpful to the work I did in government. What's also interesting about this is the fact that I have always believed that fiscal and social responsibility must coexist if we are to achieve the quality of life that most of us strive to achieve.

The dimensions that can often give government its slow-moving character include the need for extensive consultations. I learned that the process is at least as important as the outcome. As is the case in business, good government must be about the exercise of good judgment, the development of sound policies, and the effective delivery of the right solutions.

Whether or not we are successful in any aspect of our lives will have a lot to do with our personal commitment to ourselves. We must avoid the temptation to expect more of others than we are prepared to do ourselves.

I have heard some young people complain that they have no role models. Ron Fanfair is a highly respected journalist who has long been committed to showcasing the outstanding achievements of Black people, particularly young Black women and men, true role models for our youth. I am tremendously grateful to Ron for doing that. I admire his professionalism, the research he does for all his articles, and his obvious love for all things Caribbean. His work can be found on his website, ronfanfair.com, and also in the *SHARE* newspaper, sharenews.com, which boasts the largest circulation among Black and Caribbean readers in Canada, having been created by its publisher, Arnold Auguste, more than forty years ago.

I also believe that we need not look to well-known people for inspiration. We need not look beyond ourselves. We must have the conviction to establish personal goals and we must have confidence in our abilities to achieve the goals we set for ourselves. It has been said that if you believe in yourself, you are already a winner.

When I have focused on doing the right things, doing things for the right reasons, and doing those things well, my performance has exceeded the expectations of others, and my career has benefited. Striving for success and helping others to achieve success has always given me satisfaction and a sense of accomplishment.

As a young child, providing others with the opportunity to be successful meant being a summer-school teacher for children living in poverty. As a young woman in my early twenties, volunteering to provide others with the opportunity to be successful meant teaching men, factory workers, to read and write and to do arithmetic at the end of the workday.

As an executive at Scotiabank, it meant providing personal and technical development opportunities for my staff, involving them in the determination of how we could improve productivity while serving our customers better, and pursuing a variety of ways to reward them for exceeding their performance objectives.

It also meant being thoughtful, understanding, and supportive when their personal challenges created anxiety and made it difficult for them to carry out their responsibilities at work. It meant remembering that they also had obligations to their families. And it meant being honest and constructive when their performance fell short of expectations. It also meant being respectful and appreciative of everyone, regardless of the positions they held or the roles they played.

I was always blessed with teams of talented, dedicated, loyal, hard-working staff and I had tremendous respect for them. Just before the busy Christmas shopping season one year, a commercial customer of the bank who had been verbally abusive, repeatedly, toward relatively junior members of my team told the manager of that area that he would be calling me, the senior vice president, to file a complaint. When I was told about the situation and the call I should be expecting, I decided to be proactive. I called him. I told him I had heard he was unhappy with the service he was receiving from us, and that I had also heard that there seemed to be nothing that we could do to satisfy him. I told him that I thought it best that he find another bank to provide him with the merchant services our bank had been providing and I would be sending someone to collect our point-of-sale payment terminals. He told me I couldn't do that because it was his busiest season and he wouldn't be able to make arrangements with another service provider in time. I told him I couldn't afford to pay my staff enough for the abuse to which he had been subjecting them. He agreed never to be abusive toward my staff ever again. He remained true to his word. It had not escaped me that he knew I wouldn't allow him to treat me the way he had believed he could treat my staff. I had flexed the full weight of my proverbial muscle, the authority I had assumed as senior vice president, to protect the well-being of staff who did not have the same ability to defend themselves.

In my work as a board member, providing the organization with the opportunity to be successful has meant being conscientious, carefully reviewing materials prepared for meetings, asking questions meant to improve the organization's outcomes, providing constructive feedback, and being critical while being enabling.

It meant working to protect the brand when I chaired the board of the United Way of Canada, a charity with more than 120 member organizations across Canada, well known for its workplace fundraising campaigns and its community-building approach and impact.

It meant being willing to listen carefully to the diverse and sometimes conflicting views of students, faculty, staff, and the senior administration when I served as a governor and vice chair of the governing council of the University of Toronto and a member of the board of governors at the University of Guelph.

It also meant going back to university to do a third-year political science course that would help me understand the complexities of policies and practices in the health sector when I was asked to join the board of two hospitals in the Rouge Valley Health System. My responsibilities at the bank provided me with the flexibility to attend classes on Friday mornings before going into my office. On the first day of the course, the professor asked each student to share why they had chosen that particular course. The other students looked like third-year university students. I certainly didn't. They stated reasons related to their chosen programs of study. When it was my turn to share my reason for doing the course, I told them that I had recently been appointed to the board of a hospital and I knew nothing about Canada's health system. The students laughed. The professor obviously observed that I wasn't amused. To his credit, he suggested we work together to ensure that I was one of the strongest board members. That was music to my ears. A year or so later, I was asked to chair the clinical quality committee and not long after that, I was appointed vice chair of the board.

Everything I have just described served me well in my two ministerial roles. Stakeholders expressed surprise and appreciation because I listened to them, apparently an unusual experience in their long-standing relationships with governments. I was not always able to do exactly what they asked, but I listened to them because I needed to understand their challenges. And while I sometimes disliked their tactics, I had no difficulty separating unpleasant approaches from the issues they needed me to understand and to address.

As someone who believes that conscientious politicians and democratic governments can positively impact more lives through thoughtful public policy than most other professions can, I reached out to the views of ancient political philosophers who believed that politics should be about serving the public good. I also recognized that the crafting of effective public policy requires an understanding that policies which might be good for some people might be detrimental to others. I would suggest, for example, that in the area of criminal justice, the creation of public policy for the protection of public safety should not ignore the complexities of human and social psychology, the risks of implicit biases in predictive policing models, or the possible impact of factors such as the social determinants of health. Similarly, public policy that might be seen as unnecessary or burdensome by some might be essential for the basic existence of others. Breakfast programs exist in some schools because children who are hungry or undernourished are likely to perform poorly and perhaps behave antisocially.

It's also important to understand that politics is not the sole domain of people who hold political office. We each have the ability to serve the public good by making constructive contributions toward a better life and better opportunities, particularly for the most vulnerable and marginalized among us. I encourage others to understand that they have the ability to influence public policy.

One of the people high on my list of committed advocates is Lillie Johnson. In my roles as MPP and Ontario's minister of children and youth services, it was a real pleasure for me to recognize Lillie Johnson, a native of Jamaica, as the determined and longest-serving advocate for support for victims of crippling sickle cell disorders.

The occasion was the announcement in 2005, at Rouge Valley Health System's Centenary Hospital in my riding, of the government of Ontario's decision to expand newborn screening to include the most comprehensive suite of early screening for diseases in Canada. This was another progressive move during George Smitherman's time as Ontario's minister of health. Sickle cell is included in the diseases for which newborns are now screened. Centenary Hospital was chosen for the announcement because it hosted a sickle cell clinic in partnership with Toronto's Hospital for Sick Children.

Lillie Johnson is acknowledged as the primary advocate for recognizing the importance of newborn screening for sickle cell disease in Ontario. Dedicated to the provision of health education and health care, she worked as a registered nurse and director of public health for Leeds–Grenville and Lanark District in Ontario before her retirement. As a public health nurse, her front-line exposure to the detrimental effects of sickle cell disease gave her a good understanding of its painful and debilitating nature. Her own research and formal training informed her conviction that, with early detection and appropriate interventions, people afflicted with sickle cell disorders can live productive lives without the frequent and seemingly unpredictable but characteristic crises that can lead to early death for some, severely limited physical abilities for others, and periods of absence from the workforce and the education system. In 1981, Lillie Johnson founded the Sickle Cell Association of Ontario, initially conducting its work from her home.

Miss Lillie, as she is lovingly and respectfully known by many, also volunteered with Cuso International, and served on two assignments in Jamaica from 1989 to 1995, fulfilling a promise she had made to return to Jamaica to help improve the provision of health care there. During her last four years as a Cuso volunteer in Jamaica, Miss Lillie opened and ran a medical clinic. But it was her ongoing concern for victims of sickle cell disease that continued to have her unabated commitment, volunteering in clinics, organizing conferences, distributing literature, counselling individuals and their families, and bringing others together to improve the lives of those afflicted with this terrible, poorly understood, and significantly under-resourced disease.

For more than four decades, Lillie Johnson has devoted her life to the education of sicklers and their families, health practitioners, policy-makers, educators, governments, and the general public about the symptoms and implications of sickle cell disorders. Lillie Johnson was named the 2009 public health champion by the City of Toronto Board of Health for her "outstanding contributions to protecting and promoting the health of Toronto's residents." In 2010, she was appointed to the Order of Ontario.

———

When I announced that I would not be seeking re-election, my deputy minister hosted a reception in my honour. We had accomplished a lot of good things together. The deputy and each assistant deputy minister said a few words about their experience working with me. The assistant deputy minister who was responsible for the administration of the ministry's finances, along with other files, said she had quickly learned that if what I wanted seemed impossible, she would have to find a way to make it happen because I wouldn't be backing away from my request simply because it would be difficult to accomplish. The lawyer in charge of the ministry's twenty-three legal counsels said that when his friends or associates asked him to describe his minister, he would need only one word for his response. The word was *integrity*. I recall feeling good about that for about two seconds before wondering if perhaps he had not always been able to describe the other ministers he had worked with in that way.

The day I was sworn in as a cabinet minister, one of my sons visited my mom and told her that I would now be referred to as the Honourable Mary Anne Chambers. Without hesitation, my mother responded that she had always known I was honourable, but now everyone else would know.

I arrived at Queen's Park with my integrity intact and left Queen's Park with my integrity intact, content that in my four years there as an MPP and a cabinet minister, I had served the public good. There is no other kind of work or service that can impact the lives of so many people. I still miss the public policy work.

In the early days of my life after government, I reflected on my empty schedule. The feeling was different from being on vacation and the luxury of being able to get out of bed later in the morning. It felt different because there was no end in sight to the absence of routine. Unlike the plans that I had had in anticipation of my early retirement from the bank, I had given no thought to what I might do when I left government. It was an uncomfortable feeling that caused me to start doing sudoku puzzles every morning after breakfast to keep my mind functioning at an acceptable level. I knew there would have to be more to my life going forward.

The ever-thoughtful and kind Dr. Sheldon Levy, then president and vice chancellor of Ryerson University, as if he knew what I might be going through, invited me to accept an appointment as a distinguished visiting professor at the university. I accepted Sheldon's invitation, but only for a year and on the basis that my involvement would not be heavy. Over the years, Sheldon has made similar gestures to others who find themselves in transition mode, helping them to remain vibrant while giving students the opportunity to learn from their experience and insights.

I had known Sheldon from before I served in government and he had been very helpful to me while I was minister of training, colleges, and universities. In 2005, when he called to let me know he had two job offers under consideration, I didn't hesitate in suggesting that he accept the offer to be Ryerson's president. I knew he would be perfect for the role. I was right. The Ryerson community loved him, quite the achievement in the complex world of university dynamics. During his years as president, Sheldon calmly elevated the university's urban image as a centre for innovation in the city of Toronto.

Although I was feeling a bit restless, I was also exhausted. My announcement that I would not be seeking re-election was intentionally made just shortly before the end of my term. I had a list of things to get done before I left, including important new legislation for the establishment of the regulatory college for early childhood educators and the independent provincial advocate for children and youth, and I didn't want an early announcement to disrupt any of that. It was a race to the finish line but with the strong support of my bureaucrats and my minister's office team, I was successful in getting everything on my list done.

I also anticipated that I would receive a number of requests for my involvement in support of various organizations. I didn't want to say yes to everything that others had in mind for me to do. I had always believed it to be wise to remember that saying yes to a particular opportunity might mean having to say no to other opportunities. The life plan I had developed while I was at Scotiabank included sections on my goals, what was important to me, and how I wanted to be able to spend my time, resources that might be helpful in achieving those goals, particular areas of interest, and financial considerations. I updated my life plan to help me focus. Consistent with being the lifelong learner I consider myself to be, I did the chartered directors' program offered by the Directors College, a partnership between McMaster University's DeGroote School of Business and the Conference Board of Canada, to refresh and certify my governance skills.

In the years that followed my departure from the government of Ontario, I accepted invitations to join the boards of YMCA Toronto, CAMH, the University of Guelph, PACE Canada, Cuso International, GraceKennedy Limited and its Canadian subsidiary, and the advisory board for YCEC. For five years, I also served as a member of the grants review committee for the youth opportunities fund administered by the Ontario Trillium Foundation. In the interest of doing my part as a responsible neighbour, I served on the board of my condominium corporation for three years. This actually represented a deviation from my personal preference for focusing on work I could feel passionate about.

Chapter 20

The Only Ones Among You Who Will Be Really Happy Are Those Who Have Sought and Found How To Serve[6]

I AM IMMENSELY PROUD OF my son Stefan. When he chose to become a police officer, he helped me to get accustomed to the idea by telling me that no one could grow up in the Chambers household without having a social conscience. I must admit that I had not previously thought of policing in that way.

Stefan introduced me to the nine policing principles defined by Sir Robert Peel, Britain's home secretary, when he established the London Metropolitan Police in 1829. Peel's principles emphasize the importance of the relationship between police and the public. The second principle resonates the most with me: "To recognize always that the power of the police to fulfil their functions and duties is dependent on public approval of their existence, actions and behaviour, and on their ability to secure and maintain public respect."

6 Albert Schweitzer (philosopher, Nobel Peace Prize recipient for altruism, reverence for life, and tireless humanitarian work).

Some years ago, a chaplain with the Toronto Police Service, a very sweet older man, and I conducted a little exchange of inspiring spiritual verses. He gave me one of the coins he carried in his pocket. I believe he usually gave these coins to officers who sought his support. The coin carries two hands formed in prayer on one side and on the other side, there is the "Serenity Prayer": "God grant me the serenity to accept the things I cannot change, the courage to change the things I can, and the wisdom to know the difference."

I in turn showed the chaplain the card I was carrying in my purse. It contained words of the prophet Micah, which have long been a source of inspiration and a conscience for me. In Micah's words, "This is what the Lord asks of you, only this, to act justly, to love tenderly, and to walk humbly with your God."

I prefer the words of the prophet Micah because they tell us very clearly how we must conduct ourselves in our relationships with each other. In my view, the "Serenity Prayer" might give us excuses for not doing what we should be doing. Sometimes we decide we are not able to make change where change is exactly what is needed, because we are afraid that the task might be too difficult or there might be risks involved. Feelings might be hurt, the status quo could be challenged, comfort zones might be disturbed.

It is important to recognize, in a constructive and objective way, the reality that when we are in positions of authority, we have a greater responsibility and bear a heavier burden for how we interact with others. Police officers are perceived, by the general public, as being in positions of authority. That perception can influence the nature of the interaction, sometimes causing resentment rather than respect. A heavy police presence, supposedly intended to keep the peace, can lead to discomfort and incite conflict when people are gathered in peaceful protest of issues that concern them. When a young person, for example, exhibits anti-social behaviour or mouths off at a police officer, they might feel this is their only line of defence, the only recourse they have. A show of mutual respect might be the key to success in these interactions, and it's likely easier for the person in the position of authority to be able to take the lead in that regard. With mantras like "to serve and protect" and "good deeds speak," police services ask us to hold them to a high standard. Fortunately, in Canada, we are usually able to see that as the reality. What I do know is that young people, just like older people, can sense when they are undervalued. They can also usually tell when others care about their well-being. It's important, I think, that we be conscious of how we conduct ourselves and how we treat others. We should all expect to be held accountable for our behaviour.

Actions that are rooted in systemic racism, or reflect implicit bias or an abuse of power, undermine the intentions of those who carry out their duties professionally and even compassionately. I have encountered both sides of this coin.

Who would have thought that decades after my experience with Ida's daughters in Jamaica, I would hear from youth living in certain neighbourhoods that they could not get jobs? It had also been my observation, while in the world of business, that youth who had the benefit of a parent or a friend with influential management-level connections were more likely to get the summer jobs.

Summer job opportunities, with the support of subsidies to participating employers for youth in underserved or marginalized communities, became a component of our government's youth opportunities strategy. One such initiative is the extremely successful, fully government-funded Youth in Policing initiative, which has the added benefit of helping to improve relationships between police and youth in Ontario. Thousands of youth have benefited from these initiatives, and employers have spoken highly of the strong work ethic they have observed among youth who really just need a chance to show what they are capable of and to be defined by that rather than by where their family has been able to afford to live.

More than thirty years ago, I suggested to the principal at my sons' high school that it would be good for the students if there were police officers involved in the life of the school. I thought it would be an opportunity to establish constructive relationships under positive circumstances and a great way to build trust and mutual respect between the students and the police. I believed it would certainly be better than the possibility of the first encounter between police and a young person being a negative confrontation. The principal dismissed my idea as impossible because the police did not have the resources to enable them to be engaged in schools.

I never abandoned my conviction that it is both preferable and possible to have positive relationships between police and young people in the communities they serve and protect. In 2005, not long after my appointment as Ontario's minister of children and youth services, the Toronto Police Service Chief Bill Blair invited me to attend a meeting with police and community members in the auditorium at their headquarters on College Street. The team in my minister's office had already been working on the development of a youth opportunities strategy, one component of which was to be an initiative to provide youth in the most marginalized neighbourhoods in the province with the opportunity to have summer employment experiences with their local police services.

I asked Chief Blair why he had invited me to attend the meeting at headquarters that night. His response was that he had told the premier's office that he wanted someone from Queen's Park at the meeting who would be willing to act, not just to talk. As I observed the community members and the police making little or no progress toward any kind of common ground, I invited Chief Blair and Dr. Alok Mukherjee, then chair of the Toronto Police Service's board, to meet with me at my office. A few weeks later, Dr. Mukherjee, Deputy Chief Keith Forde, whose responsibilities included human resources, and Peter Sloly, who would later be appointed a deputy chief for the Toronto Police Service, came to meet with me.

I realized very quickly that we were on the same page. They told me they wanted to hire fifty youth but they did not have the money to make that happen. I learned after the meeting that they had actually hoped I would give them money to hire twenty-five youth. They thought that if they asked for fifty, I would bring the number down to the twenty-five they actually wanted. To their surprise, or perhaps shock would be a better word, I asked them if they would be willing to hire one hundred youth if I was able to secure the funding. They didn't know that this was what my team's youth opportunities strategy had already planned for Toronto, along with proportionately lower numbers for other police services in the province. I gather that the three men who had come to meet with me headed back to Toronto Police headquarters, somewhat nervously, to deliver the news of the possibility of hosting one hundred youth, to Chief Blair.

In 2006, the Toronto Police Service launched the official pilot with one hundred youth in the Youth in Policing program. I knew that the likelihood of expanding the program to Ottawa, London, Hamilton, Windsor, and Thunder Bay in the following year, as defined in my ministry's youth opportunities strategy, rested firmly with Toronto Police Service making the first year a success.

As soon as the Youth in Policing program was announced with Toronto as the pilot, I received a telephone call from Vernon White, chief of police for Durham Region. He told me that as Toronto's immediate neighbour to the east, his region was experiencing challenges similar to those perhaps better known as existing in Toronto. He asked me to extend the program to Durham in its first year. He promised that his board would match whatever funds my ministry could provide. It is my recollection that Durham hosted twenty-three youth in that first year. The chief invited me to visit while the program was under way, and it was obvious his team was doing a great job.

Vernon White, who had previously served as an assistant commissioner with the Royal Canadian Mounted Police, was new to the Durham Region when he was appointed its chief of police in 2005. He quickly immersed himself in learning about the community and demonstrated a commitment to reflecting the rich diversity of the region in his police officers. Chief White's stay in Durham was relatively short, ending with his selection to lead Ottawa's police service in 2007. The Youth in Policing program was in place in Ottawa by that time, and Chief White invited me to attend the program's graduation ceremony that year. It was heartwarming to hear police officers offering to continue their mentorship of the youth with whom they had spent that summer.

In 2012, I was pleased to learn of Vernon White's appointment to the Senate of Canada by then Prime Minister Stephen Harper. In October 2019, Peter Sloly's appointment as chief of the Ottawa Police Service was viewed very positively by many who had seen him as deserving of that role in Toronto.

I recall Toronto's Chief Blair sharing with me some of the internal resistance he was receiving to the new initiative, but he confidently took the steps necessary to address those concerns. I also recall that community members were very skeptical, to put it mildly. They told us that young people would not apply. They declared that youth from their communities would not want to work with the police. Given long-standing concerns about anti-Black racism in policing, I wasn't surprised by that reaction.

In the midst of all of this, I knew of police officers in Scarborough who were competing against each other to see who could get the most youth to apply. They even helped youth to complete their application forms. Within three weeks after the initiative was announced, 1,300 applications had been submitted for the one hundred positions.

The chief threw his full support behind the Youth in Policing initiative, and staff at the Toronto Police Service put their hearts and minds into the design of Toronto's program. I have been told that the chief would boast about the program at meetings with chiefs of police from jurisdictions across Canada. Chief Blair spoke publicly, proudly, and frequently about the Youth in Policing initiative. He spoke about the positive impact the youth have had on the women and men in the Toronto Police Service who have had the opportunity to work with them and observe their abilities and their potential. Chief Blair also advocated for the creation of similar employment opportunities for youth in the private sector. I will always be grateful for his committed leadership and support for the young people of Toronto through the Youth in Policing initiative. In the third year of the program, when the government of Ontario announced that, in recognition of the program's huge success, the decision had been made to fund the program in perpetuity, Chief Blair told me he was so excited that he looked up "in perpetuity" in the dictionary just to be sure.

Some years ago, the capacity of the program was expanded. Now, more than one hundred and fifty young people participate in Toronto Police Service's summer Youth in Policing initiative. After-school programs in the fall and in the spring have also been added, a tangible illustration of the program's success. And because of the success of the initiative in Toronto as the pilot location, the initiative is now in place in more than twenty police services across the province of Ontario.

It has often been observed that for an organization to be truly successful, the right tone must be set at the most senior levels of its leadership. When Bill Blair retired from the Toronto Police Service, his successors, Chief Mark Saunders and later Chief James Ramer, fully embraced the program. Following his retirement, Bill Blair ran successfully for the federal Liberals and was appointed Canada's minister of public safety and emergency preparedness.

The Youth in Policing initiative would not be the success it is without the support of women and men who work in police services throughout Ontario. Scott Mills is one of those who will always have my appreciation. Following the first graduation for the program in Toronto, I was leaving the event when I heard a voice calling, "Minister, minister." It was Scott, in uniform, a tall man with what could be an intimidating physical presence. As he caught up with me, he reached into his pouch for a note he wanted me to see. It was from a female participant in the program, who had written to express her appreciation for his mentorship. Scott beamed as he told me he planned to keep that note. He has continued to support the program and, for the many years he remained with the Toronto Police Service, I looked forward to seeing him at each year's graduation event. I have also used those events as opportunities to greet and thank other officers whose participation has enriched the lives of Toronto youth even as the young people have enriched the experiences of those officers.

The Toronto Police Service has demonstrated what can be accomplished when governments find willing and able partners to deliver on their quest to serve the public good. It also helped showcase the ability of our young people to excel when given a fair chance to do so. It is my sincere hope that the Youth in Policing initiative and the constructive and mutually beneficial relationships it has fostered will become the model for all interactions between police and youth. This approach to every aspect of police and community relations takes commitment. The possibilities of the legacies the program has been creating are infinite.

My relationship with members of the Toronto Police Service has not always been positive. One night about ten years ago, I had a rather negative experience on my way home from an event at Ryerson University. When I made an entirely legal left turn at a traffic light, carefully changing lanes when I discovered that the ramp from the right lane to the Don Valley Parkway was closed, a police cruiser, lights flashing and siren blazing, caused me to pull over and stop by the side of the road.

A slim, youthful-looking officer came to my window, yelling that I was driving carelessly and that was the kind of driving that caused accidents. He told me I obviously didn't care about the safety of others and cared only about myself. He repeated those comments a few times, yelling at me the entire time. He continued yelling at me even when, in response to his request that I give him my driver's licence and my insurance information, I reached over to the glove compartment where those documents were kept. He then took my documents and returned to his cruiser where he sat with the interior light of his vehicle on, while I watched through the rear-view mirror in my car. He must have been in his cruiser for at least fifteen minutes. The time seemed like forever.

When he returned to my car, he handed my documents back to me and, in a softer voice, told me he had decided to let me off with a warning. I told the officer I certainly did not feel like I had been let off with a warning. I told him that in my almost sixty years on this planet, no one had ever spoken to me like he had.

I don't know what he had found when he looked me up in his database. I wondered if what he saw had caused him to adjust his approach. My hands shook and I could feel my heart racing as I continued my drive home.

The next time I attended an event at Toronto Police headquarters, I happened to be seated next to one of the deputy chiefs whom I had come to know and appreciate in his previous role as unit commander of 42 Division in Scarborough when I was in government. Beyond a number of interactions at events in the community, he had willingly attended and spoken at my career fairs for youth in Scarborough, and he had visited my constituency office and made thoughtful recommendations when I sought advice on how to address security concerns related to unwelcome activity. He had also increased police patrols when residents in the area raised complaints about solicitation, prostitution, and evidence of illicit drug use. He had been a breath of fresh air compared with his predecessor, who had dismissed my requests for support. That day, when I was with him at Toronto Police headquarters, I asked that deputy chief, "Who is in charge of the command responsible for traffic enforcement?"

"I am," he said.

The conversation came to an end at that point, as the master of ceremonies went to the podium to get the event started. At the end of the event, I stood and said my goodbyes to those around me, including the deputy chief responsible for traffic.

"Do you want to tell me why you asked about traffic enforcement?" he asked as I was walking away.

"No," I responded without hesitation.

"Come with me to my office."

I did as the deputy chief asked and I told him about the incident. I shared with him my concern that it was individual officers like that who could give the entire police service a less than positive reputation.

"Did you make a note of the officer's name or the number on his cruiser?"

I thought the conversation would end there because I had not taken any identifying information. I had not given any thought to following up on the incident. The experience had been upsetting enough that I really wanted to make it go away, erase it from my memory, if possible, but I guess I couldn't. Maybe that's why I had asked the deputy chief who was in charge of traffic enforcement. I certainly hadn't planned to do so. The conversation didn't end there, as I thought it might have.

"That's okay. If you tell me the date, time and location of the incident, I will be able to determine who the officer was."

I told him the location and when I got home, I provided him with the date and approximate time.

The following day, he called to tell me he had identified the officer. "Do you want to file an official complaint or would you prefer me to take care of the matter for you myself?"

I asked him to address the issue on my behalf. A few days later, he called to let me know he had dealt with the matter.

Chapter 21

Back to Business

I RETURNED TO THE WORLD of business when, in 2011, Douglas Orane, then chairman and CEO of the GraceKennedy Group, invited me to join the group's board of directors. Since then, as a non-executive member of the board of directors of GraceKennedy Ltd., a food and financial services conglomerate traded on the Jamaica and Trinidad and Tobago stock exchanges, I have been travelling to Jamaica several times each year.

Shortly after my appointment to the board, and with Doug's retirement approaching, the dual roles of chairman and CEO were separated. The transition toward a new group CEO and an independent chair resulted in the appointment of Donald Wehby, who had served as chief financial officer for the group, as group CEO. Professor Gordon Shirley, then pro-vice-chancellor and principal of the Mona, Jamaica, campus of the University of the West Indies, was appointed chairman. Gordon Shirley had previously served as ambassador for Jamaica to the U.S.A. Douglas Orane served as an independent senator for four years and Don Wehby currently serves as a senator in the government of Jamaica. Beyond the passion that Doug, Gordon, and Don share for the GraceKennedy Group, the commitment of these three men to Jamaica is unmistakable and unrivalled. They have each been recognized with national honours reserved for those who have served Jamaica with the utmost distinction, and I see that in evidence consistently and constantly. It has truly been a pleasure to know them and to work with them as colleagues. We have become good friends.

Jamaica is one of the most beautiful places in the world. Whenever my flight starts its descent for landing and I see the blue Caribbean Sea and the green, undulating mountains, goose pimples surface, my heart beats a bit faster, and I know I will soon feel the caress of a warm breeze and welcoming people.

As soon as my airplane touches down on the runway at Kingston's Norman Manley International Airport, I phone Mr. Smith, the driver the company provides for me for the duration of my visit. He is usually in the taxi parking lot, awaiting my call. I will be one of the first passengers to leave the aircraft and, because I am travelling only with carry-on luggage, I will ask him to meet me outside the arrivals area in about fifteen minutes.

As I am leaving the airplane, I know it's time to breathe deeply and psych myself down because I might be the only person in a hurry to get to wherever so that I can do whatever. If I am smart, I will remind myself of Bob Marley's promise that every little thing will be all right.

Other drivers, mostly men, stand in the partially covered pick-up area just outside the terminal building, hoping there will be arriving passengers who need their services. They wear white shirts and black pants. A few who recognize me from previous occasions greet me with warm smiles and say, "Hello, Miss." They don't ask me if I need a drive. They know Mr. Smith and they know he is my driver.

Mr. Smith is not a tall man. I would guess he is at least a few inches shorter than I am. I think he is probably in his late sixties. He is slim and soft spoken. When he sees me, he is going to greet me with a hug before he puts my small suitcase on the floor of his van, just behind where I will be sitting. "Hello, Mrs. Chambers, welcome."

"How are you, Mr. Smith?"

"Giving thanks, Mrs. Chambers, giving thanks," Mr. Smith will respond.

"And how is the family, Mrs. Chambers?"

Along the way to my hotel, Mr. Smith will update me on how his wife, daughter, and grandchildren are doing. He will also bring me up to speed on the major political happenings and other important local matters. We might stop to pick up dinner at a popular jerk-food place close to the hotel. I will order pork and Mr. Smith will order chicken. Or we might go to Devon House, where I will struggle to decide which I will choose of the several mouth-watering flavours of the richest, creamiest ice cream in the world ever. There are no low-fat options among the ice cream flavours. I will usually settle for a scoop of real rum and raisin and a scoop of grape nut in a cup. I will get more than enough calories without adding a cone. The two scoops are generous enough to satisfy me for dinner. Mr. Smith and I will sit outside, under a massive poinciana tree with its stunning red flowers, to enjoy our special treat before it melts in the soothing warm air.

My frequent visits are short, usually no more than four days in duration. They are not vacations. Board and committee meetings fill most of my time there but I very much enjoy my colleagues and I am proud to be involved with the company, which is well recognized for its extensive youth-focused initiatives, mainly in education and sports, as well as a variety of other community support efforts. The company is an exemplary corporate citizen.

I look forward to indulging in authentic Jamaican food and I am sometimes able to spend a few hours in a shaded area on the patio of my hotel. The colourful bougainvillea shrubs that line the perimeter of the large and beautifully maintained Emancipation Park across the road from my hotel bloom profusely and constantly. The staff at my hotel welcome me "home" when I arrive, and throughout my stay, several hug me and update me on happenings in their personal lives.

The people of Jamaica are unapologetically proud and remarkably resilient. "No problem" is the typical response to situations that are, in fact, problems. The little children are irresistible. They are affectionate and smile easily. Their smiles are beautiful. I am saddened by the fact that so many live in poverty. A former high commissioner for Canada to Jamaica once told me that he had observed that the children who live outside the cities, in villages where everyone else lives like they do, are happy. They don't realize how poor they are. That realization occurs when they become teenagers, old enough to leave the rural or more confined areas in which they have been living, and start to discover the stark contrasts in how other people live and the privileges some have. Yet, those inner-city communities and rural villages are not without their success stories. As is the case elsewhere in the world, access to high-quality education is often the most reliable path to success.

More than forty-four years after choosing Canada as my home, Jamaica is still very much a part of who I am. I bristle at any suggestion that after all these years I should be classified as an immigrant, but when I am told that I haven't lost my accent, I say, "I hope I never do."

My Canadian passport shows Kingston, Jamaica, as my place of birth, and that triggers a "welcome home" from the Jamaican immigration officers when I visit. I always respond by telling them how good that makes me feel. Occasionally they ask me why I don't, or suggest that I should, travel on a Jamaican passport. Their facial expressions indicate disappointment, sometimes displeasure, when I say, "I am Canadian."

This might all sound confusing, contradictory, or complicated, but it's all very clear in my mind. I will always love Jamaica but Canada is my home by choice. I see no conflict between my love for Jamaica and my love for Canada.

Chapter 22

Citizens of the World

HAVING BEEN INTRODUCED TO TRAVEL at a young age, it has become more than a hobby. Travel continues to be a way for me to expand my understanding of how other people live. It has enabled me to see examples of humanity wherever in the world I have found myself and it has given me the opportunity to celebrate differences and to find common ground. Travel has truly enriched my life.

Chris and I have done Mediterranean cruises with itineraries that have allowed us to see amazing architecture by Antoni Gaudí, as well as other forms of art in Barcelona; romantic places in Italy like Venice, Rome, and Tuscany; and countries filled with ancient history like Turkey, Croatia, and Greece.

In 2008, on our second visit to Greece, our friends Georgia and Bill Geropoulos were already waiting for us on the pier when our ship docked, ready to make our experience even more special than the first time we had visited the Greek Islands. They took us to their home and to an amazing bakery where we feasted our eyes on what seemed like infinite offerings and had a great deal of difficulty deciding what to select. We enjoyed an array of fresh seafood at an oceanside restaurant popular among local residents, always a good sign and the way we have often been able to measure the authenticity of ethnic restaurants in Toronto. Georgia and Bill took us to the site of the games of the XXVIII Olympiad, the 2004 Summer Olympics. They also took us to the newly opened Acropolis Museum, a stunning architectural feat with a glass floor that allows visitors to see archaeological ruins underneath the structure while also being able to view the original site of the ancient Acropolis and its Parthenon on the hill above. The newly constructed Acropolis Museum had only recently been completed, so new that it was not on the list of shore excursions offered by our cruise ship.

In Istanbul, when our tour provided us with time to explore the city on our own, our guide remained with us, giving us the opportunity to learn how his excellent English had worked in his favour. When other young men had to fight the Kurds on the front line, his mandatory military service was spent as a translator in a military office. Recognizing that work as a tour guide was unlikely to be a full-time job, I asked him what other kind of work he did. He told me he worked in merchant services for a large commercial bank in Turkey, which had me thinking that if he had done that kind of work in Canada while I was working with Scotiabank, our paths might have crossed. Merchant services had been one of my areas of responsibility at the bank. I reflected on the fact that when we allow ourselves to get to know other people, wherever they might be in the world and regardless of differences in culture and language, we can often find something that we have in common.

I would describe the two-week escorted tour Chris and I did of mainland China and Hong Kong, in 2012, as fascinating. There were twelve or thirteen people in our tour group. We had great tour guides, perfectly fluent in English and surprisingly willing to share with us information we would have thought to be too politically sensitive.

Our port of entry to China was Beijing's ultramodern airport. After getting through immigration, I went to the ladies' room, where I was surprised to find the toilet "seats" at floor level. As I squatted above the floor, thankful that the muscles in my legs were up to the task, it occurred to me that I had obviously not done enough research in preparation for the trip.

From our hotel window, Chris videoed the chaotic-looking traffic scene in the major intersection below, where large numbers of pedestrians mingled with dozens of cars and bicycles in a manner not for the faint of heart. We walked a section of the Great Wall of China, strolled through Tiananmen Square under the many surveillance cameras and the watchful eyes of armed security personnel, visited the Forbidden City across the road from the square and experienced the pearl market, where it was almost impossible to distinguish genuine brand-name items from authentic looking knock-offs. We visited a home in the alleyways of the old hutongs residential area and then, as if to emphasize the contrast, we were taken to the summer palace, located on seven hundred acres of beautiful scenery. Along the way, we stopped at the Olympic stadium, where a member of our group returned to our bus boasting about his success in bargaining for a great deal on some large kites, only to later discover that there were no lines for flying the kites in the packages. I didn't need to wonder who had had the last laugh.

We flew to Xi'An from Beijing, where we saw the famous Terracotta Army and stopped at a centre nearby where the production of delicate threads by silkworms, for use in the manufacture of beautiful products from scarves to comforters for beds, was on display along with various forms of art depicting the history of the silk trade, museum style. After Xi'An, we flew to Chongqing for the leg of our tour where we would cruise the Yangtze River in awe of the scenic mountains of the Three Gorges and visit the museum on the site of the massive hydroelectric dam, a project that had involved displacing more than one million residents from areas around the river, an extremely sensitive subject, we gathered.

It was on the Yangtze River cruise that a few members of our group became ill, seemingly from something we had eaten. By the time our flight arrived in Shanghai, I was so sick I couldn't complete the tour of the city. Instead, I headed to the row of seats at the back of our tour bus and lay on my side with my knees pulled up as tightly as possible against my stomach. As everyone else left the bus to walk around in cosmopolitan Shanghai, our bus driver, who didn't speak English, opened the windows to let the air in, closed the doors of the bus, and stood outside as if he was guarding the bus and me, his fragile passenger. I was most appreciative of his thoughtfulness and I fell asleep feeling well protected.

Even the smallest city, by their definition, that we visited had a population larger than the city of Toronto. Residential construction projects involved multiple towers, not a few of a magnitude far greater than what we were accustomed to seeing at home. We also heard from our tour guides that many new apartments sat empty, financially out of reach for most of China's citizens.

Hong Kong was next on our itinerary, and after our tour guide took us by tram to Victoria Peak for a breathtaking view of the skyline, and to Stanley Market, where I shopped for linen clothing to my heart's content and bought beautiful exotic kites — complete with lines — for our granddaughters, we were left with lots of time to explore on our own. My friend Cynthia D'Anjou Brown showed us around the city, a bustling business centre that appeared to be home to every financial institution of note in the world, including those where Cynthia and her husband, Richard, worked; open-air markets that sold birds and many varieties of exotic flowers that I had never seen before; Buddhist temples; an island we got to by ferry, where we ate delicious fresh seafood on a picnic bench by the harbour; and a quaint fishing village where the villagers lived side by side in small homes on the water with their fishing boats tied up alongside them. Cynthia and Richard took us to dinner at the exclusive China Club and also loaned us their passes for the MTR (Mass Transit Railway), a transit network that included a rapid transit system that made Toronto's subway system seem archaic. Hong Kong definitely had a different feel to mainland China.

Our travels also took us back to Aruba and Barbados where Chris and I had previously visited, tourist style, staying at resorts on those earlier trips. On our return trips, we stayed with our friends Margaret and Tony Brathwaite, feeling more like locals than tourists, and of course seeing and enjoying so much more of what those islands have to offer, including new friends that we had the opportunity to meet. In Aruba, Tony was working as deputy managing director for Caribbean Mercantile Bank N.V., a subsidiary of Maduro and Curiel's Bank Curaçao N.V.. In Barbados, Margaret and Tony were enjoying the winter months at their home on the island. It had never been our preference to stay with friends when we travelled. The fact that we stayed with Margaret and Tony on two trips to Aruba and then in Barbados speaks to the close relationship that we have with each other, as well as the wonderful hosts that they truly are.

In marking International Women's Day in 2015, the then secretary general of the United Nations, Ban Ki-Moon, said that "To be truly transformative, the post-2015 development agenda must prioritize gender equality and women's empowerment. The world will never realize 100 percent of its goals if 50 percent of its people cannot realize their full potential."

Also in 2015, when Justin Trudeau promised that if chosen by Canadians to form the next government of Canada, his cabinet would be composed of an equal number of women and men, detractors accused him of playing politics by putting gender ahead of qualifications. How often have we heard it suggested that equity initiatives, in whatever setting, would result in less competent people being appointed to senior roles? Sometimes women, even those with impressive credentials, need champions to enable the realization of their full potential.

In the first year of its mandate, the Trudeau government also announced its Feminist International Assistance Policy. A message from the Honourable Marie-Claude Bibeau, then minister of international development and la francophonie, stated: "Canada is adopting a Feminist International Assistance Policy that seeks to eradicate poverty and build a more peaceful, more inclusive, and more prosperous world. Canada firmly believes that promoting gender equality and empowering women and girls is the most effective approach to achieving this goal."

My appointment, in June 2016, and reappointment in June 2019, as a governor of the International Development Research Centre (IDRC), a Crown corporation of the government of Canada, has given me the opportunity to support the achievement of sustainable development goals in the developing world. It is my view that investment in the transfer of knowledge and the building of capacity that enables developing nations to do well for themselves equates to nation building in ways that lead to more peaceful and mutually respectful relationships.

When I was on a field visit with fellow governors to Uganda, the women involved in the Fermented Food For Life project told us that their contribution to their family's income gave them respect they had not enjoyed before. Getting married meant the husband received cattle, a very valuable gift from the bride's father. But once married, the woman had no claim to the cattle and, for that matter, no say in the operation of the household. She had no seat at the table, literally. The floor, in a corner of the room, was where she was allowed to sit. Milk from the cattle served the needs of the family. The woman's opinion, not deemed to be of value, was never sought. But the cattle produced more milk than the household could use. The situation, not unique to one particular household, changed when a few women learned about a project that would give them the opportunity to use milk along with a probiotic culture to produce yogourt. With the approval of their husbands to use each day's excess milk, these rural women formed a cooperative, became entrepreneurs, made enough yogourt to sell to schools and hospitals, and hired youth to do the deliveries. The money they made was, of course, shared with their husbands but most importantly, these women became respected and valued members of their own households, entitled to sit on chairs in their homes and contribute their ideas to discussions with their husbands. This was women's economic empowerment in action. And it gave these women privileges that they had not enjoyed before.

I have always known I would have to be financially independent. I had no desire or need to be wealthy. I just needed the sense of security that would come with knowing I would be able to look after myself. It still surprises me to hear about women who rely entirely on their husbands to manage the family's finances. Some have dedicated their lives to raising their children and supporting their husbands' careers while depending on their husbands to take care of them. Unfortunately, in some cases, when the husbands of many years passed on, the wives have found themselves in difficult situations financially.

In Andahuaylillas, about an hour's drive from Cusco, Peru, the stories shared by Andean women who travelled for three days by bus and by foot to tell us how the financial inclusion project Proyecto Capital had improved their lives reinforced how I think about financial literacy and financial independence. The project included teaching the women about the value of the alpaca that they raised, not only as a source of milk for nourishment and wool to keep them and their families warm but also as an asset, something that they own and could use as collateral for loans to support and expand the scope of their farming. The project also included an introduction to banking. The women had previously had to travel large distances to collect, in cash, their monthly support from their government. Apart from the inconvenience, there was also the risk they could fall victim to thieves and lose the cash on the way home. If they were fortunate enough to return home with the cash, they would then have to find hiding places to keep the money safe. Working in partnership with the government and several financial institutions through Proyecto Capital, bank accounts were opened for each of the women and the government's monthly support payments were deposited electronically. Banking machines were located in places like local convenience stores where the women could withdraw cash or deposit money they were saving for future use. So new was the concept to these women that their first action would be to withdraw cash just to prove that it really was available to them and then they would put it back into their accounts with the confidence it would be there for them when they needed it. Rather than these women simply existing from day to day, their quality of life had improved significantly, enabling them to become more independent and also more influential in the lives of their families.

In Medellín, Colombia, researchers at Universidad EAFIT, some of whom are graduate students from Canada, are improving educational outcomes for young children through the introduction of computers in local schools and the training of older children in those schools to act as teaching assistants. With a focus on prevention, research on diabetes and vector-borne diseases like malaria is helping to improve health conditions in Colombia and Peru.

A graduate student at Universidad de los Andes in Bogotá, Colombia, told me she felt her research project, *Overcoming Violence through Local Institutions: A Comparative Study of Households and Communities in Colombia*, might have failed. When I asked her to explain why she believed this to be the case, she told me her project had helped women in a rural community to acquire skills that would prepare them to access employment. But when they left their homes to take up those jobs, their sons were recruited by gangs and their daughters were raped by men in the community. The women also found that their male partners were not supportive of their employment and believed that the women's rightful place was in the home, caring for their men and their children. I offered the researcher the suggestion that she consider how the men could be included in her project in order to help them to see its value to the entire family and how they could help to mitigate the risks identified.

It is my opinion that while women should not require men's approval, the engagement of others close to them, most specifically the men in their lives as well as their children, will often help the women to achieve greater success. I recall making that observation many years earlier, when I chaired a United Way of Greater Toronto Freedom from Violence Grants committee, reviewing proposals for projects to address violence against women. If a project proposal did not reference the inclusion of programming for men and boys, it did not receive my support.

I have also seen IDRC's work in action in Vietnam, helping children have better health outcomes thanks to the results of research on food security. The little children at the school we visited called out to me with smiles on their faces as they ate their nutritious cereal, produced using locally grown vegetables. I asked the teachers what they were saying as they called out to me. The teachers told me that they were saying, "Hello, Grandma." I found myself thinking about all the money that was spent on the Vietnam war and how many lives were lost. Wouldn't it have been better for those resources to be directed to programs such as these that serve to build stronger relationships between countries?

In Nepal, climate change takes its toll as water security in many areas is a problem. There are encouraging signs from the work that IDRC is enabling in partnership with local researchers.

The huge informal sector in India creates challenges that are particularly detrimental for women.

I have seen evidence of all of this and much more as a governor of IDRC, all of which has served to reinforce my great pride in being Canadian.

———

The citation that accompanied my Order of Ontario in January 2016 said that I had "served the people of Ontario with a profound dedication." The Order of Ontario, the province's highest honour, was created in 1986, and approximately twenty-five individuals are appointed to the Order each year. I am humbled to have the privilege of sharing that honour with some truly outstanding Canadians, including some who are also daughters, granddaughters, sons, and grandsons of Jamaica. They each serve to illustrate that ordinary but special people can accomplish extraordinary things and, in doing so, make life so much better for others. It has been a source of inspiration and pride to know many of these special people. The list includes Kamala-Jean Gopie (public service), Lloyd Seivright (community service), Dr. Mavis Burke (social service), Dr. Avis Glaze (education), Dr. Inez Elliston (education), Delores Lawrence (health care), Alvin Curling (public service), Lillie Johnson (health care), Ucal Powell (community service), Joseph Halstead (public administration), Beverley Salmon (public service), June Girvan (community service), Dr. Anna Jarvis (medicine), Dr. Upton Allen (health care), Donovan Bailey (sports), and Michael Lee-Chin (philanthropy/business).

In the early 2000s when I served on the board of the Rouge Valley Health System's Scarborough Centenary Hospital and

Ajax-Pickering Hospital, the chief of surgery and chief of staff, Dr. Naresh Mohan, the chief of paediatrics, Dr. Rosemary Moodie, and the chief of psychiatry, Dr. Ken Sealey, were all graduates of the University of the West Indies. And when children in Ontario needed a more advanced level of care than their local hospitals could provide, they would be rushed to the world-renowned Hospital for Sick Children in the city of Toronto, where the head of emergency services, Dr. Anna Jarvis, was a graduate of the University of the West Indies. Graduates of the University of the West Indies are also faculty members and professors at the University of Toronto's medical school.

Clearing the path for practitioners from the Caribbean as a pioneer in the field was Dr. Douglas Salmon, the late husband of Beverley Salmon, herself a trailblazer as Toronto's first Black female city councillor and the first Black female to serve as a commissioner on the Ontario Human Rights Commission. A registered nurse and daughter of a Scottish-Irish mother and a Jamaican father who attended MIT before serving in the Canadian military, Bev Salmon was appointed to the Order of Ontario in 2016 and the Order of Canada in 2017. Her citation for the Order of Canada describes her as "an exemplary model of civic engagement" and "a dedicated champion for the social and educational well-being of Black communities in the city." Dr. Douglas Salmon practised surgery at Scarborough Centenary Hospital from 1967 until he retired in 1995. For some of those years, he also served as president of the hospital's medical staff and chief of general surgery. Born to Jamaican parents in 1923, Douglas Salmon was orphaned at the age of six, during the time of the Great Depression. Tough times. Douglas Salmon was also an accomplished pianist, and in the 1940s led a group of musicians known as Doug Salmon and his Orchestra. He and friends fought discriminatory practices that prevented Black people from attending performances by highly acclaimed Black

American musicians at Toronto's Palais Royale. In 1967, when Dr. Salmon joined the staff of Centenary Hospital, Scarborough wasn't nearly as racially diverse as it is now. After having to fight to be allowed to attend concerts at Toronto's Palais Royale just twenty-five years before, Dr. Douglas Salmon, Canada's first Black surgeon, would make an outstanding contribution to the quality of life every Canadian seeks to enjoy.

Both graduates of the University of the West Indies and members of the Order of Ontario, Dr. Dorothy Anna Jarvis and Dr. Upton Allen are just two examples of Canadians of Jamaican ancestry whose impact in the field of children's health in Canada and internationally has been exceptional.

An alumna and fellow inaugural inductee to the hall of fame of Immaculate Conception High School, our high school in Jamaica, Dr. Jarvis is recognized as being one of the first Canadian paediatric emergency physicians and Ontario's first paediatric emergency medical services physician. Her special concern for children living in underserved communities also established her as a leader in the provision of a continuum of pre-hospital paramedic care for some of the sickest and most seriously injured children from their homes and the streets through to community or paediatric emergency departments. Dr. Jarvis has served as director of the division of emergency services at the Hospital for Sick Children in Toronto and director of the Child Health Network. She also held appointments at the University of Toronto — including that of professor, director of the office of student affairs for the faculty of medicine, and associate dean, health professions student affairs — in the faculty of medicine. Dr. Jarvis has repeatedly served as an external examiner for medical programs at the University of the West Indies in Jamaica and Trinidad, the University of Kuwait, and the Kuwaiti Board of Medical Specialists, and for the sub-specialty of paediatric emergency medicine as a member of the Royal College of Physicians and Surgeons of Canada's examination board. Having dedicated more than forty years to the provision of emergency paediatric medicine in Canada and around the world, Dr. Jarvis has created a tremendous legacy through the impact she has made and continues to make in inspiring students and health professionals to excel, and in helping to build the capacity of systems to care for children in the Middle East and Asia. She has been described as the mother of paediatric emergency medicine in Japan, a giant of Canadian paediatrics and emergency medicine, a medical ambassador for Canada, and an exemplary citizen of the world. Dr. Jarvis is now a professor emerita in the department of paediatrics at the University of Toronto and has retired from clinical practice.

Dr. Upton Allen, a professor of paediatrics and health policy management and evaluation at the University of Toronto, is also the division head for infectious diseases at Toronto's Hospital for Sick Children. He was the first paediatric infectious diseases physician to be specifically recruited in Canada with a mandate to address infections in children with weakened immune systems outside the setting of HIV. The year was 1995. Since then, Dr. Allen's work has included the training of specialists from Canada, the United States of America, the United Kingdom, Switzerland, Germany, Nigeria, China, Japan, India, Pakistan, Australia, Latin America, the Middle East, and the Caribbean, creating an exceptional legacy in the field of infectious diseases in Canada and around the world. In 2013, Dr. Allen became the first Canadian to receive the American Society of Transplantation Clinical Science Established Investigator Award, recognition granted to individuals considered to be the best in the field. The American Society of Transplantation is the largest professional transplantation society in the world with an international membership of over four thousand professionals who are working to advance the field of transplantation through research, education, advocacy, and organ donation. Dr. Allen has also been awarded an honorary fellowship by the Royal College of Physicians in the United Kingdom for his work in training specialists around the world. In Saudi Arabia, former trainees of Dr. Allen have established visiting professorships in his name.

Jamaicans have long had a notable presence in the provision of health care in Canada. Long-term care facilities in the Greater Toronto Area, like the one where my mother spent her last few years, have many Jamaican nurses and personal support workers on their staff. That was to become a source of great comfort to me. Mommy had peaked earlier in life at a height of five feet four inches and had gradually lost a couple of those inches as she aged, but she could be feisty and had little interest in editing what she would say to her caregivers. Even so, they treated her as though she was theirs. They took very good care of her, they would hug her warmly, and they often brought Jamaican food they had cooked at home to share with her. They also ensured that I kept her supplied with gin, her favourite drink, which they served her with ginger ale at lunch every day. When Mommy passed away at the age of ninety-four, I took the staff on her floor of the nursing home two dozen long-stemmed red roses in appreciation for the love they had shown her.

Chapter 23

The World Is Brought to Its Knees

IT IS THE YEAR 2020, a year we will not soon forget.

While Chris and I we were on our winter vacation in the Hawaiian islands, an elderly couple on vacation from mainland U.S.A. joined us as we sat having lunch at a picnic table in a beachside park while directing our gaze toward the ocean in anticipation of another whale sighting. We were being treated to performances by these massive creatures as they breached, raising a large portion of their bodies out of the water as though reaching to the sky, so majestically and seemingly so close to swimmers. It doesn't matter how often I see the whales in whatever act they are engaging, I continue to be amazed. I am not alone. I usually know where, along the Maui coastline, I will spot them. At other times it will be the in-concert movement of people rising from their lounge chairs on the beach or coming to a sudden halt on their stroll along the boardwalk, all to face the ocean in awe, that will draw my attention to the show that is being staged by these incredible mammals.

As we shared stories about our various travel experiences and favourite restaurants, the friendly couple who joined us at our picnic table told us not to be surprised if we were to see lots of people wearing masks while in transit through the San Francisco airport on our way back to Toronto. We had seen television news coverage about the virus that, it was believed, first surfaced in Wuhan, the capital city of Hubei province in China. We had also heard health professionals in the media making comparisons to the annual flu virus, reminding viewers that influenza kills large numbers of people around the world every year. As the days went by, they started comparing transmission rates, the coronavirus versus the annual influenza.

We left the Hawaiian islands on February 15 and arrived home on February 16. On February 24, I left Toronto for board meetings in Jamaica and returned home on February 27. In the international arrivals hall at Toronto Pearson Airport, I had to respond to a new question about whether or not I had recently been in China. The question was displayed on the screen of the kiosks where passengers insert their customs declaration forms. Apart from that, life still seemed relatively normal in my sheltered world. That was about to change as concern about the movement of the virus began to rise.

On Saturday, March 8, Chris and I attended an International Women's Day event at the Jamaican Canadian Association. There were individually packaged hand-sanitizer wipes positioned with the place settings for lunch. I tried, unsuccessfully, to avoid being hugged by several people who were happy to see me, people who are also accustomed to being hugged by me. Chris and I left that event to attend a concert by Anderson & Roe, an American piano duo, at the Markham Theatre. I was happy that no one was sitting in the seat immediately next to mine.

On March 11, the World Health Organization declared the Covid-19 outbreak a pandemic. That evening, Chris and I attended a scholarship awards ceremony at Centennial College. The master of ceremonies announced that members of the administration, scholarship recipients, and scholarship sponsors should not shake each other's hands but rather use alternative ways of greeting each other. Some did the elbow-to-elbow move, some tapped shoes, others bumped hips. I used the namaste greeting.

The following afternoon, March 12, I attended a colloquium at the master's in public and international affairs program at York University's Glendon College. Ontario's lieutenant governor, the Honourable Elizabeth Dowdeswell, was the guest speaker. We greeted each other using namaste rather than shaking hands. Before the event ended, someone from the university told me that the Ontario government had just announced the immediate closure of all schools in the province. The situation was obviously escalating as more became known about the public health risk that the virus presented.

The following day, Chris and I had lunch at a sushi restaurant a few minutes from where we live. There were very few other customers and Sam, the manager of the restaurant, expressed concern that business had fallen off significantly.

Since that week in March, very little else has seemed newsworthy. The numbers are being updated daily, confirmed cases, hospitalizations, deaths, people who have recovered.

As the wicked virus has moved from country to country indiscriminately, washing over each place like a giant wave, it has served to illustrate that markings on maps are man-made boundaries that become much less important when stressed by disease or human failings or when made irrelevant by human achievements and technologies with global reach.

Governments, which have sometimes been viewed as unnecessarily intrusive, are being called upon to help their citizens get through the crisis, and the expectations are enormous.

Whenever I leave my apartment to dispose of the garbage or to go to the mailbox, the supermarket, or the drug store, I am armed with a paper towel that I use to protect myself when I touch the elevator buttons or the handles of doors. I hope I will not encounter any of my neighbours in the hallway because public health departments and leaders of government have told us to practise social distancing or, to be more accurate, physical distancing. Physical distancing means maintaining a distance of two metres from other people except those with whom we live. Also as advised, I wear a face mask when I go to places where physical distancing might be difficult to achieve.

Social distancing, the term commonly used, is certainly not happening. Technology is not only bringing news of the situation to us constantly, it is also allowing those of us who have telephones or access to the internet to maintain contact socially. People in non-essential services or occupations that do not require in-person, face-to-face contact with clients are working from home. The rest of us have been told to stay home except for accessing essential services. Until September, school buildings were closed with teachers supporting students through online learning. Video conferencing has become the universal approach to holding meetings.

Even so, I feel truly fortunate. Chris and I have each other's company. We have food and other necessities. We have been keeping well. Our apartment is comfortable; staying home is not a hardship. We have access to all the technology we need to keep in touch with, and can even see the faces of, other members of our family when we get together. And, as retirees from the regular workforce, we have no jobs to lose as the economy tanks and many businesses have reduced staffing levels or shut down as a result of the restrictions and protocols that have been introduced. Chris's bridge club is closed so he and his regular partners are playing bridge online, almost every day. I know for certain that we are among the more fortunate.

Our apartment looks out onto a forest with a tributary of the Don River that flows year round. It is home to deer, black and grey squirrels, reddish-brown chipmunks, racoons that keep to themselves and are not a nuisance, a small red fox with a long tail that hangs close to the ground, who visits from time to time, the occasional rabbit, several varieties of birds, small and large. From spring through to the fall, Canada geese fly over in formation, making the unique loud cackling noises that identify them even if we are not actually seeing them. Blue jays and cardinals tend to come by in pairs. A great blue heron visits, gracing us with its massive presence as it perches for several hours on branches close to the top of the tallest tree in the forest. Our forest provides privacy and the abundance of nature soothes our souls.

When I am told to stay home, I might find that inconvenient, even frustrating. People have complained of having cabin fever. When people in any country who are homeless or live under high-density or otherwise precarious conditions are told to stay off the streets, their reality is different to mine. For them, having a home in which they could safely shelter in place would be considered a blessing.

What I have missed most is being able to hug members of my family. It pains me not to be able to be with them when they are not well. I worry when I try to contact someone and they don't respond as quickly as I think they used to. What troubles me most of all is that I have no idea when this will all end. The increase in the numbers of cases reported in Ontario each day threatens a return to the most severe restrictions that were imposed during the first wave, with no obvious end in sight.

And then I wonder how I will behave when we are no longer being told to wash our hands frequently with soap and water, or to use hand sanitizer before we enter a public place, or to keep a distance of two metres away from others, or to wear a mask whenever we leave home. Will I ever shake someone's hand again? Should I return to greeting people with a hug? Is namaste the way of the future for me? It made a lot of sense when I was in Asia, last year. It seemed more thoughtful and practical from a personal hygiene perspective. It also seemed more universal a practice than hand-shaking. I quickly adapted to that way of greeting others and I liked the fact that I greeted everyone the same way. It seemed to me to be more respectful of everyone, regardless of their perceived status. I noticed that the heavily armed, no nonsense–looking young police officer was watching me as I left the airport terminal upon arrival in Kathmandu. It felt really good that he smiled when I acknow-ledged him with my hands in the namaste position and bowed my head gently. And while I would smile and say "hello" but wouldn't necessarily shake the hands of hotel porters anywhere in the world as they would stand ready to relieve me of my luggage, they re-turned my namaste with a smile when I greeted them that way in Nepal and in India. How civilized, I thought.

Inequities as defined by the social determinants of health are resulting in some people being disproportionately impacted by Covid-19. An area in Toronto known for its high-density, low-income housing and racialized population has been identified as being the area hardest hit by the virus. In contrast, people who can afford to purchase lakeside cottages outside of the city have con-tributed to a record increase in sales of those kinds of properties. In a recent interview, Toronto's chief medical officer of health, Dr. Eileen de Villa, thoughtfully observed that, "The fascinating thing about Covid-19 is that it has actually really laid bare where the health inequities are in the city, in a way that frankly all the reports that we have done over the years just haven't done as effectively."

People over the age of seventy and those with pre-existing respira-tory conditions and diabetes are deemed high risk for contracting the virus with severe health effects, particularly pneumonia. Those physical health–related conditions place some members of society at higher risk, but Covid-19 does not seem to discriminate. People of all ages are easy targets even if they might react differently. Beyond that, there are socioeconomic factors that affect people's ability to protect themselves. People who live in crowded accommodations find it more difficult to practise physical distancing, staying the prescribed two metres away from others. People with limited access to clean, running water are not able to wash their hands with soap and water frequently, as recommended by public health officials. And then there are people who lose their jobs or are laid off temporarily even as their obligations to care for themselves and their families remain. Front-line workers in essential services like health care are at great risk, not only for themselves but also for their families, but must soldier on because they are needed more than ever.

Steps that have been taken in an attempt to contain the spread of the virus impact some people more than others. Some fast-food restaurants that had to close their dining areas and were limiting provision of their service and access to their menu items to their drive-through windows have been reported to have turned away would-be customers who, not having vehicles to carry them through the drive-through lane, have tried to walk up to the window. A Public Health Ontario notice advises people experiencing symptoms of Covid-19, "When you visit your health care provider, avoid using public transportation such as subways, taxis and shared rides. If unavoidable, wear a mask and sit in the back seat." I am reminded that some years ago, a social worker told me that when instructions for the use of medications say "take with meals three times a day," the assumption is that the patient can afford to eat three meals per day. For others, those of more independent means, this is not an issue.

Privilege matters less when conditions beyond our control take charge of our lives. Around 80 percent of deaths in Canada during the first wave have been among vulnerable seniors in long-term care homes, a heartbreaking and shameful situation. Some of their caregivers have also been falling victim to the virus. On a day when it was reported that a City of Toronto long-term care home had recorded 100 positive cases among residents and forty-two among staff, I heard an interview of a worker on his way into the home.

"Aren't you worried?" the reporter asked.

"I have to go to work," the man responded in a distinctive Jamaican accent. "I need to take care of my residents."

On a percentage basis, deaths in the privately owned and operated long-term care homes in Ontario have been reported as significantly higher than those in publicly operated homes. Staffing in the privately owned homes has been reported as being 17 percent lower than in government-operated homes. This has me recalling arguments that I heard against for-profit child-care centres, while I served as the minister of children and youth services. The concerns were about the risk that the quality of care might be compromised in favour of higher profits. Around the world, healthcare workers are being hit hard.

We are being forced to re-evaluate how we have traditionally assigned value to certain kinds of work and those who do those kinds of work, day after day. They are now recognized as "essential." Some are at the minimum-wage level of compensation. Others have simply been disregarded or taken for granted until recently, when we realized that without them we would not have food to eat. We now have a much better understanding and appreciation of what it means to be an essential worker, the risks and the demands that go along with being essential, not only for the individuals but also for their families.

Priorities have changed, at least for the time being. The invisible virus is forcing us to value personal protective equipment, and factories that previously did manufacturing for the automobile industry and for the racing car industry have been repurposed to make face shields and ventilators. A company that manufactured high-end down-filled jackets for those able to afford such luxuries has repurposed its factories to produce face masks. A distillery that normally produces gin is now producing hand sanitizer. These are just a few examples of many innovations that have surfaced in response to the crisis.

Many of my young friends who had been living independently have moved in with their parents. They are the more fortunate ones. For others, home might not be a safe place. There are reports of an increase in domestic abuse situations. Victims of violence feel trapped, unable to escape to places where they can feel safe. Uncertainty is leading to financial distress and a rise in mental illness across people of all ages.

As the price of gas has fallen owing to an oversupply and lower demand while people are staying home and all forms of travel have been substantially reduced, the air has cleared in highly industrialized cities where manufacturing plants are closed and the exhaust from vehicles has been substantially reduced. This has certainly been a positive side effect of Covid-19 and has served as evidence of messages that environmentalists have been trying so hard to deliver for many years. If only this could last, people who survive the virus would be much healthier. Some years ago, when Chris and I visited China, our tour guide in Beijing had told us it had only been when she had won a trip to a rural province that she had realized the sky was actually supposed to be blue. When I visited New Delhi, India, a year or so ago, I was provided with an anti-pollution mask.

Covid-19 has caused severe hardship. Millions of jobs have been lost, some temporarily, others permanently. It has been particularly hard on already vulnerable people and precarious informal sectors. Governments have been in high gear, pumping out billions of dollars of subsidies through a wide range of grants to individuals and organizations in an attempt to help them cope and to help resuscitate the economy.

Life, when things settle down, will be different. Work will be done differently. Hopefully, we will be able to preserve at least some of the good, including the humanity that has surfaced among so many people who have come to appreciate who and what we had been carelessly taking for granted.

I do worry that the interests of institutions that have traditionally weighed decisions in favour of prevailing economic imperatives will again be the interests that rule our lives going forward, leaving socioeconomic considerations and far-reaching public health concerns behind. Many of the jobs deemed essential and unable to be carried out under work-from-home arrangements are done by people at lower income levels. While some have had their wages temporarily increased during the crisis because they were deemed essential, some employers have already announced that the temporary increases will be eliminated as the emergency comes to an end, as though those jobs will no longer be considered essential.

While policy-makers might mean well, some public policies might work a lot better for some sectors of society than for others. If we are to emerge from this crisis in better shape than we were before it, we will need to have a reckoning of what we have traditionally valued and undervalued.

―――――

As if Covid-19 hasn't been enough to test our fortitude, and as if we needed yet another reminder of the evil of racism, on May 25, 2020, a white police officer in Minneapolis, in the U.S.A., kneels on the neck of a Black man for almost nine minutes, demonstrating to the world that racism against Black people is very much alive and continues to destroy lives and cause despair. The man,

George Floyd, dies. The ripple effect of that unconscionable display of hatred, recorded with both video and audio even as the police officers involved boldly display their perceived right to do harm with impunity, results in protests in and beyond cities in America and Canada, bringing people, literally, to their knees. Unlike the novel coronavirus, Black people have been afflicted by the racism virus for centuries.

I watched the video, a video that no one should ever have to see, the video that it seems everyone needed to see. The video is not a movie "based on a true story." The viewer is actually watching a man die, over a period of approximately nine minutes, in real time. This is as graphic as it gets, totally void of humanity except for the ignored and dismissed outcries of witnesses who are watching and recording with their cellphones as the horror happens.

A few days after George Floyd's death, a successful Black businessman tells me that while out for a walk in his upscale Toronto neighbourhood, he saw that an elderly white woman had fallen on the sidewalk. He wrestled with what he should do. He imagined how the picture would look: a physically fit younger Black man, standing over an elderly white woman. Should he reach out to help her? Could this cause him to be accused of terrible things that he had not done? I told him I hoped he helped the woman. He told me he had, but only because his white wife was with him. I told him I was happy that he had helped the elderly woman because I believe that we must never lose our humanity. But I could certainly understand the reason for his caution.

Racism, unlike Covid-19, did not suddenly arrive in 2019 or 2020. For centuries, horrendous acts against humanity as well as no end of micro-aggressions have been the experience of Black people, Indigenous people, and other people of colour. Some of these experiences have been meant to deprive people of their dignity and exert dominance over and oppression upon those who are deemed to be of lesser value to society. Such actions, whether imposed by individuals or institutionalized within public policy and enforced by individuals, have also served to protect the power and influence of those in positions of dominance over those in society whose voices and opinions are more often ignored or dismissed.

Those at the receiving end have sometimes resigned themselves to the existence of discrimination and other manifestations of inequity, whether based on their race or their socioeconomic status or their lack of privilege, as being their fate.

On a day more than twenty-five years ago, Chris and I had just left York University after helping our son Stefan, a first-year student, move into his residence. We stopped at a nearby restaurant, one of the locations of a world-famous fast-food chain. It was an off-peak time and except for staff, ourselves, and four young Black boys sitting together playing cards, the restaurant was empty. There was no evidence of food or drink on the table where the boys were seated. This was obviously a safe place, a comfortable place, an oasis in an area that appeared more industrial than residential, but an area that could be referred to as a neighbourhood, the boys' neighbourhood, given the high-rise, rent-subsidized apartment buildings that could be seen all around.

Apart from the fact that there were no other customers who could have been disturbed by their presence, the boys' behaviour was certainly not offensive, certainly not disturbing. Yet shortly after we took our seats with what we had purchased, the boys were asked to leave. And they left. And I did nothing. I could have claimed the boys were with me. I didn't. I could have ordered ice cream for each of them, thereby making them legitimate customers with the right to remain seated in the establishment. I didn't. Instead, I sat silently as they left obediently and in as orderly a fashion as they had been sitting, chatting with each other before they were asked to leave. The boys seemed resigned to that being their fate, likely not an unusual experience, the story of their lives. That experience and my inaction have haunted me ever since. Life happens with or without our interventions. The choice is ours whether to be observers or advocates.

My personal experiences with anti-Black racism pale in comparison to what I have read or heard about. At Scotiabank, for example, I could not say with any conviction at all that my career was impacted, whether negatively or positively, by my race. There was one particular experience, however, that could without any doubt be described as racist, one which I will never forget. It involved John, a colleague. I shouldn't have had to tell my boss to get out of my office after John had complained to him that I had just given him, John, the same "instructions." That was more than twenty years ago. I was a vice president at that time. John had a habit of saying things to me that I found offensive. An American, he had previously told me that the Black woman who believed herself to be fortunate because she worked in his parents' home when he was a boy would describe herself as an Oreo cookie: "Black on the outside and white on the inside." John had also watched all the television coverage of the 1989 Dubin Inquiry into the use of steroids by athletes. The inquiry was launched by the Canadian government after Ben Johnson, a Jamaican-born member of Canada's Olympic team, lost his gold medal in the 1988 Seoul Olympics after testing positive for steroids. The inquiry didn't focus only on Ben Johnson. The use of banned performance-enhancing substances was determined to be widespread among athletes from several countries. John made a point of sharing with me his observation that steroids seemed to "make people's skin turn black."

It had gotten to the point that nothing John could say would surprise me anymore. In a meeting in my boss's office that day, John arrogantly and confidently proclaimed that where he had just been on vacation, I wouldn't have been entitled to have an opinion.

When I asked him where he had been, he told me he had just returned from a tour of wineries in South Africa. Another colleague who had been in the meeting left our boss's office saying that he didn't want to be present for that kind of discussion. My boss said nothing.

Later that day, John had the nerve to come to my office to ask for my help with a project he was working on. I was in no mood to help him. He wouldn't take no for an answer so I had to express my position more forcefully. That's when he went to our boss to file a complaint. Ironically, this was the first time my boss had ever come to my office. While I was more annoyed than angry with John, the racist, I was very angry with my boss for the different ways in which he had chosen to deal with the two situations. He had not responded to John's unprofessional and offensive comment to me but he was ready to stand up for the racist when I stood up for myself. I fully expected to hear more about how I had responded to my boss. I never did. In the years that followed, I was given other vice president roles with increased responsibilities and, in 1998, I was appointed a senior vice president at Scotiabank.

So deeply has the curse of anti-Black racism been entrenched in our lives that Black people have even tried to mask their blackness in order to get ahead. In early 2000, having come to the realization that my beautiful, shoulder-length hair was more trouble than it was worth, I came to the conclusion that it was time for a change. I decided to stop spending hours in the hair salon every few weeks, using a hair dryer after each shampoo, and sleeping in curlers, which in hindsight might have contributed to the arthritis I have in my neck.

I revealed my decision to my hairdresser, who, along with staff at his popular salon, had taken very good care of my hair for many years. I told him I wanted to cut my hair really short and go with an entirely natural look. To my surprise, this resulted in a lengthy argument which included a warning that corporate Canada was "not ready for a woman with an afro." I was already an executive with one of Canada's top banks. I wondered what he told the teen-aged Black girls who were still trying to figure out who they wanted to be and how to be accepted in the wider world.

I insisted that my decision be respected and then I found a new hairdresser, Robert Samuels, who has taken care of me since then, a young man who wears his own hair in natural, shoulder-length dreadlocks and takes no more than thirty minutes to cut my hair perfectly every three or four weeks. Robert has often compli-mented me on my choice as being a sign of confidence in who I am, and hugs me as I leave his salon after each appointment. I used to receive lots of compliments for my high-maintenance, relaxed shoulder-length hair. I now receive lots of compliments for my low-maintenance, natural short hair.

I also know that when a colleague I admire a lot thoughtfully reached out to check on how I was coping with all of this while telling me that she had just watched *I Am Not Your Negro*, the 2016 documentary written by James Baldwin, she certainly meant well, but I didn't really know how to respond because while George Floyd's death has shaken all of us, I was thinking about all the lives that were sacrificed before and since his, long ago and recently.

When I hear people say they are colour blind, I figure they must be approaching a hundred years of age. There was a time when that comment might have resonated in some circles, but it simply isn't enough now. Similarly, to say that one is not a racist is also not a meaningful position. Tell me you are opposed to racism, that you know racism is wrong, if you want me to have any confidence in your sincerity. Then tell me how you are going to live your life so that others can live their lives.

The hope that emanates from being able to build on the achieve-ments and progress that have been made through the efforts of many who have made huge sacrifices in the quest for human rights must not be undermined by complacency. It has been demonstrated that progress already thought to have been achieved can be eroded and reversed.

We must not forget that the work of past movements served to change and repeal abhorrent laws. This was absolutely critical for any progress to be made. Martin Luther King Jr. was branded as a radical by those determined to protect the status quo.

What we need now is a change in attitudes, and there is greater insistence that there be accountability for how we act toward each other, both individually and collectively in the form of institutionalized practices. Unfortunately, it's harder to legislate that kind of change. It might be inconvenient for some to recognize that dominant society and dominant culture continue to determine, based on their own experiences and privileges, how everyone else gets to live. While it is important to acknowledge that reality, it might be even more important to recognize that the institutionalization of public policies and how they are implemented is all within the control of human beings. I think this is important to remember when we talk about systemic racism or the social determinants of health, for example, or even simply about "the system." Perhaps when we think of systems as the problem, we should remember these systems are created by people eager to establish or protect what they deem to be their rights as opposed to and at the expense of what they think is good enough for everyone else. The commitment that we all need to make is to respect that we all deserve to be able to live with dignity and in ways that do not involve the oppression of others.

I have heard it said that the enemy of transformation is incremental change. My generation and generations before mine might have seen incremental change as a sign of progress. I don't think the young people of today will settle for anything other than transformational change.

At time of writing, scientists all over the world are working, with a great sense of urgency, on developing vaccines against Covid-19 and on treatment for those who are afflicted with the disease. For racism, there will be a lot more effort and commitment required because only extermination will suffice.

Crises can cause us to acknowledge our vulnerability. Crises can also remind us of the importance of caring for each other. It has never been more important to protect, preserve, and promote our humanity.

In all the despair, I am seeing hope. Listening to my granddaughters as they describe how they are engaging with their white friends on the issue of anti-Black racism gives me hope. Seeing the diversity in ages and races of the people who are participating in protests against racism gives me hope. The clarity of the thinking, the determination, and the fearlessness of the actions of young people of all races, give me reason to be hopeful. Never before has that been more evident or more powerful. In "Glory," songwriters John Roger Stephens and Lonnie Rashid Lynn foresaw this when they noted that elders and young people would need to bring their wisdom and energy together for the cause.

Chapter 24

A Way Forward

AFTER OUR GRANDDAUGHTERS WERE BORN, I found it even more sickening to read or hear news reports about children being hurt in any way at all. I prayed then and I continue to pray that they will never suffer harm. Alexa is now twenty-two and Ashley is twenty, and when we are out in public places together I still instinctively walk just behind them, ready to intercept unwelcome attention should any occur.

I arrived for Alexa's first soccer game just before Chris did and I put our chairs out across from centre field, the best location for viewing the action, I thought. I spotted Alexa immediately and when Chris arrived, I said, "There she is, number 5."

"All the players are wearing the number 5 on their jerseys," Chris calmly observed.

"Oh. You're right. I guess the team must have gotten a good deal on their uniforms."

I only ever had eyes for our granddaughters when they played.

Their dad, our son Nick, was one of their coaches and his manner was always gentle, encouraging, and professional. Both Alexa and Ashley became very strong soccer players, often the top goal scorers on their teams. Alexa was fast. I would hear her power as she went by where I sat. Ashley seemed to model herself on her favourite professional soccer player, the Argentinian Lionel Messi, who played for Barcelona. She would sometimes look uninterested in or unexcited about what was happening further away on the field but at the right time, she would come alive and she would be dangerous. One day when I heard a coach on the team Ashley was playing against tell his players to "get her," I also heard a few parents who were seated near to me echoing the coach's instructions. I politely but firmly told them, "That's my granddaughter."

They understood that I meant for them to stop. On our way to the parking lot at the end of that game, I asked Ashley how she felt about being targeted by the coach of the other team. She told me it made her feel good.

Chris and I followed our granddaughters around, like groupies, to their dance competitions at venues in Ontario and also south of the border. I was happy that they worked as hard at their soccer as they did at their dancing. I wanted them to be balanced.

Alexa and Ashley were obviously very proud to be chosen by the teachers at their high school to serve as members of their school's student council. They were following their dad, who had served as president of his high school's student council, and before him, their grandmother, who had served as head girl at her high school. They both served as ambassadors for their high school, appearing in the marketing material used for recruiting new students in Canada and internationally and taking prospective students and their parents on tour when they visited the school. Ashley was a "big sister" to a younger student with long red hair who was always smiling happily when I saw them at school together.

When I am told that my granddaughters are beautiful, I agree, but I respond by highlighting other characteristics that I admire about them, like their thoughtfulness and their confidence and their determination, characteristics that reflect the goodness and wisdom and strength of character I see in them. They must know how much they are loved.

When my parents seemed to agree on little else, they agreed that I was wonderful and they often told me I was wonderful. I have no recollection of them telling me I was beautiful. Knowing how much they loved me worked for me as a child, a young woman, and even now in my senior years. That was, and still is, powerful.

———

Public health and social science practitioners know that a person's well-being is influenced by socioeconomic factors known as the social determinants of health. Poverty is usually found at the top of the list of the social determinants of health, which also include such factors as early childhood development, unemployment and underemployment, substandard housing, quality and level of education achieved, race, gender, disability, and social exclusion. Researchers quantify the impact of social determinants of health as 50 percent of what makes people sick. The remaining 50 percent is composed of access to quality health care, genetics and biology, and the environment, such as the quality of air we breathe. Social determinants of health impact not only how the world around us sees us but also how we process that world and where we dare to believe we belong in that world.

I believe we are each born with potential. I think we have different gifts and talents. Each person's ability to achieve their potential depends not only on the particular individual but also on that individual's environment and the opportunities that exist to enable the achievement of that potential.

The natural but unfortunate tendency that we have, as human beings, to classify, value, and treat others in ways that reflect our opinion of their socioeconomic status is evident in our everyday lives. So natural is that tendency that we often don't even realize it is happening. The saying "dress to impress" is a simple illustration of the reality that physical appearance matters — first impressions are made before we even give ourselves a chance to get to know more about each other.

When we work together to bring our different strengths to bear on addressing problems and creating solutions, for example, the outcomes are likely to be more sustainable because we have made space for each other at the table. We have given ourselves the opportunity to hear and learn from voices that often go unheard because we had not recognized that those voices mattered. We might have assumed we knew what would be good enough for others but that's simply not the same because we have not walked in their shoes.

Having a true appreciation of the impact that the social determinants of health can have on the likelihood of an individual to succeed in life can help us to better understand how to assess situations and the kinds of steps that can be taken to mitigate these challenges. We have the opportunity to make a difference, to matter, when we are willing to strengthen our understanding of others' circumstances before we pass judgment and when we are willing to advocate for what we have learned from those who live those realities. Social determinants of health and the stark inequities we see played out in so many aspects of life go hand in hand.

I didn't learn any of this from my time in the world of financial services. When people tell me they want to be appointed to boards of corporations rather than boards of charitable and not-for-profit organizations, or when they ask me for help with networking to further their success in the business world, I think of all I have learned because of my willingness to be of service to others. I think of the rich experiences I have been privileged to have and the relationships I have been fortunate to build by working with others who care for much more than their personal interests.

I grew up knowing I was fortunate. I knew that not because we had everything we needed and more, but because I had parents who allowed me to pursue my curiosity about how other people, less fortunate than we were, lived.

The children in Trench Town whom I taught during my summer breaks in my elementary school years, the bus conductors with whom I argued because my height had them believing I should be paying the adult fare before I had actually turned twelve, accepting the reality that Vera would donate my clothes to her adopted family and friends when she felt I had worn them enough ... these early experiences were all unplanned and unscripted but fortuitous lessons in my development. They kept me grounded and served as the true foundation of my privileged life.

So, my story is truly one of gratitude for all that I have had the privilege to learn from others. This awareness has provided me with the motivation to do my part in helping to provide opportunities that could enable children and young adults to have better lives. I have learned that everyone has abilities. I have learned that everyone has potential. Along with realizing how fortunate I have been, I have also learned the importance of self-esteem and resilience, believing in ourselves.

A young Indigenous leader once told me that people in his community believe that it takes seven generations to establish sustainable social change. That may be why it sometimes appears that progress can be slow. It's also important we realize that social evolution can be very fragile. Even as we think we are moving forward, there remains the constant risk of setbacks that can be triggered by what might seem like an infinite variety of events, often unpredictable, globally, locally in the communities where we live, or even personally in our families. To further complicate things, the fragility of social change is not necessarily based on rational thinking. Unfortunately, we have even seen that manifested where we would have expected leaders to rely on evidence and science to influence the decisions that impact people's lives in significant ways. All of this serves to demand vigilance and determination and commitment.

I have learned the value of making a conscientious effort to work well with others, showing respect for what they have to offer, and recognizing that there is often more that can be accomplished with them than without them. I sometimes wish it was not so easy for me to detect insincerity and hypocrisy when I encounter those behaviours in people. Unfortunately, I think it might be the downside of not taking people for granted and genuinely wanting to understand what they are thinking rather than simply absorbing what they want me to believe. I have also learned how important it is to be willing to acknowledge that there are many things I do not know, and to take steps to acquire that knowledge, a commitment to lifelong learning.

It's important to believe in ourselves and to take personal responsibility for our actions and the achievement of our goals. When I tell young people to dream big, I am telling them not to settle for the easiest path or the path that others might define for them. Most importantly, I am hoping that they will realize that their destiny is what they aspire to for themselves. I tell them they are the ones who should be determining their future, and how successful they will be. I advise them to take charge of their lives.

It makes me uncomfortable to be referred to as an exception. Yes, I am the Black woman, not Canadian-born, Jamaican, married, mother, and Roman Catholic who shouldn't have been disappointed when I didn't get too far. But I had a few secret weapons. I came from a supportive environment where any barriers to my success resided primarily within me. My environment included the love and high expectations of parents who were not themselves struggling with challenges that would have crippled their ability to raise me up. Each little success gave me additional confidence to reach further.

Some people don't need much more than a supportive hand in order to confidently take their own steps and to make their own way through life. I believe that if policy-makers were to apply that kind of thinking to providing enabling supports that help people to get on their feet, the results would be amazing. Instead, there is too often a tendency to see some segments of society as unwilling to do for themselves.

I recall, many years ago, the United Way of Greater Toronto asking homeless men in Regent Park how the organization could best assist them. The men said they really needed a voice mailbox so that when they applied for jobs they would be able to provide prospective employers with a telephone number where they could be reached. It had been their experience that the stigma of being recognized as homeless was enough to prevent them from being considered even for jobs that required the minimum of skills. The United Way funded their request and the results were so positive that before long, the community service agency with which the men were associated assumed responsibility for provision of the service, covering the cost by charging their clients a small fee for its use. In my view, there were two obvious takeaways, the first being that people often know what kind of help they need, and the second being that people would prefer to not have to depend on others in order to be able to look after themselves.

I have never been able to predict how or when someone will enter my life in a way that has impact or influence. I do know that the experiences I have had throughout my lifetime have profoundly influenced the person I am.

The inequities I have seen in my life, whether close up or from a distance, are what I think about every day. I know, by a variety of definitions beyond those to be found in dictionaries, that my life has been one of privilege. I am unsure how that has come about. Why me? Why have I had access that others have not had? Why has my voice been heard, even sought, when so many voices go unheard? Why has my life sometimes seemed to matter more than the lives of so many others? What might we be able to learn from all of this and how can we use what we learn to make our lives, our presence in this world, truly matter?

We are each a work in progress, yet to be perfected. Most of us have yet to achieve our full potential. We should never stop trying to be better human beings and, as the socially responsible beings I believe we were created to be, this must include being each other's keepers, taking care of each other to the very best of our abilities and making our privilege matter, not only for ourselves, but also for the good of mankind.

Acknowledgements

ACCORDING TO A WISE AFRICAN proverb, if we want to go fast, we go alone. If we want to go far, we go with others.

As a first-time author, I could not have come this far without the advice and support of many people.

Denham Jolly was one of several people who encouraged me to write. He told me it was important that I record my story for my family, especially for my granddaughters. His book *In the Black* is dedicated to his grandson. Denny told me about the process and the people he had worked with on his biography.

I reached out to Fred Kennedy, author of three books, *Daddy Sharpe: A Narrative of the Life of Samuel Sharpe, A West Indian Slave Written by Himself, 1832; Huareo: Story of a Jamaican Cacique*; and the soon to be published biography of his father. I also reached out to Bernice Carnegie, the daughter of hockey legend Herb Carnegie, whose story is told in *A Fly in a Pail of Milk: The Herb Carnegie Story*. Fred and Bernice generously shared valuable experiences with me about the world of publishing.

Lawrence Hill, author of several successful books, including the award-winning, bestselling *The Book of Negroes*, which has been described as a masterpiece, took the time to help me understand how to use bridges effectively to glue scenes together. He told me to slow down a little to achieve greater depth.

Zanana Akande and Warren Salmon saw an early version of my manuscript. Their feedback was extremely thoughtful. It was obvious that they had done a careful and thorough read. When I wondered if I would find a publisher interested in working with me, Warren told me publishers sometimes missed the boat, failing to recognize the value of a story. He suggested I get in touch with Itah Sadu, owner of the popular Toronto treasure A Different Booklist. Itah connected me with Scott Fraser, publisher at Dundurn Press, who welcomed the positive (contrary to many stereotypes) story that he believed people needed to know.

Jamaal Myers, a corporate lawyer, liked the preface that I shared with him and provided legal guidance on how to interpret the terms of the publisher's contract.

My husband, Chris, has told me to keep writing. He thinks there is more for me to share. Chris, Nick, and Minka read an early version of the manuscript in record time. Minka said it was as though she was hearing my voice. Nick suggested I say more about a few of the people he thought I had mentioned too briefly. My granddaughters, Alexa and Ashley, told me that they had wondered why I hadn't written my story before and inquired often as to how the work was coming along. Chris, Minka, Stefan, Katrina, and Nick checked in from time to time for updates, hoping that I would soon have a publication date to share with them. My family was also my focus group, and their energy fueled me along the way. I couldn't disappoint them. They obviously wanted this to happen.

So many people cheered me on. I think it is best that I do not attempt to name them all, because I wouldn't want to forget anyone. Let me simply say that they all enabled this work. I humbly offer them my sincere appreciation for the confidence they placed in me and their belief that others might be interested in, and perhaps even benefit from, knowing my story.

I have saved my final reflections for the wonderful team at Dundurn Press, Scott Fraser and every member of his team. They each made me feel like I was the only author they were working with and that my book was the book they had been waiting for. I am truly grateful to them for helping me to make *From the Heart* a reality.

About the Author

JAMAICANS BY BIRTH, as a young couple, Mary Anne Chambers and her husband, Chris, decided Canada would be a good place to raise their two sons. Mary Anne made a personal commitment to herself that her family would be good for Canada and Canada would be good for them.

A graduate of the University of Toronto Scarborough, Mary Anne majored in commerce and political science as a part-time mature student.

After retiring early as a senior vice president at Scotiabank, one of Canada's largest financial institutions, Mary Anne ran successfully for political office and was appointed a cabinet minister in the province of Ontario. For more than three decades, she has served on the boards of several not-for-profit organizations with a primary focus on education, health, community building, and international development, sometimes at the level of chair or vice chair. In April 2022, Mary Anne was named the University of Guelph's 10th chancellor. She is also on the board of GraceKennedy Ltd., a global food and financial services group of companies with Jamaican roots.